D1330857

TEA
WITH
HITLER

TEA WITH HITLER

THE SECRET HISTORY

OF THE ROYAL FAMILY

AND THE THIRD REICH

DEAN PALMER

The
History
Press

For Mum, Freddie
and Dylan

First published 2021

The History Press
97 St George's Place, Cheltenham,
Gloucestershire, GL50 3QB
www.thehistorypress.co.uk

British Library Cataloguing in Publication Data.
A catalogue record for this book is available from the British Library.

ISBN 978 0 7509 9564 1

Typesetting and origination by The History Press
Printed and bound in Great Britain by TJ Books Limited, Padstow, Cornwall.

Trees for Life

CONTENTS

PREFACE

The Second World War divided the Anglo-German British Royal Family. In 1939, brothers, sisters and cousins suddenly found themselves on opposite sides. This dilemma was Queen Victoria's fatal legacy: she had wanted to secure peace in Europe through a network of royal marriages. Her eldest daughter, Vicky, helped realise this ambition by marrying the future German Emperor Frederick in 1855. By the time the Queen died in 1901, six of her eight children had married German royals. Her forty-two grandchildren resided in palaces and castles across the continent. Victoria wanted this soft power to foster sensible constitutional government based on the British model, but this backfired with two world wars.

This book focuses on three family relationships to tell this remarkable story. The first is between Duke Charles Edward of Coburg and his devoted sister, Princess Alice, Countess of Athlone. The Duke was born and raised in England, until Queen Victoria withdrew him from Eton as a 14-year-old and exported him to Germany to rule Coburg. After the First World War, he became an ardent Nazi, and Hitler used the Duke as a secret diplomatic channel directly to the heart of the British Establishment. Charles Edward played a crucial role in organising the Duke of Windsor's notorious visit to Nazi Germany in 1937, and he was aided by Princess Alice, who entertained senior Nazis at her Sussex home. Alice shared her brother's anti-Semitic views, and later helped to whitewash his reputation at the post-war denazification courts set up in 1946 to rid Germany of Nazi ideology.

The second centres on the tripartite friendship between Edward VIII (later Duke of Windsor), his sybaritic younger brother the Duke of Kent, and their playboy Nazi cousin, Prince Philipp of Hesse. The three men admired Germany's rapid economic recovery under Hitler, and they viewed the Nazi Party as a barricade against Communism. They advocated peace at any price and flirted with fascism and unhelpful amateur diplomacy.

The final one is Prince Philip of Greece (who became the Duke of Edinburgh) and his sister Princess Sophie. The pair were very close, and after Sophie married Prince Christoph of Hesse (Philipp of Hesse's brother) in 1930, the teenage Prince Philip stayed with them, in Germany, during his school holidays. When Philip started his career in the British Royal Navy, under the patronage of his uncle Lord Mountbatten, Christoph became the protégé of Hermann Göring, the man who founded the Gestapo. Christoph was quickly promoted, becoming head of the *Forschungsamt* (Research Office): a secret Nazi wiretapping unit. Had Christoph not died in a plane crash in 1943, Philip would have endured the ignominy of seeing his sister's husband face a war crimes trial. Such a scandal could have ended his chance of marrying the future Queen of the United Kingdom.

At the centre of this family network sat the ardently pro-German Edward VIII (later Duke of Windsor), whose love for Wallis Simpson forced his abdication in 1936. Afterwards, the former king made world headlines by taking his new bride to visit Adolf Hitler for tea at his Alpine retreat in Berchtesgaden. In private they also expressed sympathy for Hitler's regime. Since then, there has been a tendency to target him, a foolish man who made a mess of his kingship, as the lone Nazi sympathiser in the family. It is a mistake to hold this narrow view.

During the 1930s, British aristocratic circles were culturally and ethnically closer to Germany than to any other nation. Traumatised by what they saw on the First World War battlefields, most members of the 'Establishment' did not want to start another conflict and ignored the Nazi atrocities. They viewed German anti-Semitism as a purely internal concern. The British upper classes, not famed for their racial tolerance at the best of times, vilified wealthy Jews as flashy arrivistes, while they condemned poor Jews for spreading socialism. George VI and his wife Queen Elizabeth (who later became the Queen Mother) held the conventional view of being more afraid of Communist Russia – guilty of murdering their Romanov cousins – than of the Nazi Party. Initially, anti-Churchillian George VI was as much an ardent appeaser as his brother Edward.

Society was changing rapidly in the 1930s. The aristocracy complained about their downturn in fortune, and the spectre of class war threatened Royal privilege. Understanding this history today is critical, as the rise of populism in modern society sometimes echoes a chilling familiarity with the 1930s. The Great Depression destroyed prosperity and produced deep anxiety which Hitler exploited. He understood the people's fears and anger better than the urban elite. Hitler delighted in the outrage his speeches caused abroad and had contempt for the press who attempted to hold him to account. He lied often and shamelessly.

Ideally, the world's Establishment would have coached the Nazi Party towards civilisation, or Hitler and Stalin would turn on and destroy each other in a war on the Eastern Front. Most people in Britain did not want to listen to Winston Churchill's erratic and unsound warning regarding Hitler. He was considered a warmonger. Most preferred the calm reassurance of Neville Chamberlain, considered a reliable man. However, the Nazis created a breed of true believers who obeyed them without question. When the people cast their votes in the ballot boxes in Germany, the Nazi count increased. Voting became about protesting against the complacent status quo. A divided opposition in Germany allowed the Nazis to launch their power grab, despite much evidence of corruption and thuggery. The rest of the world turned a blind eye: they hoped Adolf Hitler would protect them against communism, not realising that he was possibly the greater evil.

INTRODUCTION

Bamberg POW Camp, Allied Occupied
Germany. November 1945.

Everywhere, the smell was putrid. Sixty years old and crippled by chronic arthritis, Charlie Coburg staggered around a rubbish dump, digging into refuse to find an old tin can to use as a food bowl. He pulled up grass growing inside his prison pen and added it to the thin soup ration his American captors allowed him for sustenance. For a man who had once enjoyed the luxury of owning seventeen castles, life was now a simple checklist: food, tobacco, warmth.[1]

Prince Charles Edward, Duke of Saxe-Coburg and Gotha – Charlie to his friends – was an inmate at Bamberg, part of a network of American prisoner-of-war (POW) camps that held 5 million German soldiers who had surrendered on 7 May 1945. It was an unmanageable number.[2] The prison pens – some of them containing 100,000 inmates – were a mass of grey-clothed, faceless prisoners, surrounded by barbed wire.[3] Few German prisoners had tents, so they had to dig holes in the earth to protect themselves from the winter climate. The only currency in the camps was nicotine – Lucky Strike and Camel – and a new race of men appeared: the *Kippensammler*, 'the collector of butt ends'.[4]

Outside the prison, anarchy prevailed. The German people lived amongst the ruins, and bomb craters pocked the roads. Rivulets of people walked in a dazed indolent fashion, going nowhere. Like a nomadic tribe, they carried the remnant objects of their old lives in sacks or crates. There was an oppressive, almost visible, disquiet. People were starting again from nothing and scavenging an existence from the rubble.

Defeated by the Allies – America, Britain, Russia and France – quadripartite Germany was divided into four occupation zones by the victors. Bamberg fell inside the American zone in Bavaria. Most of King George VI's German relatives – including both the Hesse and Coburg families – now lived under American control. In 1945, General George S. Patton's Third Army had overrun southern Germany, and President Roosevelt appointed Patton as the region's military governor. While the German people suffered, the American occupiers lived well.

'I came away with a sense of sheer horror,' wrote George Kennan, a high-ranking US State Department official, 'at the spectacle of this horde of my compatriots and their dependents camping in luxury amid the ruins … oblivious to the abundant evidence of tragedy all around them … flaunting their silly supermarket luxuries in the face of a veritable ocean of deprivation, hunger and wretchedness.'[5]

Driving around in supercharged Mercedes which had been seized from their Nazi owners, the Americans stationed in Germany treated the autobahns as racetracks and relished living in requisitioned castles and villas.[6] Arthur D. Kahn, a former Chief Editor in the Intelligence Office of Information Control in Frankfurt, censured his fellow countrymen for creating an American raj:

> We became an 'Indian Service' – 'poohbah sahibs' – masters of the conquered people, rulers of an occupied Colonial State. Little people from the States haughtily ordered mayors and governors to appear before them … The most beautiful women in Germany we had at our price. There were servants to minister to our every need … And in the streets, before the opera, groups of Germans gathered to fight for our cigarette butts.[7]

Coburg Castle. April 1945.

Seven months earlier, in April 1945, American troops had surrounded Coburg after General Patton's 11th Army Division first spotted the 'Disney-like' castle up on the hill.[8] They attacked the fortress with howitzer shells and an aerial bomb until Major General Pickett advanced under a white truce flag. A man wearing hunting clothes marched out of the castle gates, and speaking with a cut-glass British accent, the gentleman asked the Pickett what he wanted. The Major's ears were startled by the plummy sound of his received pronunciation and he replied, 'I wish we could stop the fighting.' 'I think that's a good idea,' said the man in tweed plus fours. He was Charles Edward, Duke of Saxe-Coburg and Gotha. The Duke then commanded the German troops stationed at the castle to surrender and asked Pickett if his men could help extinguish the fire: 'Your aeroplane dropped a bomb into the area where we had put the art treasures.' For the next hour, German and American troops formed a 'bucket brigade' to rescue both the art and the castle.[9]

Charles Edward had been expecting the Americans' arrival for days. As soon as he saw them approaching, he removed his officer's uniform with its shiny Nazi insignia and put on civilian clothes.[10] The transformation was a tactical move: this Anglo-German Royal, whom everyone at Windsor Castle had called 'Uncle Charlie', precipitously switched back to his English identity, posing as a harmless and slightly eccentric British aristocrat. He declared himself a prince of the United Kingdom and a grandson of Queen Victoria. Although it had been forty years since his school days at Eton, he name-dropped important pre-war connections, such as Neville Chamberlain, Anthony Eden and, of course, his cousin, King George VI.[11]

The Americans were unaware that nationalistic Coburg, the first German town to vote the Nazi Party to power, had been one of Queen Victoria's favourite residences. With its English gardens and picturesque architecture, Coburg was the birthplace of her beloved husband Prince Albert. 'If I were not who I am, this would have been my real home, but I shall always consider it my second one,' wrote the Queen.[12] Infatuated with Albert, Victoria had declared the British Royal Family the House of Coburg, and in private, Queen Victoria was far more German than British. She was a direct descendant through her father's side of the German House of Hanover and her mother was also a German princess. Young Victoria's upbringing at the red-brick Kensington Palace was mostly German; the cradle songs that lulled her to sleep were German and sung to her by a German governess.

At first, General Patton permitted the Duke of Coburg to remain at his castle under house arrest, living in bomb-damaged rooms with a cut-off water supply.[13] The Duke and the General had met before when Charles Edward visited the United States in 1934, while acting as Hitler's ambassador-at-large. The two men were on friendly terms, until Patton let slip to reporters that he was using former Nazis in his military government. He told the press that, in his opinion, there was not much difference between the Nazis in Germany and the political parties back home in the United States who favoured segregation.

Patton may have been a legendary military tactician and war hero, but he was also an anti-Semite with little empathy towards the Jews living in the displaced persons' camps that fell under his command. Conditions in these facilities were appalling, and after one critical report of Patton's camp supervision, he complained that the inspectors mistakenly believed 'that the Displaced Person is a human being, which he is not, and this applies particularly to the Jews who are lower than animals'. Patton went on to say that the Jews had 'no sense of human relationships' and likened them to locusts.[14] The Americans even made Jews bunk with former Nazis appointed to positions of authority in camp administration. Patton's oversight was so cruel that President Truman wrote in a letter to General Eisenhower, the Supreme Commander of the Allied Expeditionary Forces in Europe, on 31 August 1945: 'We appear to be treating the Jews as the Nazis treated them except that we do not exterminate them … One is led to wonder whether the German people are not supposing that we are following, or at least condoning, Nazi policy.'[15]

Heated exchanges occurred between Eisenhower and Patton on 28 September 1945. Firing one last shot, Patton told journalists that he did not see the need for this 'denazification thing' and stated that communism was now the greater threat.[16] Eisenhower immediately sacked Patton, and Charles Edward lost an ally.

The Americans put the Duke of Coburg on their official list of wanted Nazi war criminals, so it was only a matter of time before they would interrogate and arrest him. The Allied code-breaking unit at Bletchley Park in England had intercepted a telegram from Hitler. It stated that 'on no account' should the Duke fall 'into enemy hands'.[17] This implied that Charles Edward had knowledge about 'the most secret actions of the Nazi regime and should never be allowed to provide evidence to the Allied governments'.[18] As secretary of the German nuclear research centre, the Kaiser Wilhelm Society for the Advancement of Science in Berlin, Charles Edward knew where the Third Reich had hidden its skeletons.

American soldiers escorted Charles Edward to the POW camp at Bamberg in November 1945. His chauffeur gave him his own food rations, saying, 'You'll need them.'[19] When his wife, Duchess Victoria Adelaide, appealed to the guards at the prison gates to talk to her husband, they told her that she would 'never see him again'.[20]

The US military intelligence officers questioning the Duke were all members of a specialised unit called the 'Ritchie Boys' because of their training at Camp Ritchie in Maryland.[21] Many were German-Jewish émigrés to the United States who had fled Nazi oppression. Some had arrived in the US as children, without their parents, as part of a group called the One Thousand Children, rescued between 1934 and 1945 by refugee agencies. The Ritchie Boys were first-hand witnesses to the horrors of the concentration camps at Bergen-Belsen and Auschwitz and most were determined to treat their Nazi prisoners with the utmost severity. The catchphrase – 'The only good German is a dead German' – was as appealing in the immediate aftermath of the war as during it. In this atmosphere, most Germans seemed to wear the face of a death-camp guard, and many of the Nazi inmates at Bamberg were dying of ill-treatment.[22]

Stefan Heym, the German socialist writer, was one of the Ritchie Boys who interviewed Charles Edward in 1945. He found the Duke 'badly informed and arrogant' regarding Nazi atrocities.[23] For powerful men like Coburg, crimes were something that others committed: men of his station thought themselves above the law and untouchable. The Duke of Coburg had been the first German aristocrat to support Adolf Hitler after hearing him give a far-right speech in a Coburg beer garden on 14 October 1922.[24] This event was the first ever Nazi rally. Ten years later it was celebrated as *Deutscher Tag* (German Day) in Coburg. A Coburg Badge, struck to memorialise the event, was the highest-ranking Nazi medal. Made out of bronze, it featured a sword and a swastika within an oval wreath. At the top of the wreath was Coburg Castle and the inscription: *Mit Hitler in Coburg 1922–32* (With Hitler in Coburg 1922–32).

Under interrogation, Charlie insisted that Adolf Hitler had done an excellent job for Germany and although the policy to eliminate Jews was harsh, it was essential to destroy Jewish influence. Drawn to the Nazis by their anti-Semitism, Charles Edward viewed the Jews as catalysts for communist agitation. It was a stance motivated by racial, as well as political, factors. During his visit to America in 1934, the Duke was appalled by Jews playing an 'unrestricted' role in society, and he felt they 'abused it'.[25] When Heym hypothetically asked him if he would be ready to partake in a new German government, the Duke, still unwilling to accept Germany's defeat, accepted the hollow offer. He then insisted that his entire personnel must come from the Nazi Party and that the Allies should not charge any German for war crimes. Heym concluded that he was deluded and would soon face the consequences.[26]

Five categories of war criminal existed: Major Offender, Offender, Lesser Offender, Follower and Exonerated Person. In November 1945, the Duke's military prosecutors charged him as a Major Offender with 'crimes against humanity' for his complicity in Hitler's Final Solution. One of his many roles within Hitler's regime was President of the German Red Cross and he had used this position to collaborate in the Nazi programme of forced euthanasia.[27] Asked about the concentration camps, he disingenuously claimed to know nothing: *Ich bin nur ein kleiner mann* (I am just a little man).[28]

Charles Edward's performance did not fool his interrogators: they found his new outward transformation into an Englishman absurd and his wilful amnesia a blatant lie.[29] His denial of the death camps was implausible since German Red Cross trucks had often been used to transport victims to the gas chambers: a deliberate manipulation to keep people from reacting to their impending deaths.[30]

Used to being obeyed, the Duke of Coburg demanded notepaper from his captors to write to his British sister in London, Princess Alice ('Tigs'), the Countess of Athlone. The moment she discovered Charles Edward's arrest, Alice started mobilising courtiers at Buckingham Palace to pressure the Foreign Office into rescuing her brother.[31] The Princess also contacted a family friend, Sir Miles Graham, a Major General in the British Army. He, in turn, contacted Sir Brian Robertson, the Deputy Military Governor in the British Occupation Zone, who expressed a minimal desire to assist:

> Of course, I haven't the slightest idea what the man has done, or whether it is possible, even desirable, to alleviate his lot … Coburg is the brother of one of our royal princesses, there might be in the event of a trial undesirable publicity.[32]

Alice requested Robertson use his contacts with American officials to impose pressure on the relevant people.[33] She boarded a train in London and travelled across war-torn Europe to Bavaria in order to plead for his release. She even confronted General Lucius D. Clay, Eisenhower's deputy, who had started to investigate Charles Edward. Clay, a West Point graduate from Georgia, was described by Alice as a 'charming man', doubtlessly because he let her travel between Frankfurt and Coburg in his private train.[34]

Clay was often soft on the former Nazis. He attracted controversy by commuting the death sentences for Nazi war criminals such as Erwin Metz and Ludwig Merz, commanders of the Berga slave labour camp, where 350 US soldiers had been beaten, tortured and starved by the Germans because they were Jewish.[35] He also reduced the sentence for Isle Koch, the 'Beast of Buchenwald', convicted of murder at Nuremberg, whom the press infamously accused of making lampshades from prisoners' skin.[36] Clay viewed Germany as essential in the new Cold War that had started between the USA and the Soviet Union and their respective allies. By releasing Nazi offenders early, he boosted German public opinion towards the United States.

Despite the revelations in the newspapers about the horrors of the Holocaust, Princess Alice had not changed her opinion about the Jews since the 1930s. Before the war, she had entertained her brother's visiting Nazi friends, including Hitler's Foreign Minister, Joachim von Ribbentrop, at her Sussex home, Brantridge Park.[37] Hitler had plotted before the war to utilise the Royal Family's German connections to help convince Britain that peace with Germany was in their self-interest. Cosy back-door diplomacy between sympathetic British aristocrats and Nazi Party members had occurred in country houses, such as Cliveden in Berkshire and Mount Stewart in County Down. They were a breeding ground for anti-Semitism.

CLAREMONT

Claremont House, Surrey. 19 July 1884.
Twenty steps led from the drive to a giant portico supported by four Corinthian columns. Claremont is a vast Palladian-style mansion set in leafy parkland designed by Lancelot 'Capability' Brown. Prince Charles Edward, Queen Victoria's twenty-eighth grandchild, was born here on 19 July 1884. He was named after the romantic, failed Scottish rebel, Charles Edward Stuart ('Bonnie Prince Charlie') because his father, Prince Leopold, Duke of Albany, was obsessed with Scottish history.

Leopold never held his son in his arms; he died from a cerebral haemorrhage caused by haemophilia four months before Charles Edward was born, leaving behind a 13-month-old daughter, Princess Alice, and a German wife, Princess Helen of Waldeck-Pyrmont. Resultantly, at the moment of his birth, Charles Edward immediately became His Royal Highness, Prince Charles Edward, the Duke of Albany.

Princess Helen was from an insignificant German principality near Darmstadt. Pictures show that the princess was tall with a beautiful figure, very dark hair, deep-set dusky brown eyes and a sweet smile.[1] Growing up in Waldeck, she excelled academically and worked as the superintendent of the local infant schools, where she devised the curriculum. Helen was never told of her husband's illness until the Royal Family announced their engagement. Her family, particularly her pushy mother, was so overjoyed about the prospect of an advantageous marriage into the prestigious British Royal Family that health details did not matter.[2]

At 25 years old, Helen became a dowager, with two small children and reduced status. Her annual income was cut from £25,000 to £6,000 and suddenly she was a poor relation.[3] However, Helen's biggest problem was the constant interference from her mother-in-law. Queen Victoria pried into every aspect of Helen's life. The Queen refused to allow Helen to install central heating at Claremont and she even appointed the children's nanny, Nanna Creak, feeling that Helen was too young to decide such matters. Nanna Creak doted on Alice but could not handle Charles Edward's temperament, which was 'delicate, nervous and tiresome'.[4] His jumpy behaviour frustrated her so much that she left, and Queen Victoria felt distinctly annoyed by her disloyalty.

As was customary with aristocratic Victorian children, Charles Edward and Alice saw their mother at set periods only, usually in the late afternoon when they ate their supper at a little table in their mother's sitting room. When the children finished their food, they stayed with her until bedtime. The family would sit there in the gaslight, their mother reading while the children worked on painting or knitting. Even little Charlie learnt to knit. By way of incentive, the Duchess would hide a small bronze animal in a giant ball of yarn which the children could have on finishing the wool.[5] Helen kept the animal curios in tins decorated with pictures of *Alice in Wonderland*, gifts from Lewis Carroll who had been at Oxford University with her late husband.

For the most part, Alice and Charles Edward enjoyed an idyllic English childhood – picnics in the woods at Claremont, visits to their grandmother at Windsor Castle, and summer holidays on the Balmoral estate. To Charles Edward and Alice, the Scottish castle was a paradise: long walks across the heath-covered hillsides and enormous teas with scones and jam.[6]

A sensitive child, Charles Edward relied on Alice, his older, more dominant sister. Both loved to play-act in classic war stories. Alice always chose to be on the winning side: she was Julius Caesar to Charles Edward's Pompey and Alexander the Great to his Darius.[7] This pattern was to continue throughout their lives.[8] At Claremont there was almost no contact from the outside world, as the class distinction between royalty and even the upper-middle classes was so enormous, it restricted the pool of companions severely. A lady-in-waiting told Princess Alice not to partner so often with two girls at her dancing class, because they were not quite 'U'.[9] Alice remained home-schooled, but Charles Edward went to Sandroyd, a preparatory school nearby, riding there each day on his Shetland pony called Puck. Later, he was sent to Lyndhurst to prepare him for Eton.

At 14 years old, his life suddenly changed when his syphilitic and drunkard cousin, Prince 'Affie' of Saxe-Coburg-Gotha, shot himself with a handgun over a failed love affair with a young Irishwoman called Mabel

Fitzgerald on 22 January 1899. The blast from the pistol echoed throughout the palace-fortress in Coburg, leaving the household in shock, but the suicide was botched. With guests arriving to stay at the castle, the lovesick prince was quickly bundled into a carriage and dispatched on a bumpy 350-mile journey to the Martinsbrunn Sanatorium in the South Tyrol, where he died on 6 February.[10]

Coburg Castle, Germany. 22 January 1899.

Affie's father was Duke Alfred of Edinburgh, Queen Victoria's second son, who inherited the Dukedom of Saxe-Coburg-Gotha in August 1893, when his uncle, Prince Albert's older brother Duke Ernest, had died. Victoria's dynastic masterplan was for the Prince of Wales to succeed her, while Duke Alfred, as son number two, would be sent to Germany to rule his father's ancestral homelands. By 1893, Alfred, once a shy and handsome young man, full of early promise, was a silent, moody, friendless drunk.[11] Family members tactfully referred to his 'intemperance' as code for his alcoholism.[12] The sudden death of his only son exacerbated these dark moods.

For Queen Victoria, the question of Coburg's succession was now critical as she regarded the town as the cradle of her dynasty. Duke Alfred had throat cancer, too severe for any medication or treatment, and Victoria was determined to keep the duchy within her family's direct ownership.[13] Legally, the next heir to Coburg was Victoria's third son: Prince Arthur, Duke of Connaught. Arthur was his mother's favourite, and the Queen proclaimed his inheritance without consulting the German Emperor, Kaiser Wilhelm II, who was her eldest grandson.[14]

Germany had changed since Victoria had visited Coburg as a young bride, and Wilhelm understood the new tide of nationalistic feeling occurring on the continent. The Kaiser now insisted that whoever became the next Duke of Coburg must move to Germany and join the German army. Under the German constitution, the Kaiser was 'First Amongst Equals' with the other German princes and minor kings, but in practice, the Emperor dominated. Prince Arthur was a British general, and understandably, the German press was hostile. The *Leipziger Neueste Nachrichten* (Leipziger Latest News) adopted the slogan, 'German thrones for German princes'.[15] The German people viewed mixed Anglo-German heritage as a malignant influence, and the *Berlin Tageblatt* wrote that, as the princes were the custodians of the Reich, they had to be German: 'It is impossible to have two souls inside one's breast – a German and a foreign one.'[16] Nationalists were questioning whether international royal families, with estates scattered throughout Europe, could be capable of genuine loyalty to one country.

The Kaiser threatened his grandmother Queen Victoria with new legislation, which would declare that a foreign prince was incapable of succeeding to a German ducal throne.[17] Coburg itself was rapidly becoming the most xenophobic town in Germany, and the current Duke Alfred, considered more British than German, was highly unpopular. In any case, Prince Arthur had no wish to leave his career in the British army and his wife, Princess Louise Margaret of Prussia, had led a wretched life in stuffy Berlin and did not want to return to Germany.

Victoria, therefore, decided that Arthur would 'decline' the throne of Coburg in favour of Prince Charles Edward, who was next in line. 'The whole family is united in thinking it must be Charlie,' wrote Queen Victoria.[18] After all, Charles Edward's mother was a German, and the widowed Duchess of Albany agreed to move with her son to Coburg, permanently, where he would serve in the German army. Only just a teenager, Charles Edward was young enough to be turned into a proper German, an essential factor in appeasing both the Kaiser and the influential Chancellor Bismarck.[19]

Reinhardsbrunn Castle, Coburg. March 1899.

Drunk, alone and grieving after his son's suicide, Duke Alfred shut himself inside the remote fairy-tale castle at Reinhardsbrunn in the Thuringian Forest.[20] In this grand Gothic folly, surrounded by an English landscaped garden, he escaped the criticism of Coburgers, who believed him to be too foreign. Dying of cancer, the Duke agreed that his nephew Charles Edward should inherit.

Charles Edward was small, blue-eyed and handsome. An introverted teenager, he found the gruelling process of transformation into a German bewildering and alien. His mother shrewdly understood that in the nationalistic hothouse of Bismarck's Second Reich, the current Duke Alfred's Englishness was a significant handicap to her son's new career as a German duke. She had to convert her English schoolboy into a German: 'I have always tried to bring Charlie up a good English man. And I now have to turn him into a good German.'[21] Her son was too young to resist, but he complained: 'I've got to go and become a beastly German prince.'[22]

After an arduous ten-day journey from Claremont, Duchess Helen presented herself at Reinhardsbrunn, expecting to have tea with the family's new benefactor. However, she found Duke Alfred inebriated and aggressive.

Worse behaviour followed. Not only was Alfred unwilling to offer the Duchess a permanent home, but he also wanted to adopt Charles Edward into his own family.[23] Helen had never agreed to this plan. She had left Claremont with the sole purpose of staying with her son. Angered by Duke Alfred's unreasonable demands and bad manners, she refused to let Charles Edward move in with him. The neighbouring King of Württemberg (who had married her sister Marie) came to her rescue and provided a suite of rooms at his nearby palace in Stuttgart. This gave the Duchess breathing space to consider her options, while her entire family in both Germany and Britain hovered around her, waiting to interfere.

Duke Alfred wanted to send Charles Edward to a local village school which Princess Alice described as 'a horrid, scruffy place'.[24] Swiftly rejecting this suggestion, Charles Edward's education became a tug-of-war between the Kaiser and his liberal-minded English mother, the Dowager Empress Vicky (Queen Victoria's eldest daughter). Vicky wanted the young Duke to attend a liberal progressive school in Frankfurt. Never one to refrain from expressing her prejudices, Princess Alice wrote: 'Aunty Vicky who … was continually meddling, wanted Mother to send him [Charles Edward] to a school in Frankfurt which was supposed to be very modern but was mainly attended by the sons of rich Jews.'[25]

Alice's anti-Semitism was an attitude prevalent amongst the British aristocracy and she loathed Prime Minister Disraeli's influence over her grandmother, stating that Queen Victoria was 'mesmerised by the polished and calculating flattery of the Jew'.[26]

Charles Edward was left feeling English on the inside and German on the outside. The Kaiser's severe bullying aggravated the shock of his transition. One evening, Charles Edward was given a 'proper beating up' by the Kaiser after visiting the royal library.[27] Since his mother was German, the language was not a problem, and his German essays were soon receiving better marks than his English work. However, the Kaiser felt that he 'suffered', like Charles Edward, from having dual nationality and his desire to turn him into a proper German was a correction to his own upbringing. He pledged to make his delicate English cousin a Prussian officer and so Charles Edward was enrolled at the Lichterfelde Military Academy in Berlin.[28]

Potsdam. 1899.

While Charles Edward pursued his education, Duchess Helen and Princess Alice moved into the Villa Ingenheim just outside Potsdam. It was a large white house that looked like a wedding cake, but after Claremont the family found it suburban and crammed with ugly furniture. Princess Alice called it 'undistinguished'.[29] The outgoing Alice attended a finishing school with a relaxed curriculum and dabbled in music, art and painting, which she loved. She embraced German society and enjoyed a pleasurable existence rowing on the lakes, skating on the frozen River Havel, and playing flirtatious games of tennis with the cadets her brother brought home from Lichterfelde.[30]

Potsdam was the Hohenzollerns' summer seat, and the Kaiser lived at the 200-roomed New Palace inside the Sanssouci Royal Park. The palace guards wore starched uniforms, copied from Frederick the Great's era, and they goose-stepped under triumphal arches and past monuments to war heroes. Disraeli described it as a 'Paradise of Rococo'.[31] Rows of pseudo-Greek statues in flowing drapery stood on the edge of the roof and the terrace, although the winter frost cracked their delicate faces and fingers, making restoration a continuous task.[32]

After the quiet simplicity of Queen Victoria's household, Alice and Charles Edward found the Kaiser's lavish court overwhelming. Everyone wore court dress: the whalebones inserted into collars could bruise the neck, and the severe corsetry made the summer months unbearable. The Kaiser's throne room was the most magnificent in Europe, and the Prussian military-style pomp buttressed his fragile ego: 'At Court Balls … the Kaiser would stand like a drill sergeant on the steps of the throne while long lines of dancers performed nervously and faultlessly before him.'[33] Princess Alice and her mother were also expected to spend time with the Kaiser's dull wife, Empress Augusta Victoria (known as 'Dona'), who was a religious fanatic. Dona was entirely submissive and dedicated to her husband whose eccentricities were, in her eyes, merely manifestations of his genius.[34] The British-born Princess Daisy of Pless (née Daisy Cornwallis-West) wrote: 'I have never met anyone so devoid of individual thought or agility of brain and understanding. She is just like a good, quiet, soft cow that has calves and eats grass slowly and ruminates.'[35]

More diplomatic, Princess Alice called the Empress 'affable and kind',[36] but it was apparent to everyone at court that the Empress bored and agitated her husband.[37] Wilhelm wanted his court to be elegant, and he even chose his wife's clothes. Never fashionable or stylish, when Empress Dona wore a gold dress to a court ball, it looked 'like a cheap party cracker'.[38] The Kaiser disparagingly compared his wife's provincial German upbringing to the more sophisticated ladies in his family, brought up in London.

Nonetheless, the Empress had fulfilled her primary duty and bore her husband six boys and a girl. Charles Edward became the Emperor's 'seventh son',[39] while the Empress hoped to secure Alice as a daughter-in-law. However, Princess Alice had no romantic interest in her 'rather spoilt and very conceited' cousins.[40]

Coburg. 1900.

When visiting Coburg, Duchess Helen made a point of preserving good relationships with Duke Alfred. Stoically, she attended his excruciating musical soirées, where he drunkenly regaled his guests by playing his violin while dressed in his Scottish kilt.[41] Court sycophants in Coburg encouraged his music by applauding loudly. Such tuneless performances required a certain bravado as, in private, the Duke's cancer was getting worse. By May 1900, he had to be fed by a tube, and he died at one of his favourite homes, a gingerbread-yellow villa, at Rosenau in Coburg, on 30 July 1900.[42]

Overnight, Charles Edward, Duke of Albany, became the Duke of Saxe-Coburg and Gotha. The new situation was daunting, and he became utterly inconsolable at his uncle's funeral, overwhelmed by the responsibility that lay ahead. Sixteen was a young age to become a sovereign duke in a foreign country, and the Kaiser immediately decided his cousin was too young to rule and appointed a regent. Meanwhile, Charles Edward remained at Lichterfelde, and his life continued as before. After passing out, the young Duke joined the famous Prussia First Regiment of Guards. Later he was sent off to read law at Bonn University, where his grandfather Prince Albert had studied, but unlike his studious grandfather, he was far more interested in non-academic pursuits on offer, such as joining the Corps Borussia, an exclusive duelling club for aristocratic students.

Friedrichshof Castle. 1899.

Duchess Helen rarely visited her sister-in-law, the British-born Dowager Empress Vicky. The Empress lived in retirement at Friedrichshof Castle, estranged from both her son the Kaiser and Chancellor Bismarck. Sensible courtiers shunned her, and Helen was eager to avoid making friends in the wrong places.

Empress Vicky was ostracised because, together with her late husband Emperor Frederick, she had dared to speak out against Bismarck's xenophobic policies and his willingness to go to war. Frederick and Vicky had been an unusually progressive imperial couple, but they had not been smart enough to outwit Bismarck. When Frederick was dying of cancer, the Chancellor set out to charm their son, using a mixture of toadying, barefaced flattery and manipulation, as well as strategically applied bullying. He fed the young man's arrogance and fuelled family tensions.

The moment Wilhelm became the Kaiser, his treatment of his mother became unremittingly coldblooded and cruel; it was behaviour with deep psychological roots. Wilhelm's traumatic breech birth on 27 January 1859 had left him with a withered left arm, and his mother always viewed him as 'deformed', feeling ashamed that her first-born son was so defective.[43] Throughout his childhood, Wilhelm had to endure futile, gothic treatments, from electrotherapy to having a dead hare, still warm, wrapped around his malformed arm.[44] The little boy became fixated on his beautiful but ambivalent mother who could not conceal her disappointment in him.

The Kaiser developed into a handsome man in uniform. The famous moustache was waxed every morning by his barber, but his cold blue eyes were hard and shallow. His right hand had to compensate for the left and grew overwhelmingly strong, but he always kept his left on his hip with its fingers heavily ornamented with rings to disguise an unattractive mole. Incapable of much movement, his hand could only hold a glove or paper. Riding a horse was hard; mounts had to be specially trained to respond to knee pressure.[45] Determined, Wilhelm overcame many handicaps, but he could never win his mother's approval. In civilian clothes, he was almost unrecognisable and looked far less impressive. His daughter's English nanny, Miss Topham, wrote:

> I was reminded of those gentlemen who come on stage in loud garments at variety shows and sing songs of mingled comedy and pathos to the applause of the gallery. The clothes look like a bad disguise.[46]

After his father's death, Wilhelm's first act as ruler was to evict his mother from the royal palace at Potsdam. A squadron of Hussars, dressed in bright scarlet jackets, rode into the grounds and 'hermetically' sealed off the palace at great speed: no one could leave.[47] Inside the building, Empress Vicky was broken-hearted, her dream of a liberal Germany over. 'Power now belongs to brute force – and to cunning,' she wrote. Shocked, Vicky watched fully armed soldiers emerge 'from behind every tree and statue!' to take possession of her former home.[48] Wilhelm made it clear that he considered his British mother the enemy. After refusing to give his father a state funeral, he ransacked his mother's rooms in the hunt for documents that might incriminate her. Bismarck went so far as to suggest that the Empress had stolen state papers for publication in London.[49] He even encouraged the late Emperor's German doctors to publish a fierce attack on the treatment provided by Morell Mackenzie, his British doctor. Her British background even implicated Vicky as a conspirator in hastening her beloved husband's death.[50] Wilhelm was soon telling anyone who would listen that 'an English doctor killed my father, and an English doctor crippled my arm and this we owe to my mother who would not have Germans around her!'[51]

Vicky retired to Friedrichshof, a new home which she built for herself in Hesse. The vast castle was a faux Gothic mishmash of turrets much beloved by nineteenth-century royals since Queen Victoria and Prince Albert had built Balmoral. The surrounding Taunus Mountains had provided the stone, quarried for the walls, and massive arched windows overlooked 300,000 acres of private park and forests.[52] Here, she created a comfortable feeling of England abroad: the British Royal Family's coat of arms and English family portraits were in evidence everywhere, including a flattering image of an elderly Queen Victoria.[53] Visitors admired the castle as the most modern residence of its day, with electric lights and guest bedrooms with private bathrooms. There was also a vast royal library, and unlike many similar collections, Vicky had read most of the books. In the evening, the Empress would descend the grand staircase, trailing her black robes and veil, for dinner with guests.[54]

Although alienated from his mother, the Kaiser enjoyed a warm relationship with his grandmama, Queen Victoria, and he was adept at writing compliments to her. At first, Victoria attributed Wilhelm's *esprit de contradiction* to his youth: 'It is very likely that it will get better if no notice is taken of it.'[55] Later, the Queen fully grasped her grandson's character flaws and lamented that Germany had fallen to 'that dread tyrant Wilhelm, who makes rows about anything'.[56] Lord Salisbury, Disraeli's successor as Prime Minister, groaned, 'It is evident that the Young Emperor hates us'[57] as he attempted to counterbalance the fallout from what was primarily a family feud.

For the immediate Albany family – Charles Edward, Alice and Helen – life in Potsdam became overshadowed by this increasing rivalry between Britain and Germany. At times, Kaiser Wilhelm could be more English than the English. He made one speech outlining 'a new Triple Alliance between the Teutonic race and the two great trans-Atlantic branches of the Anglo-Saxon race [Britain and America] which would become a potent influence on the future of the world'.[58] Then he would swing erratically in the opposite direction, and the fervour of his anti-British rhetoric appeared increasingly unstable. Following a nosebleed, he stated that he hoped he was losing every drop of his English blood.[59]

Osborne House. 1901.

On 11 January 1901, Queen Victoria took to her bed, suffering from a stroke that left her confused and the right side of her face paralysed. Deteriorating quickly, she lost her sight and drifted into semi-consciousness. The Kaiser rushed from Germany to Osbourne to say goodbye to his grandmother.

None of his British family wanted the Kaiser at the Queen's deathbed, and he stayed in the background, waiting until the last moment when he pushed himself towards her bedside. For once, he was uncharacteristically silent.[60] Queen Victoria died on Tuesday, 22 January 1901, at 6.30 p.m. At the time of her death, she was 81 years old. Her body was taken in the Royal Yacht *Alberta* to Portsmouth, accompanied by the sullen roar of saluting cannons. The new King, Edward VII, followed on board the *Victoria and Albert*, while Emperor Wilhelm was behind him in his imperial yacht. As they approached Portsmouth Harbour, gigantic German battle-ships formed a guard of honour, dwarfing all the other ships.[61] When her funeral cortège made its solemn procession through London, Wilhelm's wreath of white laurel was the largest.

Among the galaxy of brightly uniformed kings and princes that followed walked the 16-year-old Duke of Saxe-Coburg and Gotha.[62] His sister, Princess Alice, found her grandmother's death incomprehensible:

> I had come to regard her as permanent and indestructible … I think it would have been easier for me to imagine England without Windsor or Scotland without Balmoral than either of them without Grandmama.[63]

Five months later, the Kaiser's mother, Empress Vicky, died of cancer. She left the magnificent Friedrichshof Castle to her youngest daughter, Princess Margaret ('Mossie') of Hesse, much to Wilhelm's vexation.

London. 1902.

The new King Edward VII strode around the state rooms at Buckingham Palace, followed by Caesar, his white fox terrier. Barking orders in his gut-tural German accent, he demanded changes.[64] He had waited for many years to become king, and he swiftly dismantled his mother's belongings at the royal residences, destroying all traces of her dowdy regime. Despite suffering from bronchitis, he puffed on his cigars in rooms where Victoria had previously forbidden smoking. Buckingham Palace was utterly transformed by the theatre designer Frank Verity, who imbued the gloomy cluttered palace with a belle époque colour scheme of scarlet, cream and gold, reminiscent of the Ritz Hotel.[65]

Edward VII relished his new role as the 'Uncle of Europe', with his three nephews, Nicholas, Wilhelm and Haakon, occupying the Russian, German and Norwegian thrones. Four of his nieces were also queens or future queens. Edward's coronation at Westminster Abbey on 9 August 1902 was spectacularly stage-managed, and his Danish wife, Queen Alexandra, dazzled everyone. Dressed in golden Indian gauze with a purple velvet train, she wore a specially commissioned new crown set with the massive Koh-i-noor diamond.[66] The day did not unfold entirely smoothly: Archbishop Temple – who, at 81, was frail and blind – placed the crown back to front on the King's head. Charles Edward and Alice sat with the family inside the abbey. Here, the young Princess caught the eye of her cousin, Prince Alexander 'Alge' of Teck, and a new royal romance blossomed.

Claremont, Surrey. 1903.

Finally free from the officious scrutiny of her mother-in-law, Queen Victoria, Duchess Helen returned home to Claremont with her daughter Alice. Charles Edward was now old enough to cope with being Duke of Coburg without his mother and the Duchess was on particularly good terms with the new King. London was quickly becoming the most sophisticated court in Europe; it was 'the' place to be.

More critical for Alice was the fact that handsome Prince Alexander of Teck's regiment, the 7th Hussars, was stationed at Hampton Court, a mere 3 miles from Claremont. Alexander was another minor royal with a dual Anglo-German identity. Despite his German title, he lived in England with a British army career ahead of him. He was also one of Alice's relations – they were second cousins once removed – and this made a good excuse for him to visit the Duchess and her daughter. Fortunately for the romance, Princess Alice bought a new horse that shied whenever she tried to mount the side saddle, so Prince Alexander offered to have the horse trained at the regimental riding school. The horse's erratic behaviour gave him plenty of opportunities to help Alice into the saddle. 'It does not require the exercise of much imagination to visualise how our friendship developed, and his courtship followed,' Alice later wrote in her memoirs.[67] When she announced her engagement that year, her brother wrote to her:

Dearest Tigs,

You cannot tell how awfully pleased I am about your engagement, although it separates us ... You really can't understand how pleased I am that my brother-in-law is an Englishman. I can't help saying this although I ought not to. Alge always was a good friend of mine so I can only say I am really happy that he should be your husband.[68]

Alexander of Teck led precisely the sort of happy life Charles Edward wanted before his grandmother sent him to Germany. Alexander and Alice's wedding occurred in St George's Chapel, Windsor, on 10 February 1904. King Edward VII, who enjoyed few things better than greeting his fellow sovereigns, organised the entire event. The ceremony was a 'spectacular affair': the groom looked handsome in his Hussar uniform, and Princess Alice's dress was a lavish confection of ivory satin charmeuse with a long train. The bride walked up the aisle on her brother's arm. While at the altar, the King waited to give her away. 'Unlike most royal brides,' one guest, Lady Violet Greville, observed, 'this bride looked the picture of happiness.'[69]

After a honeymoon spent at Brocket Hall in Hertfordshire, they moved into their first real home in the Henry III Tower at Windsor Castle, and Alexander transferred to the Royal Horse Guards nearby. Alice was now known as the Princess of Teck. Not only was she the present King's niece and the future monarch's cousin, but she was also sister-in-law to the new Princess of Wales (née Princess Mary of Teck).

While Alice sat at the heart of the British Royal Establishment, Charles Edward came of age in Germany and assumed his full constitutional powers on 19 July 1905 as the sovereign Duke of Saxe-Coburg and Gotha. Three months after his accession, he married the German niece of Empress Dona, the 20-year-old Princess Victoria Adelaide of Schleswig-Holstein-Sonderburg-Glücksberg. The Kaiser chose the bride and 'Charles Edward was ordered to propose, and as usual he did what he was told'.[70] He wrote to his sister, Alice:

Dear Tigs,

I am longing for the time when you will see Victoria, she is such a dear. I am sure that you will appreciate my choice.[71]

The Kaiser was running Charles Edward's entire life. He became a general in the Prussian Guard and the Saxon Hussars and devoted his time to the administration of his estates and duchy. He produced three German sons and two daughters with his German bride. However, for the people of Coburg and Gotha, his Britishness remained an issue: he still spoke German with a British accent. The Coburg press even criticised him for keeping Scottish terriers.

Coburg. 1913.

At 19 years old, Edward, the new Prince of Wales, was handsome in a boyish way: he was slim and rather slight with light brown hair and pale blue eyes. He mixed royal manners and a concern for ordinary people, even if this interest was often superficial and short-lived. Smart, but not particularly academically gifted, at Magdalen College, Oxford, he excelled in the subject only if it interested him.

Edward's parents, King George V and Queen Mary, had succeeded to the throne after the death of his grandfather, Edward VII, in 1910. In 1913, they sent him to Bavaria to visit relatives. It was an opportunity to complete his education, and he got the chance to show off his fluent German. However, Edward was forced to endure daily ordeals of formal court lunches with distant cousins and almost died from boredom. The teenage Prince grew jaded with endless museum visits and carriage drives. The operas were particularly interminable: *Das Rheingold* – 'such a waste of time'; *Siegfried* – 'appallingly dull'; *Der Freischütz* – 'not exciting'. Like most young men, he would have preferred golf or tennis, but duty had to come first.[72] When the Prince of Wales met the Kaiser, he was astonished to find him sitting astride a leather saddle mounted on a wooden block. The Emperor, who was wearing a rather gaudy uniform, explained that he was so accustomed to riding a horse he found a saddle 'more conducive to clear concise thinking'.[73] It was an entertaining visit for Edward, and Wilhelm concluded that his charming guest was 'a young eagle, likely to play a big part in European affairs because he is far from being a pacifist'.[74]

Charles Edward rescued his cousin from the dullness of official duties in Berlin by inviting him deer hunting at Reinhardsbrunn. 'Uncle Charlie' was only ten years older than Edward, and the pair developed a close friendship. At a house party, Prince Edward met Princess Caroline-Matilda of Schleswig-Holstein. Romance soon blossomed, and Princess Alice reported that Caroline-Matilda was 'such a nice girl … much like the others, only taller and very slim'.[75] Her brother-in-law, Prince August Wilhelm of Prussia (the Kaiser's son), was sufficiently encouraged to write to Edward in June 1914 to suggest a wedding match.

The Prince of Wales wrote a reply that he described as 'an awkward job' in his diary and avoided any engagement.[76]

After his German Grand Tour, Edward joined the Grenadier Guards, where life became predictable: riding school, sword drill, care of horses and equipment, marching. 'Not very exciting but anyhow, a definite job which is the gt [sic] thing!!' he wrote.[77] He lived a very closeted existence at the officers' training camp at Aldershot. 'When in camp I make it a rule never to open a newspaper,' he wrote to a friend, 'so am completely ignorant of all happenings in the outer World, except that the Austrian Archduke and his wife have been assassinated. I expect it has caused a stir.'[78]

Sarajevo. 28 June 1914.

Few people shed any tears over the murder of the charmless and authoritarian Archduke Franz Ferdinand of Austria (heir to the Hapsburg Emperor) and his wife Sophie, Duchess of Hohenberg. People danced in the streets of Vienna with joy when the news broke.[79] The murderer, Gavrilo Princip, a pale and thin teenage Serbian terrorist, was a nationalist who wanted freedom from Austrian rule.[80] He shot the Archduke with a Browning 9mm pistol on a bright Sunday morning on 28 June 1914.[81]

At first, no one seemed to anticipate serious fallout from the assassination. King George complained that he had to cancel his annual trip to Goodwood and was regretting the loss of a weekend's sailing at Cowes. The Kaiser was on holiday at the Kiel Regatta, racing yachts and entertaining a squadron of British battlecruisers. The German town was full of British visitors. Although he was angry at the death of one his closest friends, declaring, 'This cowardly despicable crime has shaken me to the depths of my soul,'[82] he did not seem to anticipate severe trouble and commenced his usual summer cruise on the North Sea.

At Windsor Castle, Charles Edward was visiting his sister Alice. Both understood the impact of the events that were quickly unfolding. The Duke of Coburg promptly said goodbye to his sister and returned by boat to Germany with his wife and children on 9 July.[83] Princess Mossie, the Kaiser's sister, was in London, and on 14 July attended a luncheon with George V and Queen Mary, with her two sons Prince Philipp and Prince Wolfgang of Hesse. Rumours of an imminent war alarmed the group and Mossie anxiously contacted the German ambassador in London, Prince Lichnowsky. Although he attempted to reassure them, they quickly embarked on one of the last passenger ships allowed to leave Britain before the wartime travel embargo started.[84]

The Kaiser's brother, Prince Henry of Prussia, was yachting at Cowes when he heard about Austria's ultimatum to Serbia (that the Serbian government would accept an Austro-Hungarian inquiry into the assassination). Henry made an informal visit to George V at Buckingham Palace on 26 July, asking him what England's position would be.[85] Fatally, both these two amateur diplomats misunderstood what the other had said: King George claimed that he told Prince Henry that in the event of a German war against Russia and France, it would be impossible for Britain 'not to be dragged' into conflict.[86] In contrast, Prince Henry wrote to his brother saying the King had said, 'We shall try all we can to keep out of this and remain neutral.'[87] It was an exchange that exposed the ineptitude of royal diplomacy.

Just as it seemed that the crisis might blow over, Austria declared war on Serbia on 28 July; events then unfolded with a shattering rapidity. Following years of aggressive nationalism and militarism, tensions exploded, and the complex system of defensive alliances that divided Europe into two camps became relevant. Queen Victoria's great dream had been to create a network of marriages uniting Europe, but instead, by 1914, a pattern of political alliances had emerged, cutting across family loyalties and ties. Politics was no longer a family business. Germany and Austria stood on one side, with Britain, Russia and France confronting them. 'Where will it end?' the King wrote in his diary.

On 4 August 1914, George V wrote:

I held a council at 10.45 to declare war with Germany. It is a terrible catastrophe, but it is not our fault … Please to God; it may soon be over.[88]

Outside Buckingham Palace, there was an enormous roar along the Mall as over 6,000 people waited, cheering and singing for the King and Queen to appear on the balcony with the Prince of Wales – three figures of reassurance. The following day, a team of British workmen removed the imperial eagle from its perch over the entrance to the German Embassy.[89] All Anglo-German ties that had been built up over time were severed – in culture, trade and business – as well as the Royal Family.

Having lost her brother to fight for the Kaiser, Alice then watched her husband head to Windmill Hill to be with his regiment. Three weeks later, he left for Belgium to fight against Germany on 8 October. Alice then wrote:

After much diplomatic bungling, the great powers allowed the actions of an anarchist half-wit to plunge the world into the most sanguinary war that has ever afflicted mankind since the dawn of civilisation.[90]

Charles Edward was commissioned as a general in the German army, but he never held a command. He became a 'chocolate soldier', a derogatory label denoting a soldier who cannot fight, but who looks good in a uniform. It was a term popularised in George Bernard Shaw's play *Arms and the Man* (1894). The young Duke of Coburg merely visited 'his' Coburg troops and carried out various 'research' trips that followed a certain pattern: a sightseeing trip around a trench, meeting a few ordinary soldiers, then handing out medals, photographs and a good dinner with high-ranking officers. In fact, Charles Edward spent most of his time behind the front line, dining at casinos.[91] Nonetheless, he turned his back on Britain, where he was now considered an enemy alien, to focus entirely on the survival of his German duchy, declaring in 1914:

> I have renounced my position as chief of the Seaforth-Highlanders regiment because I cannot be ... in charge of a regiment which belongs to a country that has attacked us in the most despicable way.[92]

London. 13 June 1917.

On 13 June 1917, Londoners gazed up 'wonderstruck' at the sight of the German Gotha aircraft hovering 'like hawks over a dovecot'.[93] With their giant 78ft wingspan, these planes were the first bombers with sufficient range to reach the capital and they had been manufactured at factories in Charles Edward's Gotha duchy. The first bomb was dropped on London at 11.30 a.m. in Barking. Seven more fell on East Ham, killing four people. William Walker, a commercial traveller, wrote:

> Over my head were a number of what looked like large white butterflies. Now puffs of smoke were breaking high in the air around them ... Soon came the frequent dull bloom, then a horrid crash. I ran across the street. Three people laid out at my feet. The gutters were running red.[94]

Between 11.40 a.m. and 11.42 a.m., seventy-two bombs fell from the sky onto Liverpool Street station. Two bombs burst through the high arched glass roof and blew two trains apart. Three men burned to death and others were trapped knee-deep in the shattered glass. Siegfried Sassoon, the war poet, was on the station platform at the time. As he remembered later:

> [I] stood wondering what to do, a luggage trolley was trundled past me; on it lay an elderly man, shabbily dressed and apparently dead … In the trench, one was acclimatised to the notion of being exterminated, and there is a sense of organised retaliation. But here one was help-less; an invisible enemy sent destruction spinning down from a fine weather sky.[95]

At 11.45 a.m., a 50kg bomb struck the roof of the Upper Street North School in Poplar. Six hundred pupils attended the school that day, and one of the older girls in the top-floor classroom remembered: '[A] horrible vibration shook the whole building as the bomb exploded and I was flung down several stone steps … I ran home as I have never run home before.'[96] Soldiers and police officers found 'many of the little ones were lying across their desks, apparently dead, and with terrible wounds on heads and limbs, and scores of others were writhing with pain and moaning pitifully … bodies were mutilated.' One mother could recognise her dead son only by the new button she had sewn onto his shirt the evening before. A child covered from head to foot in TNT powder was mistaken as being Chinese and was taken to Chinatown by a well-meaning adult in the hope some-one there would recognise him.[97]

Eighteen children at the school died, and another thirty were griev-ously injured but survived. On 20 June 1917, a public funeral was held for the victims. The tiny coffins lay on trestle tables in rows. It was the biggest funeral London's East End had ever witnessed. Thousands attended and lined the route to All Saints Church in Poplar and 600 wreaths filled the town hall opposite. Door-to-door collections raised £1,500 to build a memorial, and the self-possessed understated inscription read: '18 children were killed by a bomb dropped by a German aeroplane'.[98]

The Gotha planes had spent just ninety minutes in British airspace, but had managed to unload 4 tonnes of bombs on London, killing 162 people and injuring 432. London erupted with further fury: East Enders took to the streets, attacking people with German-sounding names as xenophobia escalated and the people looked for scapegoats. Wild stories spread. Lights were signalling to the German planes where to drop bombs; German gro-cers were poisoning food supplies; German nurses were murdering patients and German barbers were cutting their customers' throats. People attacked

German shops and ransacked their houses in Tottenham, Highgate and Hackney. Anti-German sentiment became a pretext for looting. The *Daily Mail* printed a 'Reprisal Map' showing all German cities within striking distance of the Allied front lines.[99] *The Times* wrote, 'If it were possible … to increase the utter and almost universal detestation with which he [the Kaiser] is held by the people of this country, he did it by bombing the school.'[100]

This raid by the Gotha G.IV bomber planes placed the King's German heritage under attack. The family surname was Saxe-Coburg-Gotha, and the Herzog (Duke) Charles Edward Academy had trained the pilots flying them.[101] Perception was everything. H.G. Wells jeered at the monarch's 'alien and uninspiring court'. George V retorted, in a rare display of wit, 'I may be uninspiring, but I'll be damned if I'm an alien.'[102]

There were rumours of a vast 50,000-strong network of German spies, called the 'Unseen Hand', operating in Britain. This paranoia intensified, and by January 1917 there was an ugliness to the capital as the war was going badly for the Allies at this point. Conscientious objectors had always been heavily criticised, but the net widened to include any social outsider: artists, homosexuals, poets and foreigners (not just German) suspected of disloyalty. One article appeared claiming that the German Secret Service had identified a group of Jews, dissolute aristocrats, intellectuals and painters as targets for blackmail. Lord Kitchener 'had solemnly to assure the Cabinet that the lights seen flashing near Sandringham during an air sortie were caused by the car lights of the rector returning home after dinner' and not by a fifth columnist.[103]

Duchess Helen quietly stayed out of the public eye; she had never been a Prussian and detested the aggressive Prussian policy that had led to war.[104] Determined to fight back against the mistrust surrounding her, she quietly immersed herself in war work at Princess Beatrice's War Hospital Supply Depot in Cavendish Square,[105] and with the help of a nun called Sister Agnes, she converted Claremont into an officers' convalescent home.[106] However, John Swift MacNeill, a constitutional scholar and Member of Parliament, condemned Duchess Helen's son in the House of Commons, and demanded to know what steps would be taken to ensure that the Duke of Coburg and the Royal Family's other German cousins 'shall no longer retain United Kingdom peerages and titles and a seat in the House of Lords?'[107] At first, Prime Minister Asquith, supported by his successor, David Lloyd George, was reluctant to attack the King's relatives, but another MP, Horatio Bottomley, editor of the tabloid magazine *John Bull*, contributed relentlessly to the campaign and made himself the self-appointed spokesman for the 'man in the street'.[108] Finally, Parliament passed the Titles Deprivation Act of 1917 and Charles Edward was declared a traitor peer in Parliament and lost his British title, Duke of Albany, and property in England, with Claremont House confiscated. George V gave a very grateful Duchess Helen a new home at Kensington Palace.[109]

As families started to mourn their casualties, this wave of anti-German feeling continued. A crisis gripped the Royal Family's Anglo-German identity. In what historian Kenneth Rose termed 'a momentary loss of nerve',[110] George V decided to create a smokescreen around his German origins and ordered a change in the family name from the House of Saxe-Coburg and Gotha to something that sounded British. Lord Stamfordham, the King's trusted Private Secretary, was instructed to come up with a new family name. He probed the archives and history books but struggled to find a name untainted by the Crown's bloody past: this discounted Tudor, Stuart and Plantagenet. In a memorandum from 15 May 1917, Stamfordham wrote: 'The King bars Plantagenet and does not care about Tudor. Tudor-Stuart has been suggested.'[111] At Windsor Castle, Stamfordham struck inspiration and wrote to the Prime Minister: 'I hope we may have finally discovered a name which will appeal to you, and that is that Queen Victoria will be regarded as having founded the House of Windsor.'[112] In Germany, Kaiser Wilhelm ridiculed his cousin's change of name, declaring he was looking forward to a performance of 'The Merry Wives of Saxe-Coburg-Gotha'.[113]

Such family rebranding almost immediately had its desired effect and the British people were delighted with the pronouncement. One member of the public, Colonel Unsworth, wrote to Lord Stamfordham on 18 July 1917:

> Their strong efforts to remove, in every possible way, the German influence and power from the Court will have its fruit in the affection and loyalty of their devoted subjects.[114]

Queen Victoria's tremendous extended Royal Family of Europe was – on the surface – now collapsing, and her grandson Kaiser Wilhelm II, who had so wanted to be feted and admired in Britain, instead found himself depicted in propaganda posters as a blood-soaked tyrant hunched over dead bodies.[115]

SEPARATE WAYS

London. June 1914.
The First World War split the Windsor–Coburg family.

While the Duke of Coburg fought for the Kaiser in Germany, his cousin, Prince Edward of Wales, joined the British army. Like many the patriotic youths who had volunteered at the beginning of the war and eager for 'glorious adventure', Edward never questioned the realities of war.[1] His father, George V, signed his commission for the Grenadier Guards in June 1914, waiving the height requirement of 6 feet. Being the King's son was compensation enough for Edward's modest 5 feet 7 inches. He described himself as 'a pygmy amongst giants' amidst the group of hardened soldiers.[2]

After ten days' training at the spartan Warley Barracks in Essex, with its garret rooms, Prince Edward quartered at the Wellington Barracks near Buckingham Palace and was grateful for the comfort of a two-room suite. Edward deceived himself into thinking that he would receive the treatment of an ordinary officer; he even told himself that was what he wanted. When his regiment left for France without him, he wrote, 'It is terrible being left behind!'[3]

Haunted by the notion of not being able to fight, Edward confronted Lord Kitchener, the Secretary of State for War. In the grim formality of the War Office, he came face to face with that terrifying warlord with the steely blue eyes. The diminutive Prince made a plea to fight.

'What does it matter if I am killed?' he argued. 'I have four brothers.'[4]

Kitchener was not for budging. 'If I were sure you would be killed, I do not know if I should be right to restrain you. But I cannot take the chance … of the enemy taking you prisoner.'[5]

As Secretary of State for War, Kitchener's decision was final.

Due to his lack of combat experience, Edward felt a stark sense of inferiority when in the company of fighting men. He wrote disparagingly in his diary that Kitchener was a 'great fat bloated man',[6] but five months later, Edward finally received the overseas posting he wanted.

In November 1914, Edward arrived in France, a mixture of regal manners and immature, childish jokes; an ex-public schoolboy who delighted in dirty stories. Unlike ordinary enlisted men, Edward took his valet, driver and a convertible Rolls-Royce. This car was discreetly parked in a garage and used for weekend trips to Paris when he had leave. Occasionally, he did bits of paperwork – poorly – and conducted cursory inspections. To keep him out of danger, his superior officers contrived things for him to do. These visits, particularly one to a front-line hospital, left unforgettable impressions. When doctors hid one patient out of royal sight because of his terrible disfigurement, the Prince drew back the curtains that concealed him and kissed what remained of the man's forehead.[7] These public shows of empathy endeared the future King to his subjects. In 1914, it was unprecedented for a Royal Family member of his status to have this common touch.

Prince Edward felt frustration at having no real function. 'I feel I'm the only man here in North France who is unemployed and without a job.'[8] After yet more lobbying, Edward joined the Guards Division as they prepared for the Battle of Loos in September 1915. These endless, hideously costly attacks produced nothing but the occupation of a few extra feet of trenches, and thousands died.

Passchendaele. June 1917.

Prince Edward never stopped wanting to be in the front line, although he hated it when he was there. In June 1917, he rose at 4 a.m. to go to the trenches, 'and how I loathed it!!! But frightened tho' [sic] I am, I should honestly loathe it still more if I never went forward!!'[9]

On 5 November 1917, when Edward was at Passchendaele, three shells whizzed overhead: two near misses in one morning that could have been fatal. He dived from his observation post into the safety of a dugout among the bombed-out leftovers of Langemarck Church. Panic gripped him. The third shell fell: a direct hit.[10]

Crouched and hidden in his foxhole alongside men from the Welsh Guards, Edward escaped the bombardment – but only just. The noise overhead was harsh and without music, unremitting torture to the eardrums; so loud that it was impossible to hear the voice of the man standing

beside him. The shelling gave off the burnt whiff of detonation, but the
overpowering odour of unwashed bodies, impossible to avoid at such
close quarters, was more suffocating. Added to this was the toxic smell
of the battlefield – a lingering odour of gas, stinking mud mixed with
open latrines, putrid corpses, the stench of chloride and lime laid down to
eliminate infections.[11]

By 1917, military ambition had sunk into a sea of mud and the
task now became the futile act of trying to capture the ruined village
of Passchendaele. It rained every day, and the mud became ever deeper.
Soldiers even drowned in mud on the battlefield.[12] Tanks and horses
sank beneath it; the dirt became mixed with blood. Injured soldiers, both
British and German, cried out to stretcher-bearers for help; the lucky
ones remained unconscious. Shells ripped men to pieces; there were no
neat bullet holes in tunics.[13] Only the fools were not scared. Edward lost
many friends in those wartime months: Lord Desmond Fitzgerald, Major
Cadogan and Prince Maurice of Battenberg, his cousin.[14]

And still, it rained and rained; water flowed along the bottom of the
trenches. Soldiers stood on ammunition boxes until they sank into the
mud as though it were quicksand. Then they would put the second box on
top and stand on that.[15]

After Prince Edward narrowly avoided being hit by shells, headquarters
assigned him to His Majesty's Brigade of Guards. Edward knew most of
the officers from childhood dancing classes, from Oxford, from country-
house shooting weekends, fox hunting and London parties. Everyone
called the Brigade 'the best club in town': elite, snobbish and fixed rigidly
by tradition. Even in the trenches, they ate plovers' eggs, foie gras, roast
woodcock, cold partridge and Port-Salut cheese.[16]

Edward's duties became confined to collecting materials for reports and
inspecting ammunition dumps. With his Rolls-Royce hidden away, he
took to using a more classless bicycle as transport. The top brass's automo-
biles frequently honked infantrymen off the road into ditches and splashed
them with mud; it was an irritating reminder of class and rank. Keenly
aware of the troubles of ordinary people, Edward avoided such displays
of inequality. He boosted his popularity in the mess room by democrati-
cally sharing the contents of his weekly Fortnum and Mason hampers.
Consequently, the Prince's departure was a cause for sincere regret amongst
his fellow officers.[17]

Edward spent nine months of 1917, through the coldest winter of the
war, living in a camp of canvas huts.[18] He wrote to his father while on

night duty on 31 July 1917, describing life on the front line as 'the nearest thing possible to Hell, whatever that is!!!'[19]

There had been moments of escape. Back in May 1916, he had visited a brothel in Calais with fellow officers and watched naked prostitutes performing an erotic tableau. The Prince, a 'late developer', found the scenes 'perfectly filthy and revolting sights, but interesting for me as it was my first insight into these things!!!'[20]

Claud Hamilton and Joey Leigh, his two equerries, decided that Edward needed to lose his virginity. After much wine, the pair delivered him into the arms of a prostitute called Paulette in Amiens. 'She brushed aside his extraordinary shyness,' recorded Lord Esher, to whom the Prince described the incident.[21] Later on one of his regular trips to Paris, in July 1917, he spent a 'day's bliss' in the arms of a second prostitute called Maggy. He wrote her love letters which he would later regret:

> Oh! Those bloody letters ... How I curse myself now, tho' if only I can square this case it will be the last one, and she's the only pol [prostitute] I've written to and the last!! ... I'm afraid she's the £100,000 or nothing type, tho' I must say I'm disappointed and didn't think she'd turn nasty.[22]

London. 1917.
Back at home, George V and Queen Mary threw themselves into an austerity drive. King George closed Balmoral, turned the gardens at Frogmore into a potato patch, and switched off the heating at Buckingham Palace. Boiled fowl and mutton replaced poussin and lamb. These right-minded gestures saved money to hand back to the Treasury, although the country at large did not experience much rationing until the last year of the war.[23]

There was also the unrelenting slog of new royal obligations: 450 military inspections, 300 hospital visits, 50,000 medals and decorations personally pinned on, four trips to the Western Front and seven naval reviews. After one outing to the French front line, George V wrote of driving through 'ruined villages and towns, utterly destroyed by shell fire'. It was a 'harrowing sight', recorded Lady Airlie, Queen Mary's lady-in-waiting:

> A vast stretch of land that had once been fertile and smiling with crops, but was now only a tumbled mass of blackened earth fringed by sparse and splintered trees ... We climbed over a mound composed of German dead ... all that was left of a whole regiment who had died in wrestling a strip of land from Our troops, only to lose it again ... We stood there

speechless. It was impossible to find words. The Queen's face was ashen, and her lips were tightly compressed. I felt that like me she was afraid of breaking down.[24]

Distrust and widespread suspicion towards Germany and anything remotely German remained pervasive in Britain. All the King's Anglo-German relatives living in London and the home counties followed George V's lead of changing the family name from Saxe-Coburg and Gotha to Windsor. Each branch of the family picked a new surname that sounded less alien.

Queen Mary's two brothers, both senior officers in the British army, dropped the German name of Teck and were awarded British peerages in compensation. Prince Adolphus, the Duke of Teck, became Adolphus Cambridge, Marquess of Cambridge; and Prince Alexander of Teck morphed into Alexander Cambridge, Earl of Athlone. Alexander declined the higher title of Marquess because he felt it sounded too foreign. His wife, Princess Alice, the Duke of Coburg's sister, became Princess Alice, Countess of Athlone. Privately, Adolphus regarded this new 'camouflage' as 'stupid and petty'.[25]

Prince Louis of Battenberg, the Admiral of the British Fleet, was also transformed into the Marquess of Milford Haven. He also anglicised the family surname to Mountbatten. Princess Victoria, his wife, stopped using her German title, Princess of Hesse, and adopted the title Marchioness of Milford Haven. Louis found his new name 'a terrible break with one's past', and while staying as a houseguest wrote in the visitor's book, 'Arrived Prince Jekyll. Departed Lord Hyde.'[26] After false whispers circulated that the Admiral-Prince was the Kaiser's spy, this paranoid anti-German gossip forced him to resign from the British navy. George V wrote: 'I feel for him deeply, there is no more loyal man in the country.'[27] In a show of public support, the King appointed him to the hollow distinction of the Privy Council.

Finally, two of Queen Victoria's granddaughters, Princess Marie Louise and Princess Helena Victoria of Schleswig-Holstein, dropped their territorial designation 'of Schleswig-Holstein' and were know entirely by their Christian names.

Berlin. January 1918.

By 1918, Germany had started to lose the war as the Allies broke through the front line. On 29 October 1918, Kaiser Wilhelm, who was now personally powerless and cut off from reality, left Berlin for the Imperial Army headquarters at Spa in Belgium. Day after day, he sat by the fireplace in his gloomy, fog-shrouded lodgings, occasionally venturing out for brief walks and then returning to argue with his generals. General Hindenburg replaced the Kaiser as Supreme Warlord, and Prince Maximilian of Baden became the new Chancellor. Wilhelm complained, 'I may as well abdicate.'[28]

On 3 November, sailors stationed at Kiel mutinied. They demanded political reform and the removal of the Royal Family. A general strike broke out in Berlin, and members of the communist Spartacist League shouted revolution. After weeks in isolation, the Kaiser was shocked by the notion that the German people wanted him removed. He wavered about what to do next. Frustrated by Wilhelm's unrealistic outlook, Prince Maximilian announced on 9 November, without warning, that the Kaiser had abdicated. Wilhelm shouted, 'Treachery, treachery, shameless, outrageous, treachery!'[29]

Back in Berlin, the insurgents fittingly stole the Emperor's clothes from the Kaiser's wardrobe. Wholly crushed and broken, the Kaiser seemed terrified of being left alone. Only after a long argument with his generals did he finally agree to board a special train for neutral Holland, where Queen Wilhelmina of the Netherlands offered him political asylum. His first words on arrival in Utrecht were, 'How about a cup of good, hot, real English tea?'[30]

King George V wrote that he regarded his cousin as 'the greatest criminal known for having plunged the world into this ghastly war', although he opposed Lloyd George's proposal to 'hang the Kaiser'.[31]

In Parliament, MPs suggested that he be put on trial at Dover Castle or exiled to the remote Falkland Islands.[32] Eventually, the Kaiser bought an elegant manor house, surrounded by an English garden, at Doorn, in Holland. He was permitted to travel only within a 15-mile 'free-zone' surrounding his house, or he had to give notice to a minor local government official. After moving in on 15 May 1920, he rarely journeyed outside the 'free' limit because he disliked having to kowtow to anyone. Train wagons transported around 30,000 objects from Wilhelm's former palaces in Berlin and Potsdam, including silver, porcelain and baroque art, to ensure the former Emperor enjoyed a lavish lifestyle in his new house.[33]

Further misfortune struck when the Kaiser's youngest son, Prince Joachim of Prussia, shot himself at the family's hunting lodge in Potsdam. After his father's abdication, the 29-year-old Prince felt dejected and unable to accept his new status as a commoner. *The New York Times* reported that he had been in financial straits and suffered from 'great mental depression'.[34] The Prince had run up enormous gambling debts, and his wife had divorced him – both contributing factors to his suicide.[35] Following her son's death, the Empress rarely left her bed, scarcely slept and was semi-conscious most of the time. She finally died, broken by grief, on 12 April 1921. There were no letters of condolence from Britain, except a message from Wilhelm's aunt, Princess Beatrice, whom the Kaiser had always disliked.[36]

In exile, the Kaiser shocked visitors with his bitterness towards his English cousins. Still looking for a scapegoat, he maintained that the 'betrayal' of the German people in November 1919 was caused by 'a rabble of Jews'.[37] He even said it was right that the German people faced starvation after everything they had done to him.

Coburg. November 1918.

The carnage and slaughter of the First World War destroyed forever the myth that the interrelatedness of royal families prevented conflict in Europe. Eight million people were dead, and Europe was traumatised. Across post-war Germany, workers raised red flags and sang the 'Internationale'. The old ruling classes shuddered at the thought of what might happen. The downfall of the Tsar and the murder of the Romanovs in Ekaterinburg on 17 July 1918 showed how vulnerable the ruling families were to political upheaval. The German troops, on their return from the front, had become infected with Bolshevik ideas as they found famine and unemployment prevailing in many parts of Germany.

The German press called Charles Edward 'Mr Albany': a notice from both socialists and communists that they regarded him as an unwanted foreigner. Pressures amplified on 11 November 1918, when 1,000 citizens paraded through Coburg demanding Charles Edward's abdication. Hermann Quarck, the Prime Minister of Coburg, skilfully charmed the mostly middle-class Social Democratic Party into remaining loyal. However, the political landscape was entirely different in left-wing Gotha, where the population was primarily working class; there, collapsing living conditions had led to starvation. A radical SDP splinter group, calling itself the Independent Social Democratic Party, demanded strike action. Gotha ousted the Duke and declared itself ruled by a Workers' and Soldiers' Council.[38]

After the House of Commons had removed Charles Edward's British titles, sold Claremont House, and declared him a traitor, he had nowhere to turn. His only connection to Britain was a discreet correspondence to his sister, Princess Alice, who sent him his belongings from his old home. Charles Edward thanked her in a letter:

> It was so nice to have the old furniture and pictures about one, although it makes one very sad to know, one will never see dear old Claremont again as it was. I can only always repent this damned war.[39]

Struggling with the realities of post-war Germany, Charles Edward suffered painfully from arthritis. When Lieutenant Colonel Stewart Roddie, a British officer, visited him in November 1919, he was walking on crutches:

> He [Duke Charles Edward] arrived unattended in a 'Victoria' [carriage] drawn by two fat little ponies – a young man still in his 30s, grey and pathetically thin … 'Why,' I asked him … 'did you send that telegram home at the beginning of the war? You were an Honorary Colonel of one of the finest British regiments, and you telegraphed saying you were ashamed of having worn a British uniform.'
>
> Charles Edward sank his head upon his hands, and when he had sufficiently overcome his emotion, he whispered, 'That telegram. Oh, that telegram. I was an Englishman who had become a German. They knew I wasn't really one, and they would not believe that I was utterly loyal. They mistrusted me without cause. When I accepted the Dukedom of Coburg, I accepted all the obligations that went with it. Germany was now my country. But they knew what England meant to me, and in order to disabuse the army of any suspicion of wavering loyalty on my part, I was given that telegram to sign … no one will, or ever can, know what that has cost me.'[40]

It would be three years before the Duke of Coburg saw his mother Helen and sister Alice in London. A year later, Duchess Helen visited him again at Hinterriss Castle in Austria, but she was dying. She passed away quite suddenly from a heart condition on 19 September 1922, and her family buried her quietly in Austria.[41]

Friedrichshof Castle. 1918.
The British Royal Family was more forgiving towards their Hesse relatives, who had the advantage of not being Prussian. King George sent them a message to Friedrichshof Castle, saying 'how glad they were to be in contact again', and 'their warm feelings for Hesse had not suffered because of the war'.[42]

Princess Margaret (Mossie) of Hesse had sat out the war in the imposing surroundings of Friedrichshof Castle, which she had inherited from her English mother, Empress Vicky. Margaret was the most popular of Kaiser Wilhelm's sisters, she had been a regular guest at Buckingham Palace and led an almost semi-nomadic life between Germany and Britain before the war. Always quick to emphasise her British connections, the Princess had employed English nannies to raise her six sons: Friedrich William, Maximilian, Philipp, Wolfgang, Richard and Christoph.

Prince Philipp of Hesse was an artistic bisexual who travelled throughout the war accompanied by his pet dog.[43] Despite not being promising soldier material, he joined the Grand Ducal Hessian Prince Dragoon Regiment after Germany invaded Belgium. His younger brother Maximilian followed his example. Wolfgang and Friedrich William joined the Sixth Ulan cavalry regiment, while Richard and Christoph were too young to enlist.

Prince Maximilian was the first to be killed, at St-Jean-Chappel near Bailleul, in Flanders, on 12 October 1914. He was only 20 years old and his mother's favourite. After being severely injured in machine-gun fire, Maximilian was taken to the nearby monastery at Mont des Cats, where the monks cared for him until he died. Prince Friedrich William had his throat cut by a bayonet during close fighting at Curu Orman in Romania on 12 September 1916. Comrades found him dead, with a blood-speckled dagger resting on his chest.[44]

Now the war was over, visitors to Friedrichshof Castle found the gates kept shut and locked. The French were coming, and the family privately mourned their dead, bitter from grief. Under the terms of the Armistice, French troops marched into the Rhineland, and their castle stood in the occupied zone. Soon, foreign soldiers were everywhere – the railway stations, in town squares and billeted in homes – as a large military organisation superimposed itself on the civilian population.

Princess Margaret was now virtually under house arrest. Although closely related to the British Royal Family, she was also sister to the Kaiser. Her position in the new Republic was unenviable. Grief-struck by the deaths of her two sons, she was forced to shut down three-quarters of her home and move into the servants' wing while the Allies billeted French troops in the castle. Should any members of the family choose to leave the castle grounds, they had to proceed through a pathway railed by barbed wire. At the gate, they had to state to a guard where they were going, why, and for how long.

After visiting the Duke of Coburg, Colonel Roddie stayed at Friedrichshof. He described the Princess during this period: 'In her long, severe black dress with little collar and cuff of white lawn she made a picture of infinite sadness.'[45] Roddie felt the Princess's treatment by the French was 'degrading and unnecessary', mainly because soldiers guarding the gates were 'black'. He wrote how horrified he was to find the castle overrun by colonial troops from Senegal and viewed this as a French attempt to humiliate the Kaiser's sister. Over 40,000 black colonial soldiers occupied the Rhineland, and the French regularly organised torchlit parades of these troops to remind Germans that they had lost the war. 'I shall never forget,' one American visitor wrote, 'the looks on the faces of those silent Germans who stood watching that parade.'[46] Roddie wrote to Field Marshal Sir William Wilson:

> I believe that the utterly erroneous belief exists that the castle [Friedrichshof] is the property of the ex-Kaiser. [However] the castle was built by the late Empress to her lasting memory of the England that she loved ... a little piece of England in her adopted land ... the contents of the house were her personal, private belongings – many of them mementoes of England – and that she left all this to her youngest daughter to be kept and cared for ... The Princess to whom the castle now belongs is the devoted daughter of an Englishwoman ... She mourns the loss of her eldest sons, both killed in the War.
>
> It would be a gracious and generous act if the French would secure Princess [Margaret] of Hesse ... her uninterrupted occupation of Friedrichshof ... This would be a compliment to Great Britain, a generous and charitable consideration to a deeply suffering woman.[47]

Sir Henry had sent Roddie's message to Field Marshal Foch, who swiftly removed the troops. 'I think sometimes miracles do happen,' said the Princess.[48]

During these troubled times, the Hesse family kept a low profile as they juggled the French occupation with a new threat from local communists. The assassination of the Russian Imperial Family played on everyone's mind – the murdered Tsarina Alexandra was a former Hessian princess. At one stage, panic-stricken employees warned the family that revolutionary units were about to descend on the castle. However, all that happened was an isolated incident in which local workers stole a car and drove around Frankfurt in it, waving the Red Flag.

3

FEAR

Berlin. 1919.

During the winter, Berlin was never an optimistic place: clouds hung low, and the austere architecture looked drab and menacing. The German capital was defeated after the First World War, crowded with the remains of the beaten army and refugees from the Russian Revolution. A group of sailors occupied the Presidential Palace, preventing the newly elected President Ebert from moving in until officials bribed them to leave. Hard-left Spartacist rebels demanded that workers bring down Ebert's new moderate socialist government, and in the streets, they clashed with right-wing militias, called the Freikorps, who prowled the city.

Initially, these militias represented an attempt by professional soldiers to rebuild the defeated army, but this ambition rapidly fragmented into a collection of 200 piratical gangs. Such groups were symptomatic of the times, filled with men who felt betrayed and cheated by fate.[1] With over 250,000 unemployed living in Berlin alone, recruitment from amongst the discarded was straightforward. One function of the Freikorps was to divert the working classes away from Bolshevism towards *völkisch* (populist) nationalism. Most aristocrats and members of the upper classes supported the Freikorps.

In Coburg, Duke Charles Edward gave money to a former naval captain, Hermann Ehrhardt. He was a handsome and charismatic Freikorps leader who commanded 6,000 men called the Marine Brigade. Charles Edward hoped that Ehrhardt's brutal methods would help restore his confiscated lands and solve the problem of Gotha communists.[2]

Princess Margaret's 22-year-old son, Prince Wolfgang of Hesse, also joined the Freikorps. He was determined to protect the family, and he helped put down revolutionary disturbances in nearby Kassel. Not surprisingly, the remaining Hesse brothers joined militia units for security. Prince Philipp joined the Transitional Army (*Übergangheer*) where he met future Nazi leaders, such as SS General Karl Wolff, while Prince Christoph and Prince Richard became auxiliaries (*Hilfsdienst*), aged just 17, in projects started at their school to guard transport carriages.[3]

With more communists in Berlin than anywhere outside Soviet Russia, an uprising was inevitable. The Spartacist rebellion started on a cold Monday morning on 4 January 1919, and most of Berlin's shops, factories, transport and electricity suppliers closed down. However, the communist rebels' lack of clarity immobilised their strategy.

President Ebert's right-hand man, the sinister War Minister Gustav Noske, understood that the Freikorps was the only force that could stand between their government and this communist putsch. On 9 January 1919, he sent 1,200 militia members into the headquarters of the socialist newspaper *Vörwart*, the main Spartacist stronghold, which was defended by 350 barricaded rebels armed with rifles. It was the beginning of the end for the revolution as, street by street, the Freikorps crushed the Spartacists.[4] The two Spartacist leaders, Karl Liebknecht and Rosa Luxemburg, were arrested on 15 January by Waldemar Pabst, a Freikorps captain whose thugs tortured and beat them. One witness said: 'I shall never forget how they knocked the poor woman down and dragged her around.'[5] Rosa was left limping and dazed from a beating with a rifle butt. A lieutenant called Kurt Vogel put a pistol to her head and blew her brains out in a back alley. Troopers threw her corpse into the Landwehr Canal. Vogel also lied about killing Liebknecht, and the official declaration stated he died while struggling to escape.

The Weimar Constitution was declared the law on 11 August 1919. Drafted by Professor Hugo Preuss, a Jewish liberal, he pieced together all the best bits of other Western democracies: an elected Head of State, like the United States; minority interests protected through proportional representation, like France; a Chancellor, who like the British Prime Minister, was accountable to Parliament. However, there were two inherent weaknesses: the provincial autonomy of the state government allowed the Nazi Party to flourish, while Article 48, empowering a president to rule by decree, eventually allowed for Hitler's rise to power.[6]

Coburg. October 1919.
Republicanism did not destroy the power of Germany's old princely families. Adopting a policy of compromise, the Weimar politicians planned to

integrate the princely families into their new democracy. While Duke Charles Edward lost all constitutional authority as a sovereign ruler, he remained a duke in name, at least. However, he had to negotiate a financial settlement with the new regional governments in both Coburg and Gotha.

Conservative Coburg quickly struck a deal with Charles Edward, and he received compensation when the ducal museum, art collection and theatre passed into state ownership. He could still occupy Coburg Castle (the official residence of the Coburg dukes) and he kept valuable farming estates, as well as two other castles, Callenberg and Rosenau, as his private possessions. He also held onto various Austrian properties, including a third castle in Hinterriss. However, in 'Red Gotha', the situation was radically different. Gotha capped the Duke's compensation at 1 million marks (£3.2 million), which would have seen him lose 96 per cent of his assets. When Charles Edward rejected their offer, the Gotha government nationalised the Duke's entire estate.[7] Charles Edward picked up his pen and wrote angrily to his sister in London, Princess Alice, in October 1919:

> Gotha continues to behave disgracefully, but they are driving it to such a point now, that the Bauern [peasants] have at last woken up and are preparing to fight the government there. It is too disappointing after all the trouble one had to bring Gotha on. The word 'thanks' is at present unknown in Germany. I never thought that German civilisation was so near the surface … I get on quite well with the present blighters in power here in Coburg, which is a great help. One even asked my advice the other day … what do you say to that?[8]

Eventually, the German courts declared Gotha's actions unlawful. Charles Edward became a rich man again when the courts restored 37.2 million Reichsmarks' (£122 million) worth of land and art to him in 1925. Despite this reversal of fortune, he continued to fear a communist take-over, as his letters to Alice reveal:

> I only hope our winter will remain quiet, but the Russians seem to be getting our communists on the move … In different parts of Germany, they have begun attacking our nationalists, but have luckily been beaten off with cracked crowns. If only the leaders would leave the workmen in peace. They are so sensible when they are not poisoned.[9]

Versailles. June 1919.

Ebert's first task as president was to negotiate the peace terms with the Allies. The Armistice signed in 1918 had been only a cease-fire, nothing more. Germany's Foreign Minister, Count Ulrich von Brockdorff-Rantzau – a thin, bloodless aristocrat with a monocle – was dispatched by Ebert to negotiate at the peace conference in Versailles. Crossing the French border in a private train, Brockdorff could see the devastation the German troops had inflicted on the French countryside. When they arrived, the French isolated the German party in a remote hotel surrounded by barbed wire. The unwelcoming French staff made them carry their baggage upstairs.

Their uneasy confinement lasted a week until Brockdorff was finally summoned and appeared before the Allies in the famous Hall of Mirrors. There would be no discussion, and the Allies forced the Germans to accede to brutal terms. They calculated reparations at 132 million marks (£284 billion in 2018) and a war guilt clause made Germany responsible for causing all the wartime destruction. Overall, Germany lost 25,000 square miles of territory on the continent and 7 million German citizens. France got Alsace-Lorraine, Denmark and Belgium sliced off several border regions, and Poland received the important industrial area of Upper Silesia (cutting East Prussia off from Germany). The League of Nations took over the administration of Germany's colonies as mandates and distributed them among the Allies. Disarmament applied to Germany alone, and the country was forbidden to possess any warplanes or tanks, while the Kaiser's great navy scuttled fifty of its sixty-eight ships. Germany's humiliated Foreign Minister let his feelings of disgust be known. Leaning over the treaty, he lay down a pair of mourning gloves in a gesture of protest.[10]

When the Germans began to starve, 270,000 tons of American food was withheld from them because the French government objected to the policy of paying for aid out of the reparations payments the Allies received. The economist John Maynard Keynes, a British delegate to Paris, warned against continuing on the path of bankrupting Germany.[11] Across the political spectrum in Germany, members of the Weimar Parliament denounced the Versailles Treaty. Right-wing circles promulgated the notion that the fearless German soldiers, who could have won a victory on the battlefield, were 'stabbed-in-the-back' by politicians at home, especially Jews and leftish republicans bribed with Jewish money.

Coburg. 1921.

As Germany stumbled, the Duke of Coburg became a focus of far-right activity. Over 5,000 local men joined the Organisation Consul (OC), a new militia led by Captain Hermann Ehrhardt and financially supported by Charles Edward. In the sea of nationalist clubs that sprouted like mushrooms, the OC had clout and muscle; soon, it started profiteering via weapons deals negotiated with political agitators in Hungary and Ireland. Both the hopeful and the despairing joined up. When Ehrhardt supported the failed right-wing Kapp-Putsch rebellion against the Weimar government on 13 March 1920, he became a wanted man hunted by the police. Charles Edward hid him under the assumed name of 'Neumann' at Callenberg Castle in Coburg, and then later moved him secretly to Hinterriss Castle in Austria. The OC concealed massive stockpiles of armaments and weapons inside various Coburg properties. Charles Edward was now supporting right-wing terrorism.[12]

Ernst von Salomon was another critical member of the OC who, despite his Jewish-sounding name, was a staunch anti-Semite.[13] Both the Duke and Salomon had much in common: they had both attended the Prussian military academy in Lichterfelde. Charles Edward trusted Salomon enough to send him to Sweden to sell family heirlooms, including a valuable medal collection. The money raised was used to finance the OC's increasingly malicious activities, including political assassinations.

Their first murder victim was the left-wing USPD leader, Karl Gareis, in Munich on 9 June 1921. The USPD (Independent Social Democratic Party) had played a key role in agitating for the confiscation of Charles Edward's Gotha properties. The second murder – of Matthias Erzberger, the Finance Minister – took place on 26 August 1921. Erzberger had introduced wealth taxes in Germany and was therefore profoundly unpopular with the aristocracy. However, the most famous victim was Walther Rathenau, the Weimar Republic's Foreign Minister.

Although Jewish, Rathenau was a nationalistic German. With a tidy goatee beard and moustache, he proudly declared himself: 'a German of Jewish descent ... My people are the German people; my fatherland is Germany.'[14] Despite this intense patriotism, to most Germans he was still a Jew, and from the moment of his appointment, police warned him of plots against his life. He even carried a small pistol in his pocket, complaining: 'Things have got to such a pitch I cannot go about without this little instrument.'[15]

Nationalist members of the Reichstag so frequently criticised Rathenau that he became, in the minds of millions of starving Germans, the Jew who had bankrupted the German middle classes. When marching, the Freikorps started singing this chorus: 'God damn Walther Rathenau. Shoot him down, dirty Jew.'[16]

At 10.45 a.m. on 24 June 1922, a chauffeur drove Rathenau in an open NAG convertible to his office in Wilhelmstraße. A high-powered Mercedes swept past. Inside were three clean-shaven young OC members: Ernst Werner Techow, Hermann Fischer and Erwin Kern. Kern, the leader, was a good-looking but narrow-minded zealot who hated all Jews. He was the main protagonist amongst a group of thirteen conspirators, including the Duke of Coburg's right-hand man, Ernst von Salomon, who acted as a lookout and provided a getaway car.[17]

Working on a nearby building site, Herr Krishbin, a bricklayer and witness, saw that Kern was armed with a gun and that he:

> leaned forward, pulled out a long pistol, rested the butt in his armpit, and opened fire on the gentleman [Rathenau] in the other car. There was no need for him to aim; it was such a close range. I saw him, so to speak, straight in the face. It was a healthy, open face, the sort of face we call an officer's face.[18]

Meanwhile, Fischer threw a hand grenade into the car.[19] 'At that moment there was a bang, and the hand grenade exploded. The impact raised the gentleman in the back seat some way off the seat, and even gave the car a slight jerk forward,' said Krishbin.[20] The chauffeur called for help. A brave woman, a nurse named Helen Kaiser, sprang into the back seat of the car and did her best to help the dying Rathenau. Five bullets had hit him, smashing his jaw and spine. He was dead before a doctor arrived.[21] Nine empty cartridge cases and the pin from the grenade littered the pavement, along with blown-off car parts.[22]

By noon that day, news of the murder had spread across Berlin and workers began swarming out of factories, shops and offices to protest. Altogether, the police rounded up and charged the conspirators with murder: Kern and Fisher became elusive fugitives and police officers killed them while resisting arrest.

A month later, in a courtroom decorated with portraits of German Emperors, the court clerk read out the accusations against the remaining eleven conspirators. Spectators struggled to find a seat in the crowded auditorium, as the lawyers wearing shabby black robes took their seats and the women dressed in expensive clothes watched events through opera glasses. They stopped sucking sweets only when things became exciting. Witnesses wore their Sunday best, stumbling through their oaths.

Ernst Werner Techow, one of the right-wing conspirators, testified that:

> Kern told me that Rathenau belonged to the 'veiled' Bolshevik movement, that he was one of the three hundred elders of Zion who were seeking to bring the world under the rule of the Jews.

'Were you afraid of him?' asked the robed judge.

'Yes,' replied the sobbing Techow. 'Kern said to me, "If you refuse, I'll shoot you."'[23]

The courts sentenced Techow to fifteen years in prison. This was later commuted to seven, and he served only four before going back to university, where he studied to become a lawyer.

During Salomon's arrest and trial, the Duke of Coburg's position became tricky. He suffered death threats when his links to the conspirators became known publically.[24] Von Salomon served five years in prison,[25] and on his release, became a movie writer, living in Hamburg. The rest of the conspirators received light sentences and got on with their lives, moving out of the spotlight.

Political assassinations became commonplace in German public life. Between 1918 and 1922, murders committed by left-wing radical elements numbered twenty-two; of these, seventeen received severe punishment. However, right-wing extremists found the legal system extremely benevolent towards the 354 murders they perpetrated. The bias of both the police force and judiciary to the extreme right fatally destabilised the Weimar Republic. Arguably, this flaw was its most fundamental defect. Average prison sentences starkly characterised this prejudice: fourteen years for the left-wing killers, and four months for the right.[26]

Coburg. 14 October 1922.

Charles Edward's aim at this point was the unification of all the various right-wing groups across Germany.[27] To accomplish this merger, he hosted *Deutscher Tag* (German Day) on 14 October 1922. The National Socialist German Workers Party, often referred to as the Nazi Party, were invited as guests. Their leader was Adolf Hitler, a gaunt young man wearing a shabby beige coat who was a failed artist. As a soldier serving on the Western Front, he had won an Iron Cross, First Class, for bravery, and a gas attack had nearly blinded him. After recovering in a North Berlin hospital, he returned to Munich to work as an intelligence agent. Assigned to spy on the tiny German Workers' Party (DAP), he soon realised that he agreed with many of their underlying tenets. He joined them and quickly rose to the party's top post. The DAP became the Nazi Party, and Hitler designed the party's chilling banner of a swastika in a white circle on a red background.[28]

Hitler arrived in Coburg on a specially chartered train, bringing with him 800 men from his newly founded *Sturmabteilung* (Storm Detachment or SA). They provocatively entered the city in closed formation, accompanied by marching music. Violence followed, and Hitler's Stormtroopers behaved like thugs. He would later gloat, writing, 'there wasn't a trace of anything red left on the street'.[29] Supposedly, even Hitler took part in the street fighting – something he never repeated. That evening, following a speech, he sat down with the Duke of Coburg to celebrate in a pub. The two men bonded while, outside, the fighting persisted, and Nazi thugs beat up a Jewish businessman.[30] Later, this day was baptised the 'Train to Coburg' and became part of Nazi folklore. Hitler wanted to be on good terms with the Duke to exploit the social cachet such a friendship offered, while Charles Edward needed Hitler after Gotha's lurch towards communism. The Duke genuinely believed that the Bolsheviks would take over in Germany. He did not trust the police force or government to conduct the muscular action that might be required to prevent this catastrophe from taking place.

Although privately Hitler referred to the aristocracy as decadent, the Nazis and the nobility shared two common enemies: their mutual anti-Semitism and hatred of communism. Hitler's belief in a global Jewish conspiracy influenced his speeches on the Russian Revolution. He spoke of a 'Jewish dictatorship' and a 'Moscow Jew government' that was draining the Russian people. This world view struck a chord with the many Russian refugees in Coburg. They viewed Hitler as a warrior against communism who would drive Stalin from the Kremlin. Later that year, Hitler was invited to stay with the exiled Grand Duke Cyril of Russia in Coburg at the suggestion of his wife, Victoria Melita, a Coburg princess who was Charles Edward's first cousin. Since the Ekaterinburg murders, Cyril and Victoria Melita were the heirs to the Russia Imperial Throne, and in 1922 the woman who wanted to be Russia's next empress even attended an early Stormtrooper meeting.[31]

Berlin. October 1923.

As always, the Weimar Republic teetered on the verge of collapse. Hyperinflation continued to spiral as the German currency became practically worthless: a loaf of bread that cost 250 marks in January cost 200,000 in November. Charles Edward wrote to his sister Princess Alice about the German situation:

> We are tumbling and rolling down the hill faster than ever. At the cheapest pub, a plate of soup costs 1,000,000 Mark. For 1 Pound one gets 50,000,000 Marks. Work is getting scarce, the factories closing one after another, the big ones only working two days a week … The Berlin government is a disgrace.[32]

The assassination of Walther Rathenau had destroyed what little faith there was in the economy. Germany was delirious: people were paid daily and rushed to the shops with sacks of banknotes to buy anything they could get; inflation wiped out middle-class savings. Food became both a currency and an obsession. Doctors diagnosed over 15,000 children with tuberculosis. Bankruptcies became the norm and suicide was common. Upper-class landowners fared better than most: those with loans quickly paid them back with the worthless mark. Big industries tightened their control over the economy. Six large chemical companies merged to become IG Farben, and four steel companies became United Steel Works. By 1925, 2 per cent of all enterprises employed 55 per cent of all workers.[33]

There was a false belief that Jews were responsible for the ruinous exchange rate and hyperinflation. Anyone in the street who looked Jewish – particularly if they looked well fed and dressed – was seized and stripped of their clothes. Colonel Roddie, with the casual anti-Semitism of the British upper class, described these ugly crowds as 'good-natured' and wrote 'if the Jew quietly submitted, he was usually allowed to retain an essential portion of apparel. Not so the obstreperous one.'[34] Vividly, Roddie described what happened to one Jew who dared to fight back. For an Englishman, his tone is callous:

> A very fat Jew was one day held up. He proved exceptionally truculent and was therefore denuded of all but his bowler hat and very short shirt. A rope was slung over a lamp standard and a noose placed around the victim's chest under his arms. As he was drawn up, whirling rudderless round and round, the delighted crowd yelled: 'The dollar is rising,' and, as he was lowered, they shrieked: 'The dollar is falling.' This went on until the police, interfering, provided the shivering and terrified man

with a couple of newspapers, thus enabling him to depart in decency, if not in dignity.[35]

When Charles Edward visited Berlin, he patronised the sleazy Hotel Sanssouci, a meeting place for radical right-wing groups.[36] In 1923, the OC rechristened itself the Viking League with Ehrhardt assuming the leadership and Charles Edward still providing the money. When the League joined the *Stahlhelm, Bund der Frontsoldaten* (Steel Helmet, League of Front Soldiers) Charles Edward became a senior member of their national board. He soon started to network with influential right-wing conservatives, such as industrialist Fritz Thyssen.[37] The Duke's dream of uniting Germany's far-right seemed to be coming true.

When communists sought to spark an 'October Revolution' in Thuringia, 5,000 right-wing paramilitaries from neighbouring Coburg marched into the area, led by Captain Ehrhardt, to suppress the insurgents on 29 October 1923. Charles Edward's 17-year-old son, Prince Johann Leopold, marched with the militia, and the Duke proudly wrote to Alice:

> Leo is now back after playing at being a soldier at the Thuringia frontier. He was enrolled as a soldier in the Ehrhardt Brigade, and his section had a brush with the Thuringia constabulary, killing one and wounding two severely, our loss being one badly wounded … So you see we are quite warlike here. The life at the frontier and the drilling has done a lot of good to Leo and made him more manly, which was most necessary.[38]

Munich. November 1923.

The following month, with lousy timing, Hitler made his first attempt to seize power in Munich and staged the notorious Beer Hall Putsch on 8 November 1923. However, the government flexed its muscles and sent troops to ambush the uprising, making itself, momentarily, look secure and capable. Gunfire killed sixteen Nazis and three police officers. Hitler fled but was captured two days later and prosecuted for treason. With his hair slicked to the left and his moustache clipped into a square, Hitler turned the specially convened People's Court into his stage and mesmerised the country. Claiming that he had never acted out of personal ambition – 'I became a politician against my will' – the crowds believed him.[39]

Although convicted of treason, the swift commuting of his five-year prison sentence to eleven months spoke volumes about the 'compassionate' attitude of the Establishment towards right-wing revolutionaries. In

Landsberg prison, reverential visitors came to pay court to this king-in-waiting. Hitler received luxury food parcels, fine art prints, and even a gramophone from one female admirer. His cell, number seven, was large and bright with a view of the garden.

The Beer Hall Putsch had catapulted Hitler into the newspapers around the world. Sartorially, he adopted a more contemporary look: knee-high boots and a belted motoring coat. Overnight, he became a prophet, a genius who would awaken the German nation. Crucially, he shifted gears: direct action was not the way to achieve power. He knew he needed to attract the support of wealthy industrialists and aristocrats. Relishing his newfound celebrity, Hitler dictated his political manifesto *Mein Kampf* (My Struggle) to Rudolf Hess. The book was released in 1924 and gained enormous popular support, despite the fact that it was tedious and repetitive, filled with lofty, fake claims. It attacked the Treaty of Versailles and denounced communism as a Jewish-led world conspiracy. However, Hitler was impressed by Britain's empire-building ruthlessness. He pronounced that the British could preserve the empire on condition that Germany had a free hand on the Continent. Bonded by self-interest, these two Aryan nations could become allies and dominate the world.

ANYTHING GOES

Rome. 1922.

In 1922, Benito Mussolini's successful power grab in Italy encouraged the fledgling Nazis. Il Duce had 'the look of a winner'[1] and Fascism exploded because people felt it had the power to transform their lives for the better. Instead of inciting a class war, Mussolini proposed to unite classes under the common bond of nationalism, while mainstream legislators quarrelled incessantly amongst themselves. Timid King Victor Emmanuel III of Italy – always inclined to swim with the tide – benefitted enormously. When Mussolini made him the Emperor of Ethiopia, royalty throughout Europe saw Fascism confirm its loyalty to the old social order.

Soon, British aristocrats like the Dukes of Westminster and Buccleuch, Sir Oswald Mosley and Harold Nicholson all made pilgrimages to Rome to pay homage to the new Italian Prime Minister. Lady Chamberlain left impressed: 'What a Man! I have lost my heart!'[2] Even Winston Churchill was enthralled and praised Fascism: 'If I were Italian, I am sure that I would have been with you entirely from the beginning.' He heaped further praise by affirming that Mussolini's movement 'has rendered service to the whole world ... Italy has shown that there is a way of fighting the subversive forces ... She has provided the necessary antidote to the Russian poison ... the cancerous growth of Bolshevism.'[3]

The Duke of Coburg also visited Rome with seventy German soulmates. After an elaborate welcoming dinner, Il Duce gave Charles Edward a special gift of a dagger. The journalist Bella Fromme observed this bestowal with contempt: 'the unprepossessing little Duke strutted around in his fascist dagger, an honour bestowed on him by Mussolini.' She described Charles Edward as 'stooped' and 'dwarflike'.[4]

Prince Philipp of Hesse was another tourist to Italy, but in 1922, the young Prince was not yet travelling for political reasons. Philipp was doing everything possible to avoid family responsibility, including committing himself to a suitable marriage. Moustachioed with delicate features, Philipp also had a dapper sense of style. He combined this with a passion for the arts and archaeology. This colourful playboy escaped to Rome because, as a bisexual man, he wanted freedom.

Sex between men was nothing new: German society operated on an implicit code of concealment and toleration, provided it was not too noticeable. The sybaritic culture of the 1920s was determined to break this convention and destroy old taboos. Arguably, this pursuit of pleasure was a reaction to the horrors of war. A generation of young men had died. Drinking too much and ending up with unlikely bedfellows was a way of rejecting the past. There was a realisation that life was fragile: we can do anything we like today, because tomorrow we might be dead. New ideas and extreme politics were a product of too much partying, cynicism towards democracy and economic anarchy. There was resentment towards a previous generation who had allowed millions of young men to die in the First World War. As Cyril Connolly wrote: 'In those days whenever you didn't get on with your father, you had the glorious dead on your side.'[5]

Prince Philipp visited Lord Berners, the composer, novelist, painter and general all-round aesthete. He was a close friend of Diana Mitford, who would later marry British Fascist leader Sir Oswald Mosley. Berners was the inspiration for the character Lord Merlin in the novel *The Pursuit of Love*, written by Diana's sister, Nancy Mitford. He was notorious for his eccentricity, dyeing pigeons at his house vibrant colours: blue, pink, yellow and green. At one point, he entertained a horse belonging to Penelope Betjeman (the wife of the poet) with tea inside his home.[6] He planted paper flowers and booby-trapped the house with jokes, disguising pornographic books with the covers of the Bible, or a copy of the Bible was discovered inside a dust jacket reading: 'This is the hottest thing written in the last 20 years …'[7]

At Berners' house in Italy, Prince Philipp met Siegfried Sassoon, the British poet. A few days later, romance blossomed between the poet and the Prince at a picnic hosted by Harold Nicholson and his wife, writer Vita Sackville-West. After lunch under the vine leaves in the gardens of the Castel Gandolfo, they all made paper boats that they launched down a waterfall.

Sassoon was impossibly handsome with a dimple on his chin; he could also be snobbish and emotionally fickle, with a vein of cruelty beneath his attractive veneer. He had quickly established his reputation as a war poet of immense talent. His verse was a vivid post-war description of the First World War, and he made constant references to the bravery of the soldiers and the brutal incompetence of the officers. Vita and Harold were delighted by their matchmaking when Philipp moved into Sassoon's room for three days.[8] The two men shared much in common. Both fought in the First World War, though on opposite sides. Both lost brothers who were killed in combat and they each possessed a keen interest in the arts.[9]

When Philipp returned to Germany and Sassoon to England, the two men corresponded frequently. Sassoon was 36, ten years older than Philipp, and was very attracted to his royal status. Sassoon hoped that the young Prince would be his 'link with Europe' and a 'social experience'.[10] However, the war had left Philipp relatively impoverished and bitter, although he always had the funds to travel with his little dog and Greek valet.[11] Philipp wrote to Siegfried just after their Roman idyll:

> Those days at Rome mean a great change in my life & they have made me so happy – happier than I can say. That happiness shall remain in my heart & go back with me to my home where I shall keep it like a precious jewel that no one can take from me.[12]

Eleven days later, when Philipp had arrived back home at Friedrichshof, he wrote again to Sassoon:

> Home again at last finding your dear letter waiting for me here! It brought back everything more vividly than ever: you, your voice, Rome with all its beauty, the murmuring of fountains, some vague melody of Bach played by small untrained fingers, two small rooms in a hotel, & all that happiness. Yes, Sig – you are right: the gods have been very kind to us & I shall be thankful for that all my life.[13]

Sassoon asked Philipp to send a photograph of himself dressed in military uniform, and in return sent pictures and copies of his poetry books. Philipp found them 'Wonderfully clever and brilliant'.[14] Siegfried was perhaps less besotted than the Prince in the relationship. Compared to his previous lover, the artist Gabriel Atkin, he found Philipp less attractive: 'Physically I have never been really infatuated with him,' he wrote coldly in his diary.[15]

Bored, Philipp quit the Technical University in Darmstadt after two years, without completing his degree. Working for a year at the Kaiser Friedrich Museum in Berlin, he also failed to complete a catalogue of old French drawings. He travelled to Florence and Venice, then took extended vacations to Greece. His mother's sister, Queen Sophie, had married King Constantine I of the Hellenes. Philipp often stayed with the Greek Royal Family, who with the surname of Schleswig-Holstein-Sonderburg-Glücksburg, weren't Greek, but part of the extensive network of interrelated Anglo-German-Danish royal families.[16]

Despite his illustrious pedigree, Philipp needed to earn a living. Hyperinflation was crippling, and in a quest for independence, Philipp established himself as an interior designer in Rome. He specialised in decorating rooms in the grand aristocratic style, relying on family connections for clients, including Queen Victoria of Sweden. Often, Sassoon provided him with extra money to travel, and the two men met up again in Munich in the following summer of 1922, but their relationship struggled.

Although Siegfried felt Philipp's 'great assets were his charm, his really beautiful manners (always polite), and his essential amiability and kindness,'[17] he wrote in his diary: 'as much as I love P., I do not regard him as my equal in intellectual things.'[18] Philipp's promiscuity also placed a strain on the relationship. He wrote openly to Sassoon that 'R', an English boy, was coming over to see him, and 'you know what that means'.[19]

Continuing to drift from one person to another, Philipp visited Rome with a new friend called Maurice. When this affair ended, an intimate relationship started in Berlin with Princess 'Baby' Galitzine, a wealthy American divorcee who was enjoying the pleasures of Europe.[20] Philipp would telephone her in the evenings while Sassoon was in the room. Siegfried was soon describing Philipp as 'spiteful' in his diary,[21] and complaining, 'Am I only one of P's regular succession of "affairs"?'[22] He complained that Philipp was unable to 'distinguish between decent and indecent people. He is quite content to leave me after a pleasant evening, and spend three hours listening to filthy stories in a cocktail bar … P's craving for amusement and amusing people is almost a vice.' In other entries, Sassoon grumbles about the 'din of banjo and jazz orchestra' and 'people dancing', giving the impression that he was a reluctant partner in the world of Bright Young Things.[23]

Villa Demidoff, Florence. 1924.

While Prince Philipp was staying at the Villa Demidoff in Florence, a guest of Prince Paul and Princess Olga of Yugoslavia, he met his future wife,

Princess Mafalda of Savoy. An attractive woman with dark good looks and large eyes, Mafalda was the daughter of King Victor Emmanuel III of Italy. The Princess had led a sheltered life and probably did not know what she was letting herself in for when Philipp proposed marriage later that year. Naively, she accepted.

At the time, Philipp was living a louche and flashy life in Berlin, with no visible means of financial support, and sharing a flat with a 'reputedly perverse Russian prince'.[24] The affair between Philipp and Siegfried Sassoon had fizzled out. The previous year, Sassoon wrote:

> I have had some splendid times with P., but I know I shall see him getting heavier and heavier from year to year. And in ten years he shall be a bald, self-indulgent, opinionated man – living off the snobbishness of rich people. That sounds cruel and unjust, but I am afraid it will come true. I hope it won't.[25]

Philipp's father, Prince Frederick Charles, considered a pink sheep in the family an unnecessary addition. He was therefore delighted to see his artistic son married off. Both the Italian and Hesse royal families were keen for a wedding. Relations between Italy and Germany had become strained since Italy's decision to fight against Germany in the First World War. The Kaiser had called the Italian King a 'traitor' in public (and far worse in private).[26] For their part, the Italian Royal Family were delighted that the groom had connections with the royal families of Windsor, Hohenzollern and Hesse. When the German Embassy in Rome warned the King about Philipp's variable romantic history and his interest in fascism, Victor Emmanuel found the intrusion exasperating and ignored it.

The high-profile wedding took place at the Racconigi Palace outside Turin on 25 September 1925. Against the backdrop of the palace's pagoda-like roof and Gothic chapel, Philipp wore the Dragoons' uniform of his Hessian regiment with an ostrich feather in his helmet, and Mafalda was dressed in an elegant white gown and wore family jewels. The kings of Greece and Bulgaria attended, as did Prince Paul of Yugoslavia. While the event represented the old world of the ruling aristocracy, it was tinged by a robust fascist presence, with Prime Minister Mussolini as a guest of honour. Il Duce wanted to promote the impression of glamour in Italy, and this elegant royal wedding fitted with his aspirations, with Mafalda and Philipp living out a fantasy for the masses.

Although their relationship was never straightforward, it was a surprising success. The couple's home in Rome was the Villa Polissena, with its art nouveau embellishments and set in 2 hectares of gardens. Later, Princess Mafalda cashed in family bonds her parents had given her and bought the Villa Mura in Capri. Oak and orange trees surrounded the house, and there was a terrace overlooking the sea. Here, they lived the high life: yachts, nightclubs and parties.

London. 1930.

Prince Philipp of Hesse's closest friend and cousin within the British Royal Family was Prince George, Duke of Kent. George was also Prince Edward of Wales's favourite younger brother. These three playboys became leading members of the 'international fast set' who moved like a flock of migratory birds between Paris, Deauville, Saint Moritz and Cannes during the 1920s and '30s.

At the exclusive and outrageously expensive Embassy Club in Mayfair, Prince George drank heavily and danced to the latest jazz trends: the Jobrot, Shimmy and Heebie-Jeebie. The club was managed by Luigi, who knew everyone amongst the partying smart set and aristocracy. King George V disapproved, of course, which must have made it seem a lot more fun. The jazz musician Tiny Winters often saw George with Edward, drinking cocktails together and enjoying feisty pranks:

> One of them got [the other's] top hat and climbed up a lamp-post [just outside the club] and stuck [it] on the iron bar … Then the other one climbed up and got it. After that, they were chasing one another, grabbing their top hats and kicking them about all over the street.[27]

Life was a quest for a good time. George relished so many passionate sexual affairs with aristocrats, performers and strangers that 'the palace stopped counting'.[28] There was Florence Mills, a black cabaret singer and actress, whom the Prince had met in London during a run of her West End stage show, *Blackbirds*. Another was Poppy Baring, a thrill-seeking banking heiress and débutante. There was talk of marriage until an unfavourable report about her reached the ears of King George V. Romantic novelist Barbara Cartland would later claim that Prince George was the biological father of her daughter Raine, Countess Spencer. Other women included musical star Jessie Matthews, Lady Alexandra 'Baba' Curzon, who was called 'Ba-Ba Blackshirt' because of her support of the black-shirted fascists, and

Princess Stephanie von Hohenlohe, Hitler's socialite spy and recruiter in London. A handwritten letter between Stephanie and the Duke of Kent survived in the Princess's papers. It is a gushing note to her from the Prince, dated 10 November 1934, expressing 'a million thanks' for the gift of a lavish piece of furniture. The two saw a great deal of each other and held very similar pro-Nazi views.[29]

One of George's lovers, Kiki Preston – an American beauty who was a member of Kenya's notorious Happy Valley set – introduced the Prince to cocaine. She was known in society as 'the girl with the silver syringe',[30] and George soon became seriously addicted. Edward intervened and took him to a private country house with round-the-clock nursing care until he recovered, writing to his then mistress Freda Dudley Ward:

> The cure has reached a rather tricky stage … I'm carrying out the work of doctor, jailer and detective combined. The old saying 'Boys will be boys' is alright until you get too old and should know better form. He seems to lack all sense of knowing what is so obviously the wrong thing to do.[31]

Like Prince Philipp of Hesse, Prince George led a double life as a free-wheeling bisexual. As well as women, drugs and parties, there were entanglements with men. One person commented that Prince George was 'not safe in taxis with either sex',[32] and police even arrested the Prince at a gay club, the Nut House. George was held in police custody for a night until they confirmed his identity.[33]

Diplomat Sir Robert Bruce-Lockhart claimed there was a dangerously close shave in 1932 after Prince George had an affair in Paris with a blackmailing youth. Lockhart wrote in his diary: 'a scandal about Prince George – letters to a young man in Paris. A large sum had to be paid for their recovery.'[34] George had also foolishly given this youth a personally inscribed Tiffany cigarette box and Cartier lighter. The Prince of Wales made an inconvenient journey to France to recover the items but found the blackmailer had sold him copies, and kept the originals. Other reputed lovers of Prince George included the young Anthony Blunt (later, one of the notorious Cambridge Spies) and Noël Coward.[35] Coward's friends complained that he was so proud of this affair that he became 'almost a bore' on the subject.[36] There were also affairs with an Argentine diplomat and an Italian aristocrat. Prince Edward personally had one young South American man kicked out of the country for supplying his brother with cocaine. Friends noted that weaning his brother off drugs was one of the few beneficial things the Prince of Wales ever did.[37] Only in the pre-tabloid era were such secret shenanigans possible, and anyone shameless enough to leak them would have been ostracised.

Edward's partying was modest in comparison. However, by his mid thirties, he had started to look a little haunted with bags beginning to grow under his blue eyes: a casualty of reckless excesses. However, Edward did have two long-term relationships. The first was with Freda Dudley Ward, whom he met during an air raid when five German Zeppelin bombers drifted over London. Lady Cynthia Asquith described her condescendingly as 'a pretty little fluff',[38] but Freda was quick-witted, intelligent, charming and discreet. As a mistress, she was entirely safe, being a married woman who nurtured the Prince with her motherly attentions. The second was Thelma Furness, an American married to Marmaduke Furness, a viscount and wealthy shipping magnate. Lady Thurness was amusing and acerbic but very spoilt, with a smouldering dark glamour inherited from her Chilean grandmother. She wore industrial-sized diamonds and long strands of pearls.[39]

The Prince of Wales's Private Secretary, Alan Lascelles, described his boss as being 'continuously in the throes of one shattering and absorbing love affair after another. (Not to mention a number of street-corner affairs).' The two men soon came to loathe each other, with Lascelles's moral outlook too severe and unbending.[40]

All three men – Edward, George and Philipp – were 'New Men' of the 1920s and 1930s, a class of aristocratic gentlemen adventurers who flew planes, raced motorcycles, galloped horses and travelled the globe. Their idols were dashing heroes like Charles Lindberg, who flew non-stop from New York to Paris in 1927, and in 1933, Lord Clydesdale, the first man to fly over Everest. In Germany, many young aristocrats embraced the concept of the 'New Man' and many believed piloting a plane 'developed character'.[41] Flying became equated with modernity, and the fascists hijacked this image. Sir Oswald Mosley, the energetic young leader of the British Union of Fascists, even called his movement the 'New Party'. Mosley recruited men like Randolph Churchill (Winston's son) and Harold Nicholson, who both hoped the fascist phenomenon would reverse the ruling elites' decline. In truth, this upper-class clique seemed to be permanently on holiday – skiing trips to Kitzbühel, sunbathing at the Venice Lido, or piloting their new planes to fashionable resorts such as Biarritz. Most did not have the tenacity for politics, diplomacy or hard work.

Friedrichshof Castle. 1930.

On 15 December 1930, Prince Philipp's brother, Prince Christoph of Hesse, married Princess Sophie of Greece. The groom was 29 years old, and the bride only 16 years old.[42] Her 9-year-old little brother, Prince Philip of Greece, carried her train for both the Protestant and Greek Orthodox ceremonies that took place.[43]

Christoph had endured a particular kind of post-war austerity as a relaxed squire-in-training, travelling and working on the picturesque family estates in both Hesse and Pomerania on the Baltic coast. Christoph typified the 'man of action' Aryan stereotype. Passionate about horses, he laboured briefly on the family-owned stud farm, overseeing the stables, and followed this practical experience with a year studying at the agricultural university in Munich. He was a young man looking for adventure, more interested in dogs, horses, cars, motorcycles and girls. Impoverished – relatively speaking – by the Weimar hyperinflation, Christoph's network of privileged relations and cash-rich friends with dollars in their pockets offset this predicament. Colonel Roddie furnished the monies for drunken nights out in Berlin and country high society – despite cutbacks – still managed an almost obsolete grandeur. To earn more money, Christoph eventually took a job at Maybeck Werke, an engineering firm which manufactured cars and Zeppelins. Enthralled with new vehicles, Christoph would often sleep in them for the first few days after buying them.[44] However, the Wall Street Crash cost Christoph a job that interested him. Forced to move to Berlin, he worked at the suitably named Viktoria Insurance firm, selling policies to his social contacts – a role he hated.[45]

Princess Sophie was a 'Greek' princess, but in reality, her family were of German and Danish heritage. The family had to flee Athens after a military uprising overthrew the royalist Greek government in November 1922. Her mother was Princess Alice of Battenberg, sister to Lord Mountbatten and a member of both the British and Hessian royal families. Her father was Prince Andrew of Greece.

Mostly unemployable and almost utterly impoverished, Prince Andrew and his family lived as unhappy exiles amongst the cluster of White Russian and Greek émigré royals outside Paris. The family settled at a house in St-Cloud, and they were poor by royal standards. Andrew and Alice's only son, Prince Philip, a boisterous and mischievous little boy, was sent to a progressive American kindergarten. Alice fretted about finding suitable husbands for her remaining three unmarried daughters: Cecilie, Margarita and Theodora. Eventually, the three young women escaped their family's financial predicament through marriage, and they all wed affluent German princes.

The 18-year-old Princess Cecilie also married into the Hesse family, with a wedding on 2 February 1931. The groom was the handsome 23-year-old Prince Georg Donatus of Hesse, known in the family as 'Don'. He was another avid sportsman and pilot who was the eldest son and heir to the Grand Duke Ernst Louis of Hesse and by Rhine. Over fifty royal relatives attended their wedding in Darmstadt, and a large crowd of townspeople gathered outside the church and later cheered the bride and groom, who appeared on the balcony of the palace. Cecilie's new home was Wolfsgarten Castle, just outside Darmstadt. After the wedding, Lord Mountbatten, who was a guest, took his nephew Prince Philip back to his British boarding school.

On 18 April 1931, Philip was back in Germany again for a third wedding. This time, the bride was his sister, Princess Margarita. She was marrying Prince Gottfried of Hohenlohe-Langenburg, the heir to two castles: the Renaissance palace-like Weikersheim and Langenburg, which dominated a medieval town, famous for its witch trials.

The last of Philip's sisters, Princess Theodora, was married later that year on 17 August. At 25 years old, she wed Prince Berthold, the Margrave of Baden. Her new home was Salem Castle, a rambling former Cistercian monastery next to Lake Constance, now a fortress-palace after secularisation in 1803. Berthold and Theodora were the most liberal of Philip's new in-laws.

Princess Alice was excluded from all four of her daughters' wedding celebrations, although the girls sent her flowers as a token. Obsessively religious, Alice had started to become preoccupied with the supernatural, taking part in séances and dealing cards whenever there was an important decision to be made.[46] By 1930, Alice's conduct grew increasingly eccentric; she declared herself a saint and a 'bride of Christ' and attempted to exorcise the house.[47] Her mother, Lady Milford Haven (née Princess Victoria of Hesse), arrived in St-Cloud, frantic with worry.

Victoria Milford Haven was the sister of the murdered Empress of Russia. She seldom spoke about the horrors of the past and was always accompanied by her devoted lady's maid, Edith Pye, whom the family called 'The Pyecrust'. Dressed in black, with coiled snake rings on her chilblained fingers, Victoria smoked incessantly, and stuffed cotton wool into her glass cigarette holder to absorb the nicotine while conducting three conversations (or arguments) at once in different languages.[48]

Victoria now turned to Dr Ernst Simmel, who diagnosed Princess Alice as 'a paranoid schizophrenic' and determined that she was suffering a 'neurotic pre-psychotic libidinous condition'. Alice was also examined by Dr Sigmund Freud, who prescribed 'exposure of the gonads to X-ray' to 'accelerate the menopause'. It is ambiguous whether the patient consented to this remedy. However, the doctor intended to calm Alice down and subdue her libido after she became infatuated with a young Englishman.[49] After weeks of anxiety, Lady Milford Haven sent her daughter to Bellevue, a private clinic on Lake Constance in Switzerland, with picturesque surrounding parks and wealthy clientele.[50]

Alice was 'so depressed that she hardly talked at all'[51] and her behaviour became increasingly unconventional. The Princess hid things in her bedroom, walked about barefoot, blessed her teacups and, on one occasion, jumped out of her bedroom window to escape. She made it as far as the local railway station at Bellevue, where police arrested her on board the train and brought her back to the clinic. Eventually, her mother realised there was an only minimal improvement at Bellevue and Alice was moved to the more relaxed regime of the Martinsbrunn Sanatorium in Austria. By then, Alice felt let down by her family and wanted nothing to do with them.[52]

Alice's committal meant the end of family life. Although Alice and Andrew never divorced, they rarely saw each other again during their lifetimes. Prince Andrew closed the family home and abandoned the roles of both husband and father to lead the aimless life of a playboy in Monte Carlo, without the funds to pay for it. Fortunately, he quickly found a wealthy mistress, an actress going by the name Countess Andrée de la Bigne. He spent the rest of his life on her 167-tonne yacht the *Davida*, or in his small apartment, rarely bothering to see his children again.[53]

Philip's grandmother, Lady Milford Haven, took him to live with her in Kensington Palace. As a boy, Prince Philip rarely saw his mother, as the visits could become upsetting. Between 1932 and 1937, there was no contact at all, as he explained later in an interview: 'The family broke up. My mother was ill, my sisters married, my father was in the South of France. I just had to get on with it. You do. One does.'

Philip led a transient lifestyle shuttled between his English and German relatives. Many years later, he was asked what language he spoke at home, and responded with a telling riposte: 'What do you mean "at home"?'[54]

Philip's uncle, George Mountbatten, the 2nd Marquess of Milford Haven, stepped in to become his guardian and de facto father. However,

George was an eccentric with two fabled collections. The first was entirely innocent – a gigantic miniature railway. His toy trains travelled on 2 miles of railway track intricately built within an old Tudor barn at Lynden Manor, his country house in Berkshire. There were hills and valleys constructed of papier mâché, miniature goods sheds and sidings, and even Alpine mountain ranges topped with imitation ice. The second collection remained hidden behind secret bookcases inside the house: his sizeable array of pornographic books and photographs covering every possible topic: bondage, whipping, thumbscrews and incest. There was also a collection of garish adverts for dildos and the 1930s versions of vibrators. After his death, George gifted the books to the British Library, which now houses such volumes as *The Awful Confessions of Maria Monk*, a nineteenth-century anti-Catholic tract about the nefarious goings-on of a group nuns in a Montreal convent (including allegations of ritual sacrifices), and *Raped on the Railway*, a book about the violent ill-treatment of women on the 'Flying Scotsman'.[55]

Philip's upbringing was an unusual and peripatetic experience. Uncle George had married the morganatic daughter of a Russian Grand Duke, the exotic and extravagant Countess Nadejda de Torby, whom friends and family called Nada. She was a dark, slender, exquisitely dressed and bejewelled figure. Society gossiped that Nada had African blood and that one of her ancestors was an Abyssinian princess seized from the Sultan's harem in Constantinople. Grand Duke Michael was nicknamed the 'Uncrowned King of Cannes', owned three yachts, a lavish villa on the Riviera and a lease on Kenwood House in London's Hampstead Heath.[56] He was remembered in Cannes for distributing 'lovely Fabergé things' to friends[57] and Nada had infamously ordered champagne to soak her sore feet after winning a Charleston contest there. The hotel presented her with a large bill, stating: 'Champagne for Marchioness of Milford Haven's feet.'[58] However, by the end of the 1920s, hyperinflation in Germany, the revolution in Russia and the Wall Street Crash left the Milford Havens struggling for funds to support their wildly extravagant lifestyle.

Salem Castle. 1932.

Princess Theodora's late father-in-law was Prince Maximilian of Baden, the former Imperial Chancellor. After the Treaty of Versailles, he retired to his vast palace at Salem with the ambition of creating a more peaceful young elite to rebuild a new Germany. To those ends, he founded a progressive boarding school, based on Plato's philosophy, in a wing of the castle. Here, the education was strongly influenced by the traditions of British public schools, like Eton and Rugby, combined with progressive liberal schools, like Abbotsholme. The school's first headmaster was Kurt Hahn, a gaunt but brilliant Rhodes scholar who had studied at Oxford University. Hahn always wore a full-brimmed grey felt hat and strange protective sunglasses that looked more like goggles. He was also Jewish.[59]

By the early 1930s, Salem boasted 420 pupils and was considered one of the top schools in Europe. German youth, according to Hahn, was in danger from five great decays: the degeneration of fitness, self-discipline, enterprise, skill and compassion. The curriculum placed enormous emphasis on health, with pupils running a quarter of a mile before breakfast, plus regular field games and athletics practice. Two days a week, there were estate duties – farming or school maintenance. Fearful of the poisonous sexual aches of adolescence, Hahn encouraged his pupils to discover their passion with 'guilds' of student explorers, artists and farmers meeting every Saturday afternoon.[60] In many respects, Hahn's curriculum and philosophy were close to Nazi ideals and German nationalism, but without any nasty bits. That year, the school would admit a new pupil: Theodora's younger brother, Prince Philip of Greece.

Berlin. 1932.

In the German elections on 31 July 1932, the Nazi Party won 230 seats and 37 per cent of the vote. Over the following days, neither Hitler nor any other political party could attract enough support to form a majority government. Outbreaks of violence occurred across Germany, as fighting between right-wing groups and communists broke out again. It was a chaotic, bloody time.[61]

Churchill was visiting Germany at the time, touring the battlefields at Blenheim as research for a book about his great ancestor, the Duke of Marlborough. He travelled with his 17-year-old daughter Sarah, and they stayed at the Regina Hotel in Munich, where Ernst 'Putzi' Hanfstaengl, a friend of Diana Mitford and the Nazi Party's publicist, offered to arrange a meeting with Hitler.[62] Churchill told 'Putzi' that he could not understand the point of Hitler being so violent against the Jews: 'What is the sense of being against a man simply because of his birth?'[63] Hitler failed to show up at the appointed hour, so another time was fixed the following day, and Hitler stood Churchill up again. The two future leaders never met because Hitler was unshaven in his apartment and had too much to do. 'What on earth would I talk to him about?' Hitler asked. Churchill sent him a message via Hanfstaengl: 'Tell your boss from me that anti-Semitism may be a good starter, but it is a bad sticker.'[64]

On 6 November, with such an inconclusive July election result, President Hindenburg – who had remained in office – was forced to declare a second election. In the run-up to voting, Hitler gave over fifty stirring speeches, as many as six a day. The message was that he would make Germany great again. Hitler combined this with a relentless attack on the leaders of the Weimar Republic, and he screamed to spellbound crowds: 'What have they done with our beautiful, flourishing, blossoming land?'[65]

British journalist Rothay Reynolds, the *Daily Mail's* Berlin correspondent, followed Hitler on this campaign tour and was shocked by the 'stupidity' of the voters he encountered.[66] The people 'applauded him without discrimination whatever he said, good or bad, right or manifestly false'.[67] Their emotions overpowered them, and the 'sobs and indignation in Hitler's voice seemed to paralyse the reason of those who listened to him'.[68] Nevertheless, on 6 November, Hitler's share of the vote dropped to 33 per cent: down to 196 seats. As the communists gained seats, the Right became even more focused in its support for Hitler. Immediately, ex-Chancellor Fritz von Papen and Hitler engaged in tough negotiations to resolve the deadlock. Finally, Papen convinced Hindenburg to appoint Hitler as Chancellor of Germany on 30 January 1933. He was aged just 43.

Immediately, thousands of Stormtroopers marched through the centre of Berlin holding swastika banners and torches above their heads. The national anthem – '*Deutschland über alles*' – played on a loop, and Hindenburg looked down on the activities from a window in the Presidential Palace.

The stock market responded well, as business viewed Hitler as a leader who would keep the unpredictable communists under control. However, Reynolds saw one disturbing incident that was an indication of things soon to come. Celebrating Hitler's election, a parade of schoolchildren marched down the Unter den Linden. As Nazi supporters yelled out 'Judah', the watching children called for their deaths, shouting '*Verrecken!*' (die), not perhaps understanding the meaning of what they were doing.[69]

Hitler had one more card to play. On 27 February 1933, a fire erupted at the Reichstag; it was a shocking yet magnificent sight, reducing the building to a burnt-out shell. At the crime scene, the police arrested a young communist Dutchman called Marinus Van Der Lubbe. Within hours, Hitler contacted Hindenburg and asked him to suspend civil liberties to protect Germany from communism. The courts sent Van Der Lubbe to the guillotine for his supposed crime, without proving his guilt. A rumour had circulated before the fire that the Nazi Party planned to stage-manage a bogus attempt on Hitler's life in a frantic act of misinformation. Instead, it is conceivable that they orchestrated the fire as the pretext for snatching power. The German people's fear of communism overshadowed distrust of Hitler. In the 5 March elections, the party won 44 per cent of the vote: 288 seats. German democracy disappeared.

Potsdam. 21 March 1933.

The Nazi Party and the German princes sealed their alliance on the so-called Day of Potsdam, an ostentatious ceremony celebrating the opening of the Reichstag. The Nazis' swastika hovered in the breeze, alongside the black, white and blue tricolour of Imperial Germany. Joseph Goebbels, Hitler's sinister-looking Minister of Propaganda, had carefully selected Potsdam, the old Prussian capital, to stage the event. Hitler wanted to unite the country and demonstrate a link between Imperial and Nazi Germany. He understood that his grip on power was extraordinarily shaky, and he needed to legitimise his position. Although the unpopular Kaiser remained an exile, a large segment of the German population yearned for robust government, with the stability and military power embodied by the Emperor.

The Day of Potsdam's central event was a secular ceremony in the Potsdam Garrison Church where both President Hindenburg and Chancellor Hitler spoke. Hindenburg wore the uniform of Field Marshal, including a spiked helmet. His collar was high and stiff, his tunic riveted with medals 'starbursts the size of Christmas tree ornaments'.[70] His massive moustache curled into two feathery wings, and he conveyed a sense of strength that defied his 85 years. Hitler wore a dark suit, and when he shook Hindenburg's hands, his were bare, while the President wore spotless white gloves.[71] Hitler looked rather prosaic, middle-aged and middle management, with a funny little moustache like Charlie Chaplin. Photographs show him giving a slight obsequious bow, humbling himself before the great Hindenburg.

Two weeks earlier, Hindenburg had acerbically dismissed Hitler's chances of success, stating that he would make the little upstart a postmaster so that he could 'lick stamps with his head on them'.[72] Now the legendary figure had to climb down from his high horse. Together, the aristocratic President and arriviste Chancellor reviewed a parade of German troops. As Hindenburg laid a wreath on Frederick the Great's tomb, the cannon fired a 21-gun salute.

The Reichstag met at its new temporary home at the Kroll Opera House two days later. The President signed the Enabling Act, giving Hitler plenary authority: he abolished civil rights and snatched state powers. Hitler's government transmuted into a full dictatorship when Nazi thugs surrounded and threatened members who might vote against the legislation. Hitler was now the sole master and dictator of Germany.

Doorn Castle, the Netherlands. 1933.

Ignored by most of his relatives, particularly in Britain, and uninvited to the Potsdam celebrations, Kaiser Wilhelm remained in exile living on his estate at Doorn. Resentful and increasingly cut off from the world, he sipped his English tea and used outdated British expressions such as 'a damned topping good fellow'. His Savile Row suits had an Edwardian cut, and the works of P.G. Wodehouse remained his favourite books. However, Wilhelm's unlikely restoration to the German throne preoccupied him to the point of obsession.[73]

The Kaiser never bothered to read *Mein Kampf*, and he was unaware of Hitler's misgivings towards the monarchy. What united them was anti-Semitism. To Wilhelm, as to Hitler, the Jews were an alien and unworthy race, without any claims to German or even European identity. In exile, he continually blamed the ubiquitous Jewish press for their persistent hostility towards the Hohenzollern family. His interest in archaeology, which he pursued relentlessly, was also underpinned by anti-Semitism. He wanted to free Christianity from its Jewish roots, and wrote to Houston Chamberlain, the anti-Semitic British historian:

> Jesus was a Galilean by nativity; he had been born in Bethlehem and was, therefore, not a Jew, nor, being a man of uncommon handsomeness, with blond hair and with hands and arms of aristocratic stamp, did he resemble a Jew.[74]

In 1922, the Kaiser had remarried a minor German princess, Hermine von Schönaich-Carolath, described by one English visitor as a 'tough cookie'.[75] Hermine turned the castle into a hotbed of backbiting, and members of the Hohenzollern family felt her imperial aspirations were vulgar and ill-concealed: three of the Kaiser's children were absent from their wedding.

It was a constant irritation to Hermine that her passport merely read 'wife of the former German Kaiser', rather than Empress. From the start, and to her outrage, 'Empress Hermine' was curtly snubbed by the Weimar Republic whenever she visited Berlin. Doggedly, she made friends with Nazi politicians at the Berlin salons, but she lacked the required charm to be a successful emissary for the royal cause. Countess von Groeben, a striking 85-year-old who considered the Nazis all to be gangsters, asked the 'Empress' in an impeccably courteous and grand manner: 'Is it true His Majesty has made a donation to the National Socialists?' The 'Empress' just stood in embarrassed silence.[76]

At Nuremberg in 1929, Hermine tactlessly asked Hitler, always awkward in aristocratic company, why he had never married. The Führer tersely replied that he had no ambition to create a dynasty.[77] However, both Hitler's staff and the Kaiser's courtiers realised that personal contact between the court-in-exile and the Nazi Party was essential. Rather than send the oafish Hitler, the plump and rosy Hermann Göring was dispatched to visit the Emperor.

Göring was a hugely overweight man with cumbersome jowls and expensive tastes. Wounded in the failed Beer Hall Putsch of 1923, he was one of Hitler's earliest followers. Now, he was rewarded with a place in Hitler's Cabinet as the Prime Minister for Prussia and became known as Nazi Number Two. His reputation as a flying ace and recipient of the *Pour le Mérite* (Order of Merit) was useful in aristocratic circles. It helped to compensate for his lack of noble pedigree. The Order had been founded in 1740 by King Frederick II of Prussia and named in French, which was the favoured language at the King's court.

Göring impressed Hermine, who called him a 'true and respectful man',[78] but Wilhelm found the Nazis too full of themselves. He criticised Hitler's pretentiousness for using the title 'Führer',[79] while he dismissed Göring as 'a vain creature, a mere army captain who would be consigned to obscurity' once Wilhelm returned to the throne. Nevertheless, the Kaiser gave the acquisitive Göring furniture and silk hangings from the royal collections to secure his future co-operation.[80] In the Kaiser's mind, the Nazis could be used to effect a Hohenzollern restoration, but there would be no place for them afterwards.

Berlin. 1933.

Meanwhile, Prince Christoph of Hesse and Göring had become close friends after the July 1932 elections, with Göring always maintaining the upper hand in the friendship, as the Prince's patron. Christoph had initially joined the party clandestinely in October 1931, concerned perhaps that Nazi Party membership would undermine his reputation. However, on 3 July 1933, Christoph filled out his application again, receiving membership card number 1,498,608. He then backdated his entry to the party to before the Nazis' seizure of power, receiving the number 696,176 with the help of Martin Bormann, a member of Hitler's inner circle. The drastic revision in his membership number reflected the Prince's prominent position inside the regime.[81]

Prince Christoph became one of Göring's first recruits and he was commissioned as a _Sturmführer_ (SS Lieutenant) of his own company – or _Sturm_ – of 160 men, who were mostly violent thugs. Göring then appointed him a first secretary in the Prussian State Ministry and later Head of the _Forschungsamt_ (Research Office), a wiretapping and surveillance unit that was the forerunner of the Gestapo. By 1933, the Nazis had started to phone-tap citizens whose loyalty was questioned. People quickly became fearful of discussing political issues on the telephone as the country lost the freedom of the press, the freedom of assembly and the freedom of speech.

Both Christoph and his wife, Princess Sophie, were true Nazi believers and became party stalwarts. They were never opportunistic 'March Violets', the name for members who joined after Hitler's assumption of power on 5 March. Throughout the 1930s, they continued to ignore the dark side of the regime and arduously courted Göring's favour.

At Göring's wedding to the actress Emmy Sonnemann in April 1935, Christoph and Sophie were seated at the head table, with Princess Sophie in a place of honour next to Hitler. Among the guests were also Duke Charles Edward of Coburg and members of the Hohenzollern family. Royalty sat cheek by jowl with grim Nazi henchmen like Martin Bormann and Reinhard Heydrich.[82]

There was an intelligent strategy beneath Hitler's and Göring's pretentious wooing of royalty. They both realised the enormous political gains the Nazi Party could enjoy internationally with the support of the princely families. After the Beer Hall Putsch, Göring had travelled to Italy looking for new support from potential fascist enthusiasts, and found no one there willing to help them. His reception changed after he courted the Princes of Hesse, who opened the door to Mussolini for the Nazi leadership.[83]

As the King of Italy's son-in-law, Prince Philipp of Hesse rose quickly in the party hierarchy. Philipp had joined the Nazi Party in October 1930 and had a higher membership number than his brother: 418,991. Thanks to Göring's patronage, he became *Oberpräsident* (Governor) of Hesse-Nassau and a member of the Reichstag. His crucial role in the early years was to help the consolidation of Nazi rule in Germany, introducing other aristocrats to the party and lending the Nazis the aura of credibility.

In her post-war memoirs, Emmy Göring wrote that her husband 'especially cherished' the Hesse brothers.[84] The two couples regularly shared the royal box at the opera, where they sat glittering with medals and jewels, with Göring wearing his perfect white uniform. The Görings stayed with Philipp and Mafalda at their villa on Capri and soon Philipp was acting as a special envoy to Benito Mussolini.[85] Philipp and Mafalda also paid return visits to Karinhall, the Görings' fabulous hunting estate north-east of Berlin. Göring filled the house with lavish art, priceless furniture and even his desk set was encrusted with precious stones. Along the centre of the dining-room table sat a solid row of silver beasts, each one modelled on an animal he had shot. There was even a menagerie of pet lions. Princess Mafalda warned her children about the lions after 'one of the cubs leapt on me and tore the sleeve on my leopard-skin coat'.[86]

In the basement of Karinhall, Göring installed a complete Elizabeth Arden beauty unit where he could have his hair washed and waved, and exercise on a roller to remove his excess flab.[87] Ridiculously vain, Göring changed his attire according to his mood – sometimes several times during one function – and he painted his nails. Italian Foreign Minister Galeazzo Ciano was shocked to see Göring wearing a fur coat that looked like what 'a high-grade prostitute wears to the opera'.[88] However, beneath his swaggering braggadocio, he was as ruthless and unbending as Hitler himself.

Salem. 1933.

At Salem, Kurt Hahn spoke out against the savage murder of a local communist by Nazi Stormtroopers. Underestimating the Nazis' ability for vengeance, Hahn had written to the school's old-boy network, stating that 'Salem cannot remain neutral'.[89] He demanded that they all break with Hitler's thuggish regime. Payback was inevitable as soon as Hitler assumed power.

The local newspaper, *Bodensee Rundschau*, wrote about the 'sinister operations of the Jew Hahn',[90] and the police arrested him. When Prince Berthold protested, an angry Führer snapped: 'Why don't you aristocrats get rid of your *Hofjuden* [Jewish courtiers]?'[91] Only when the British Prime Minister Ramsay MacDonald made a personal appeal to the German Foreign Office was Hahn released and allowed to travel to London.[92]

The Baden family, unlike the Hesse and Coburg families, were less enthusiastic about the Nazis. Berthold persuaded Theodora to enrol her 12-year-old brother, Prince Philip of Greece, at the school at a time when many parents from abroad were withdrawing their children from the country.[93] The Nazi regime valued the Baden family's connection to the British Royal Family – a fact that might have increased Berthold's bargaining power with the new Nazi administration.

Young Philip arrived in Salem just as many in the German aristocracy were showing a dangerous inclination towards Nazism. With Hahn now in Britain, Berthold took over the school, but the day-to-day management fell to a Kommissar whose job was to promote Nazi ideology. The regime quickly changed: military athletics with tedious close-order drills became a daily routine, and the pupils joined the Hitler Youth. During assemblies, the boys listened to Hitler's interminably long speeches on the radio.[94]

Philip was habitually addressed merely as 'Greece' and never really integrated into the school. Speaking German quite badly, he became isolated.[95] Overall, Philip preferred Cheam in Surrey, and the ghastly new Salem military regime far outweighed the benefits of living with his sister. Investing his energy in schoolboy pranks, he laughed condescendingly at the Nazis' goose-stepping. As for the 'Heil Hitler' salute: Cheam boys used a similar gesture to ask permission to use the lavatory and Philip refused to participate in such hilarious arm-stretching.[96] General Sir Leslie Hollis, the former Commandant General of the Royal Marines, who knew Philip well, said he hated the Nazi overtones that had crept into the school:

> His dislike was intense for one so young. Characteristically, it found expression not in youthful political speech making but in flagrant irreverence. All the heel-clicking and saluting struck him as ridiculous … Philip would have none of it and his constant refusal to take the Nazi way could lead in the end to serious trouble, not only for himself but for members of his family.[97]

Princess Theodora and Prince Berthold quickly decided to send Philip back to Britain to resume his education. Theodora concluded: 'We thought it better for him and also for us.'[98]

HIGH SOCIETY

Grosvenor Square, London. 1933.
The Nazis, with their elaborate uniforms and their futuristic imagery, had a certain chic, particularly for the 'Ritz set' who surrounded the Prince of Wales. Drawing-room Nazis, like Emerald Cunard and Nancy Astor, were London society's most influential powerbrokers and kept Prince Edward company.

Emerald was an American hostess and the wife of Sir Bache Cunard, the shipping tycoon. Sir Oswald Mosley described her as 'a bright little bird of paradise' and her dinner parties as the stuff of legend with 'the cleverest men, together with the most beautiful women'.[1] Lady Cunard became one of Prince Edward's closest friends, and he found it impossible to be bored in her company. Her sparkling conversation was light relief compared to the purgatory dialogues endured in his parents' company at Buckingham Palace. With her guests, Emerald delighted in discussing the merits of Mussolini and Hitler, alongside her lifelong passion for the opera, interspersing her conversation with arias from Bellini, Verdi, Puccini and Wagner. Her critics were not always kind: one ungallantly described her as 'looking like a third-dynasty mummy painted pink by amateurs'.[2] Queen Mary, like many in the Windsor family, was a moribund middlebrow and banned her from the court because she displayed a 'gilded cunning and eccentric brilliance'.[3]

Nazism was also part of Lady Cunard's superficiality. Warningly, Robert Worth Bingham, the American ambassador, described her set as a 'pro-German cabal' and Lloyd George considered her the most dangerous woman in London society because she encouraged gossipy indiscretions from even the most conventional politicians. It was Lady Cunard who introduced the Prince of Wales to Oswald Mosley and Joachim von Ribbentrop, Hitler's envoy. Her attitude towards Ribbentrop was 'a mixture of flattery and being flattered, and a delight in having the arch-Hitler spy of Europe in her circle'.[4]

By 1933, the young Prince of Wales was genuinely intrigued by Nazi politics and Henry 'Chips' Channon, the politician and diarist, observed that Edward was going 'the dictator way and is pro-German. I shouldn't be surprised if he aimed at making himself a mild dictator – a difficult enough task for an English King.' His brother, the glamorous Prince George, Duke of Kent, was equally enthusiastic about Hitler's new regime. Much excited talk took place within both princes' inner circles about Mosley's extreme right-wing party – the British Union of Fascists (BUF) – and Prince Edward even corresponded with Mosley.[5]

Many within the British aristocracy felt society was in deep crisis. The political challenges facing the British Empire seemed overpowering, and the nine-day General Strike of 1926, where the working classes had almost brought the country to a standstill, had been a wake-up call. Many feared that communism had infected Britain. While most of the country's intellectual elite turned towards the extreme left, the upper classes switched to the right, towards Hitler and Mussolini. These charismatic new dictators may have been ruthless leaders, but for the aristocracy, they served a purpose: a bulwark against communism in central Europe. Only Winston Churchill shifted his opinion and started to view Hitler as a more significant menace than communism, but he was in the minority and stood almost alone.

Cliveden. 1933.

Cliveden was the elaborate Italianate party house owned by Lord Waldorf and Lady Nancy Astor. It overlooked the River Thames and stood just 5 miles from Windsor Castle at Taplow. Flanked by two giant wings and approached from the north by a long gravel drive, it would not look out of place in Rome, overlooking the Borghese gardens. Harold Nicholson described how a 'ghastly unreality' hovered over Cliveden: 'Its beauty is purely scenic ... to live here, would be like living on the stage of the Scala theatre in Milan.'[6]

Lady Astor was another capricious American in London who imposed her vivid character on the weekend house parties held at Cliveden between the wars. Her two Pekinese dogs, 'Peeky' and 'Sue-Sue', followed their mistress around the great house and their soft growls chimed with their owner's aggressive manner. Chips Channon complained he always felt '*désoeuvrè* and bored' at Cliveden. 'There is nothing so out of date as a 1900 house, which Cliveden is *en plein*.'[7]

Entertainment at Cliveden included charades, musical chairs and occasionally, to enliven the party, Lady Astor amused guests by mimicking stereotypes: dressing herself up in a Victorian hat and a pair of false teeth to perform impressions of a snobbish and condescending British upper-class lady, or donning an ill-fitting jacket for a turn as a 'low caste-Jew'.[8] Nancy embodied the prejudices of her time and class, including a deep loathing for communists and Jews. This stance was common amongst American and British upper-class society, who saw poor Jews as the carriers of communism, and the rich ones as annoying arrivistes with more money than taste. Nancy often wrote to Joseph Kennedy, the United States' ambassador to Britain. Their letters contained much anti-Semitic language: Lady Astor saw Hitler as the answer to 'world problems',[9] and Kennedy replied that the 'Jew Media' in America was problematic, for 'the Jewish pundits in New York and Los Angeles' were making noises contrived to 'set a match to the fuse of the world'.[10]

Although Nancy's anti-Semitism was not the lethal species of central Europe, it was a more discreet strain, but insidious beneath its polished society surface. Harold Nicholson, another Cliveden regular, wrote: 'Although I loathe anti-Semitism, I do dislike Jews.'[11] Lady Astor and Nicholson fell into that category of bigotry which could be tolerant of individuals but was suspicious of the group to which they belonged. Such selective prejudice allowed Nancy to be friends with Zionist leader Chaim Weizmann, but her intolerance was such that she said he was 'the only decent Jew I've ever met'.[12] British society also tended to distinguish between two types of Jew: the 'liberal European' kind and the 'vulgar, arrogant' Jew who came from Eastern Europe.[13]

The Astors' weekend hospitality also promoted their brand of politics. Lord Astor had been one of the first members of British society to meet Hitler. Lady Astor, a Conservative MP since 1918, was determined to forge Anglo-German bonds after the horrors of the First World War. The Astor family had historical family roots in Waldorf in southern Germany, so they were naturally sympathetic to Germany. Lord Astor's two newspapers, *The Times* and *The Observer*, promoted Hitler as someone of 'moderate outlook' beneath the uncouth exterior. Lord Astor felt that Hitler spoke for the discontented and rallied 'honest and earnest elements' among the 'splendid young people of the German middle class' to his cause.[14]

Most of the political guests at Cliveden were benevolent towards Nazi Germany: they included Joseph Kennedy, Charles Lindberg, Lord Lothian, Lord Halifax (Foreign Secretary between 1938 and 1940), Geoffrey Dawson (editor of *The Times*), Sir Samuel Hoare (Foreign Secretary in 1935), Neville Henderson (the British ambassador to Berlin), former Prime Minister Lloyd George and the Duke of Kent. This exclusive fraternity believed in coaching Nazi Germany into playing a responsible European role.

At after-dinner parties, Lady Astor instructed her English guests in her Anglo-American sotto voice to let her German guests like Ribbentrop, Princess Stephanie von Hohenlohe and Charles Edward, Duke of Coburg, win at the parlour games they played later.[15]

When Germany pulled out of the League of Nations in 1933, Lady Astor urged Britain to disarm to prove their desire for peace. Such a pro-appeasement stance was popular amongst the aristocracy, right-wing politicians and the diplomatic corps. Lady Astor wrote: 'It was true that at Cliveden a number of recurrent guests were in favour of appeasing the new Germany, but appeasement was by no means a bad word at the time.'[16]

Dachau. 1933.

While Britain's upper classes discussed German politics in theoretical terms, Germany's first concentration camp had opened at Dachau on 20 March 1933. This camp was the start of the Nazi reign of terror which proved indispensable in silencing their critics. Within Germany, few people cared about the fate of Dachau's first inmates – communists, gypsies, homosexuals, Jews and lunatics – who were society's outsiders. When newspapers published the details of the murder of a communist politician, Fritz Dressel, by one of the Dachau guards, furious camp officials denounced this as fake news. They complained that the writer Hans Beimler, who had witnessed the crime, was 'one of the worst peddlers of horror stories'.[17]

During that first year, vast numbers of people, estimated to be 200,000, were rounded up and placed in 'protective custody'.[18] Makeshift camps sprung up across Germany in unlikely locations, such as vacant hotels, sports grounds and castles. 'No village or city quarter is without such private martyring den,' wrote the communist journalist Theodor Balk.[19] The Nazis claimed these early camps were their method of dealing with 'wasters, idlers, social undesirables, Jewish profiteers and riffraff' by re-educating them through work.[20] The Nazis hung their infamous sign *Arbeit macht frei* (Work Sets You Free) over Dachau's entrance, but the local German people understood what was happening, as a cautionary rhyme became popular: '*Lieber Gott, mach mich stumm, Dass ich nicht nach Dachau komm!*' (Dear God, make me dumb, so I won't to Dachau come!)[21]

Extraordinarily, Dachau became a destination for many politically curious British travellers to Germany. Despite the murders, the German authorities were willing to show off Dachau to foreign visitors, particularly journalists and politicians. Victor Cazalet MP was a curious tourist who wanted to be informed about the workings of Hitler's New Germany. He described the camp in 1934 as 'not very interesting but quite well run'. Another parliamentarian, Sir Arnold Wilson, observed that the men seemed well housed and fed, but, he wrote, 'there was an atmosphere of the camp, something which revolted my soul'.[22] Visitors were not aware that the 'degenerate criminals' paraded before them were often, in fact, camp guards in disguise.[23] Vice Admiral Sir Barry Domvile visited Dachau and felt that it was splendid that the Nazis were giving the 'dregs of humanity' a new start. He penned in his diary: 'A lot of crimes against small girls, a murder or two ... went into one room full of buggers.' He praised the camp's efficiency and comfort, writing, 'The English press have been disgraceful lately with their lies about Germany.'[24] Domvile never saw the worst elements of the camp. Still, there was an element of wilful blindness that infected many invitees – or perhaps Nazi propaganda dulled visitors' senses and blurred their critical abilities.

The world stood by and watched the genesis of a terrifying new social experiment in 1933. Decades after the war, journalist Michael Burn re-read his account of his visit to Dachau. He was sickened by his apathy to the cruelty. In his memoirs, he questioned why he had not demanded to know what kind of trial the prisoners had been allowed, or how the Germans could justify the incarceration of citizens who were merely critical of the Nazi Party.[25]

Throughout this period, Hitler patiently watched for an adverse British reaction and found none even after the brutal Night of the Long Knives on 30 June 1934, when Hitler murdered his rival, Captain Ernst Röhm, the leader of the *Sturmabteilung* (SA), and eighty-five SA members who supported him.

Determined to avoid war with Britain, Hitler desired a military alliance. Hermann Göring's wife recalled how, at a dinner party for private

English visitors, Hitler remarked: 'I am so happy because I believe that we shall come to an understanding with the English, which is what I want beyond anything else.'[26] Despite making fun of the corrupt aristocracy, Hitler admired the British upper classes for their empire-building triumphs, and colleagues described him an 'anglophile romantic'.[27] The Führer, who had grown up in Austria under the Hapsburg monarchy, playfully toyed – but never with conviction – with the idea of a Hohenzollern restoration and the prospect of inviting the exiled Kaiser to return to Germany. What Hitler wanted was not another German Emperor, but an alliance with Britain. Understanding that elites preferred to do business with other elites, particularly in the instance of royalty, Hitler saw an opportunity to use the Windsors' German cousins as off-the-record diplomats.

Coburg. 19 October 1933.

On 19 October 1933, a triumphant parade of 4,000 Nazi Stormtroopers marched in torchlight through the town of Coburg. The marriage of Duke Charles Edward's daughter, Princess Sibylla of Saxe-Coburg and Gotha, to Prince Gustaf Adolf, heir to the Swedish throne, was a moment of national celebration. Hitler and Göring sent congratulatory telegrams while Coburg was decked out in Nazi flags to celebrate the two ceremonies. First, a civil service took place at Coburg Castle, and a religious service was then held in St Moritz Church on the following day. The wedding was a valuable opportunity for the Coburg family to show their Nazi credentials publicly, as Charles Edward had become a prized member of the party in March 1933 and the first German royal to support Hitler. He immediately joined the SA and later received the rank of *Obergruppenführer* (Senior Group Leader). From Charles Edward's viewpoint, Germany finally had a strong anti-communist leader, and he proudly promoted official photographs of himself in Nazi uniform taking a front-row seat next to other leading party members. The Duke of Coburg also purchased a house in Berlin, called the Villa Coburg, to be closer to the new sources of political power.[28]

Hitler now had a connection that took him into the heart of the British Royal Family. Princess Alice, the Countess of Athlone, Prince Arthur of Connaught and his sister Princess Patricia all attended the Coburg wedding. Not only was this a very public show of reconciliation with Germany after the First World War, but it was also a clear sign that Charles Edward would be received again in British society. Hitler knew that having his full support gave him money, credibility, prestige and high-level international connections.[29]

Brantridge Park, Sussex. 1934.

Understanding that great titles opened doors in diplomatic circles, Hitler selected Duke Charles Edward of Coburg as his emissary to the British Royal Family. Although many in Britain still viewed Charles Edward with suspicion, he was a grandson of Queen Victoria, and a cousin to George V. The Führer – who distrusted the German Foreign Office – tasked the Duke with wooing his British cousins. The German ambassador to London, Count Otto von Bismarck, resented Coburg's unofficial back-door manoeuvrings. Frustrated, he reported back to his superiors in Berlin:

> I told the Duke of Coburg at a reception this morning that the Foreign Editor of *The Daily Mail* visited me yesterday and asked me whether Lord Rothermere [owner of *The Daily Mail*] should receive the Duke … The Duke was very affronted by this and avoided my question whether there really was a meeting taking place with Lord Rothermere. In an embarrassed tone, he said, 'that it seemed to be impossible to carry out private trips these days.' I would like to add that I had a feeling the Duke's circle had strict instructions not to inform the embassy.[30]

Charles Edward no longer possessed his beloved Claremont House in Surrey, where he could have entertained useful friends discreetly. However, Princess Alice had purchased Brantridge Park outside Horsham in Sussex in 1922. This property was a large three-storey white house that was a conglomeration of Georgian, Victorian and Edwardian architecture, and the imposing building commanded sweeping views of gently sloping lawns and the South Downs. After a weekend house party, Charles Edward wrote a letter of thanks to his sister:

> Dearest Tigs,
>
> I do not know how I can thank you enough for all the hospitality you extended to me and my gentlemen at Brantridge. At any rate, I want to thank you once more with all my heart for all the help you gave me and for all the love you showed me. You and Alge [Lord Athlone] are really two dears. You both made Brantridge a true second Claremont for me. I felt so at home this time staying with you, that when I left Croydon [airfield], I felt quite as if I was leaving home.[31]

'My gentlemen' were Charles Edward's Nazi friends. One influential British politician, Alfred Duff Cooper, was angry at being ensnared by Princess Alice,[32] and after receiving her royal invitation to Brantridge Park he caustically wrote:

> The point of it was to meet the Duke of Coburg, her brother. It was a gloomy little party – so like a German bourgeois household. It reminded me of the days when I was learning German in Hanover. I was tactfully left alone with the Duke of Coburg after luncheon in order that he might explain to me the present situation in Germany and assure me of Hitler's pacifist intentions.[33]

Several members of London Society joined pro-German social clubs. Lord Mount Temple became chairman of the Anglo-German Fellowship (AGF) in September 1935, a group allied to Nazism. Its membership included Lord Redesdale, Diana and Unity Mitford, Ernest Tennant, Geoffrey Dawson (editor of *The Times*), the Duke of Westminster, Lord Londonderry (Minister for Aviation), Lord Lothian, the Earl of Glasgow, Lord Brocket, the Duke of Wellington, Montague Norman (Governor of the Bank of England), and Tory MPs like Edward Duncan Sandys, Sir Peter Agnew and Thomas Guinness. This elite private membership quickly grew to 450 members. Corporate membership was also available for businesses that wished to show their support for co-operation with Nazi Germany. Price Waterhouse, Unilever, Dunlop, Thomas Cook, the Midland Bank and Lazard Brothers all signed up.[34]

The AGF's sister organisation in Germany was the *Deutsch–Englische Gesellschaft* (German–English Society), formed in Berlin with Ribbentrop's support; it had the core purpose of making the Nazis seem respectable.[35] These two groups would often unite to host banquets where the guests of honour included Rudolf Hess, Joachim von Ribbentrop and the Duke of Coburg.[36] The Fellowship held a glittering dinner in Mayfair for the Kaiser's daughter, the Duchess of Brunswick, and her husband on 14 July 1936. Guests sat at tables decorated with swastikas and their choice of Bastille Day was deliberately provocative to the French.[37]

St James's Palace, London. 1935.

In London, the Prince of Wales started to plot his political path. Having seen the destruction of war at first hand in Passchendaele – the horror of the trenches and millions killed – Edward was determined to prevent such carnage ever happening again, and he became heavily involved in veterans' organisations. Old soldiers from the First World War comprised a significant number of people who visited Germany in the 1930s. A number of the highly decorated British soldiers, like Lieutenant Colonel Graham Hutchison, recipient of the Distinguished Service Order and Military Cross, were pro-German founding members of the British Legion. Hutchison founded the British Empire Fascist Party and was even on the Nazi payroll as a publicist. He campaigned for stronger imperialism and the removal of rights from British Jews. He wrote: 'We who survived the Great War are more concerned that peace shall be preserved.'[38]

While negotiations were progressing for a naval agreement between Britain and Germany, Edward gave a speech at the British Legion's Annual Conference on 11 June 1935. He asserted that the best way to ensure world peace was for British veterans of the First World War to visit Germany and 'stretch forth the hand of friendship to the Germans'. Publicly, this speech gave the impression that it was 'the seal of the friendship agreement between the two countries'.[39] It was naive and clumsy. Such remarks could not have been made at a more awkward time for the government, as discussions were under way for a naval agreement in which Germany was seeking to extend the limits of her air and sea armaments imposed by the Treaty of Versailles.

The Times reported the speech with the headline: 'Suggested Visit to Germany'. Edward's pro-German stance helped to make the Nazi Party acceptable, even fashionable, in London society and it upset both the British Foreign Office and the French government.[40] George V was furious that his son had so recklessly made a political statement that could undermine the monarchy's position of neutrality, and summoned him to Buckingham Palace to be severely reprimanded, possibly at the insistence of the Cabinet.[41] In a memo to the US State Department, Ambassador William E. Dodd wrote:

> It is difficult to conceive of any announcement better calculated to appeal to the prevalent German conception than the announcement of the Prince of Wales ... Hardly had the news been published in Berlin than statements in support were elicited from Göring, Hess and Ribbentrop ... with the greatest vitality.[42]

As well as making public statements, Edward was also privately indiscreet. The German ambassador in London, Leopold von Hoesch, reported to

Hitler that the Prince had been critical of the British Government's hard-line stance in the Anglo-German naval talks:

> The fact that he [Edward, Prince of Wales] has come to realise the rep-rehensible character of clashes of arms … by no means meant he was a pacifist. Far from it … he understood very well that the Reich Government and the German people were inspired by a similar idea. He fully under-stood that Germany wished to face other nations squarely, her head held high, relying on her strength and conscious that Germany's word counted as much in the world as that of other nations. I told the Prince that what he just said corresponded with the opinion of our Führer.[43]

For Hitler, the Prince's remarks meant a great deal. The German Führer now believed that when the pro-German Prince of Wales became king, there was a virtual guarantee of peace. He appointed Joachim von Ribbentrop to be his representative at the Anglo-German naval talks in London and sent the Duke of Coburg to accompany him. Charles Edward was very anxious about an anti-German clique in Britain who, he felt, were determined to undermine Germany. He declared:

> Has the house of Windsor forgotten that it has German roots and that Great Britain and my grandmother [Queen Victoria] owe their Empire to Bismarck's help? Are we in Germany not allowed to have the same rights that Great Britain would give any negro tribe?[44]

Charles Edward criticised King George V because 'he indulged in private hobbies and ignored politics',[45] and stated that he would discuss with the Prince of Wales the 'pitiful part the monarchy was playing in the affair'.[46] Charles Edward's behind-the-scenes interventions might have triggered Edward's unconstitutional outburst before the British Legion.

Ribbentrop was gradually becoming Hitler's unofficial ambassador-at-large, which allowed the Führer to circumvent traditional diplomatic protocols. Ribbentrop had even formed a rival Foreign Office called the *Dienststelle Ribbentrop* (Ribbentrop's Department) in Berlin, which con-ducted a foreign policy that was often divergent from the official channels. His directness and disregard for standard diplomatic etiquette chimed with what Hitler wanted for his revolutionary regime.[47]

The aristocracy and diplomatic corps always considered Ribbentrop an upstart. He was previously an ambitious businessman and champagne salesman, and they laughed behind his back at his pretentious use of the noble particle 'von' to which he had no right. Concurrently, his peers found him superficial, arrogant and a fanatic. Aside from his short legs, he was handsome with an appealing smile and arresting blue eyes. He possessed a beautiful baritone voice and was always perfectly tailored. However, his war injuries undermined his health, causing blackouts and depression.[48] As he had greater familiarity with the world outside Germany – something lacking amongst the Nazi Party hierarchy – he started to advise Hitler on foreign affairs. Soon, he became Hitler's confidant, much to the irritation of senior party officials who considered him a sycophant; he often listened intently to Hitler's pet ideas only to later present the same concept back to him. This tactic led the Führer to conclude that he was perfect diplomatic material.

As German Foreign Minister, the portly white-haired Konstantin von Neurath did not think the outcome of the Anglo-German naval negotiations would be at all favourable for Germany. He made Ribbentrop head of the delegation to London, expecting him to fail and discredit himself. At first, Ribbentrop angered Sir John Simon, who headed the British delegation, with his excessive demands, and negotiations dragged on.[49] Ribbentrop, however, was determined to succeed. He issued Sir John with an ultimatum: the British could either accept the 35:100 ratio of German-to-British ships as 'fixed and unalterable' by the weekend, or the German delegation would return to Berlin and build their navy to any size they wished. A furious Sir John was visibly angry with Ribbentrop's demands, fuming: 'It is not usual to make such conditions at the beginning of negotiations and then walk out.'[50]

To everyone's surprise, Sir John returned and accepted Ribbentrop's exacting mandate. Hitler was triumphant and declared the day that the Anglo-German Naval Agreement was signed 'the happiest in my life', believing it would launch the start of new Anglo-German co-operation. Festivities to celebrate the event took place throughout Germany.[51]

Fresh from his success in London, Hitler used Ribbentrop as a sort of diplomatic bellboy. He did all sorts of errands for the Führer, including hatching a new plan: a permanent marriage alliance between Britain and Germany. The Kaiser's granddaughter, Princess Friederike, was suggested as a suitable German bride for the Prince of Wales. In 1934, Friederike was attending an English school near Broadstairs in Kent and found herself being invited to Buckingham Palace to be inspected by George V and Queen Mary, who were the close friends and cousins of her parents, the Duke and Duchess of Brunswick.

The Brunswicks knew Ribbentrop socially; he had arranged for them to meet Hitler in May 1933. There was widespread speculation that the Duke of Brunswick would become Head of State when President Hindenburg died, perhaps even a Nazi emperor.[52] In the original German version of her memoirs, the Duchess expressed delight at the match and wrote that her daughter also wanted it.[53] However, according to a later English translation, she stated that both she and her husband were unhappy because of the twenty-three-year age gap between their daughter and the Prince of Wales. At the time, Edward was 40 and Friederike merely 17. The Duchess wrote:

> We received an astounding demand from Hitler conveyed to us by Ribbentrop. It was no more or less that we should arrange a marriage between [our daughter] Friederike and the Prince of Wales. My husband and I were shattered. Something like this had never entered our heads, not even for reconciliation with England.[54]

The marriage mission, however, was doomed to fail. The Prince of Wales was already besotted with a twice-divorced American called Wallis Simpson. More significant than this story is what it revealed about Hitler's approach to diplomacy. He continually bypassed his most experienced diplomats and significantly overestimated the political power of the Windsor family in Britain's constitutional monarchy.

THAT AMERICAN WOMAN

The Hotel Meurice, Paris. 23 October 1934.
The clicking of heels by hotel staff in the lobby at the Hotel Meurice sounded like castanets. A crew of porters scurried through the door with a mountain of luggage. The Prince of Wales's entourage then entered, led by a small, beautifully dressed woman: Mrs Simpson. Her sullen expression and the purposeful walk gave the impression that she would brush aside anyone who had the temerity to get in her way. Prince Edward followed a few paces behind her with a look of pure adoration on his face. Wallis Simpson had a 'fixed, purposeful stare and hard, determined eyes'.[1] Sir John Aird, the Prince's equerry, bemoaned that Prince Edward 'has lost all confidence in himself and follows W around like a dog'.[2]

Wallis Simpson had asserted her authority that summer. She had disposed of Edward's previous two mistresses, Freda Dudley Ward and Thelma Furness, before redecorating Fort Belvedere from top to bottom and teaching the royal butler, Finch, how to mix drinks in the American fashion – with a copious amount of ice cubes. When Finch refused to obey, the Prince fired him. Wallis then fired his successor, Crisp. Only Osbourne managed to hang on, understanding clearly where the power now lay.[3] Society was gossiping madly at the turn of events, and Chips Channon described Wallis as having the 'air of a personage who walks into a room as though she also expected to be curtsied to. At least she wouldn't be too surprised. She has complete power over the Prince of Wales.'[4]

Mrs Simpson's social elevation to the position of the *maîtresse-en-titre* puzzled many. For a generation of women, Edward was the world's most eligible bachelor and was celebrated in the popular song: 'I've danced with a man, who's danced with a girl, who's danced with the Prince of Wales.' By contrast, Wallis was no beauty, she acknowledged in her memoirs: 'Nobody ever called me beautiful or even pretty. My jaw was clearly too big and too pointed to be classic. My hair was straight when the laws of compensation might at least have provided curls.'[5] Mrs Simpson was, however, indisputably chic. Cecil Beaton noticed that she was 'alluring', her skin 'incredibly bright and smooth like the inside of a shell, her hair as sleek as only the Chinese women know how to make it'.

Edward and Wallis had travelled to Paris from Italy, disembarking the Orient Express at Domodossola, where Mussolini had provided them with a deluxe private railway carriage. It had been an idyllic summer, cruising the Mediterranean aboard Lord Moyne's yacht *Rosaura* and staying at the luxurious Hotel Villa D'Este on Lake Como. At the Meurice, the couple met up with Edward's youngest brother, Prince George, Duke of Kent, who was the only member of the Royal Family on friendly terms with Mrs Simpson. He was about to marry Princess Marina of Greece, and this impending royal wedding made him the centre of press attention. After years of rumours and scandal, the family were delighted that feckless George was about to settle down. However, just as one problem was about to be safely married off, this American disruptor from Baltimore was set to create new discord.

The following day, the two princes left Wallis in Paris, taking turns at the controls of the royal plane to attend the funeral of King Alexander of Yugoslavia in Belgrade. The new King was an 11-year-old boy, King Peter II, who was attending a prep school in England at the time of his father's death. His cousin, Prince Paul, an anglophile who often said that he 'felt like an Englishman',[6] became Prince-Regent. Educated at Christ Church, Oxford, Paul had joined the exclusive Bullingdon Club, where he first met the Prince of Wales, who was attending Magdalen College nearby. The two student princes became firm friends, and later Prince Paul forged equally close friendships with Prince George, Duke of Kent, and the Conservative politician Sir Henry 'Chips' Channon.

To add further to the infinite family interconnections, Paul was married to Princess Marina of Greece's pro-Nazi sister Princess Olga. Paul and Olga had both been instrumental in encouraging the romance between George and Marina. George had even proposed to Marina while a guest at Paul's Slovenian mountain lodge on Lake Bohinj.[7] People in London passed comment on the two princesses, that while the new 'Duchess of Kent would bring Balkan fashions to London … Princess Olga brought Hitler's emissaries to the White Palace [in Belgrade]'.[8]

Prince Philipp of Hesse and Hermann Göring were also at the funeral. Göring informed Hitler of the close friendship between Edward, George, Paul and Philipp. These four men were all kindred spirits and sympathetic to the Nazi Party. Philipp of Hesse wrote to Prince Paul immediately after the funeral, encouraging him on his first steps towards his later pro-Nazi stance:

> Göring, in whose house I am staying for a few days, came back greatly impressed from the funeral and his stay in Belgrade. He was full of admiration for you ... You have made a good friend of him which pleases me very much because you can always rely on his loyalty. His greatest wish is that you should come here as soon as you have got a chance so that Hitler can show you the new Germany.[9]

The following year, Göring and Philipp of Hesse revisited Belgrade and promised the Prince-Regent that Yugoslavia had nothing to fear from Nazi Germany. Göring issued another invitation for Paul to visit Germany for a shooting trip and the opportunity to meet Hitler. Concurrently, Prince Philipp arrived with toys for Paul's children and a gift from Hitler of two stunning Augsburg silver *cache-pots*.[10]

Buckingham Palace. 27 November 1934.

One month later, wearing a violet dress with a green sash designed by Eva Lutyens, Mrs Simpson took the hand of the Prince of Wales as he led her to the dance floor at Buckingham Palace. The Prince ignored her husband Ernest, leaving him at the edge of the ballroom looking embarrassed. Mr Simpson stood alone wearing the black knee breeches, as court custom dictated, while the gossipmongers teased: 'The Unimportance of Being Ernest.' Court snobs like Lord Curzon, Lord Derby and the Duke of Devonshire considered the middle-class Simpsons very second rate, and lamented the fact that Ernest Simpson worked for a living as a shipbroker.

The ball was part of Prince George's and Princess Marina's wedding celebrations, but that night everyone was speculating about Wallis Simpson's dazzling wardrobe and jewels which offended everyone. Unlike Mrs Simpson, all the court ladies had dressed down so as not to outshine the bride.

Society diarist Mrs Belloc Lowndes assumed the diamonds were costume pieces and those in the know 'screeched with laughter', exclaiming that all the gems were real. The Prince of Wales had given her £50,000 worth of jewels at Christmas, following it up with a further £60,000 worth at New Year.[11] A tidy sum worth £7 million today. When the King and Queen realised who she was, they watched with frosty alarm. Later, the King shouted to Count Mensdorff, a distinguished German diplomat who was also a distant relative, 'That woman in my house ... he [Prince Edward] smuggled her into the Palace.'[12]

Prince Christopher of Greece wrote in his memoirs about that evening at the Palace:

> The Prince of Wales laid his hand on my arm in his impulsive way.
> 'Christo come with me. I want you to meet Mrs Simpson.'
> 'Who is she?'
> 'An American. She is wonderful.'[13]

Edward's sister-in-law, Elizabeth, Duchess of York, thought that most Americas were vulgar and considered Wallis to be 'the lowest of the low, a thoroughly immoral woman'. The two women had met each other earlier in the year – at Fort Belvedere – with disastrous consequences. The Duchess of York had entered a room and discovered Mrs Simpson performing a very accurate impression of her: the high-pitched voice and sickly sweet demeanour. Lady Hardinge observed how 'Mrs Simpson went down badly with the Duchess from the word go. The Duchess was never discourteous, but you could always tell when she did not care for someone, and it was very apparent that she did not care for Mrs Simpson at all.'[14] In return, Wallis dubbed Elizabeth 'the Dowdy Duchess' and 'Cookie' because she looked like a fat Scottish cook. This shared antagonism eventually hardened into a lifelong animosity.

Despite the King's ban, two days later, Wallis and Ernest Simpson were seated in the front row at Westminster Abbey for the actual wedding of Princess Marina to the Duke of Kent. The bride wore a Molyneux silver French brocade dress, and Churchill remarked that she was the most beautiful woman in the country. After an extravagant fifteen-course meal, the new Duchess of Kent and her Prince embarked on a five-month honeymoon visiting Paris, Germany and a cruise of the West Indies including Trinidad, San Juan, Haiti, Kingston and Montego Bay.[15] They did not return until April the following year.

Marina made the best of her marriage; her playboy Prince was often unfaithful with both men and women, but the Princess was worldly and stayed dignified. However, it must have come as a shock when a South American homosexual inched up to her in a London nightclub and claimed, 'You don't know me, but I was your predecessor.'[16] The Duke of Kent, who had an eye for colour, entirely took over the redecoration of their new London home, 3 Belgrave Square. Throughout their marriage, he intervened a great deal in his wife's wardrobe choices, despite her impeccable dress sense. However, to the family at least, the Duke was a reformed character and no longer a high risk.

Throughout the mid 1930s, George frequently flew to Munich to socialise with his brother-in-law, Count Carl Theodor of Törring-Jettenbach, nicknamed Toto, who married Marina's second sister Princess Elizabeth of Greece. The couple owned an imposing castle, Schloss Winhöring, and were both Nazi sympathisers. Prince George – like his brother Edward – was firmly establishing warm relationships with the pro-Nazi cabal of European royals.[17]

Bryanston Court, London. 1935.

In 1935, a concerned George V asked Lord Trenchard, the commissioner of the Metropolitan Police, to investigate Mr and Mrs Simpson and the goings-on at their flat in Marylebone: 5 Bryanston Court. Not only had the Prince of Wales lavished gifts of jewellery on Mrs Simpson, but he also started to give Mrs Simpson an allowance of £6,000 per annum.[18] The King now suspected the Simpsons were blackmailers.[19] Even the Prince's unflappable and loyal lawyer, the donnish Walter Monckton, first assumed that the affair 'smacked of blackmail upon an extravagant basis' and Downing Street mused the possibility of deporting the couple.[20]

For Special Branch to investigate a member of the Royal Family was unprecedented. Trenchard chose Albert Canning, the son of a prosperous Essex businessman and a rising star at Scotland Yard, to head up this delicate reconnaissance. Canning had been promoted into Special Branch after only six months 'on the beat'. A veteran of campaigns against both the Irish Republican Army and the suffragette movement, he was sensitive and astute – a rare breed in Scotland Yard. He fully understood the boundaries under which he would be operating.[21]

Canning's first target for investigation was Wallis, and Scotland Yard officers began following her, tracking her movements, whom she was meeting and what she was wearing. The police also interviewed people she met to detect the subtleties and dynamics of her relationship with the Prince of Wales. It was clear that Special Branch was 'interested in the minutia of the personal relationship between Wallis Simpson and the Prince of Wales ... the kind of surveillance you would use for an enemy spy'.[22]

When the Prince of Wales and Mrs Simpson visited an antique shop in Pelham Street in South Kensington, Canning noted that 'they were on very affectionate terms' and addressed each other as 'darling'. Edward and Wallis made several purchases, and the couple gave orders for the shopkeeper to deliver the goods to York House, Edward's London home. However, it was noted by the antiques dealer that 'the lady seems to have the POW [Prince of Wales] completely under her thumb'.[23]

'Her patterns of behaviour,' Canning noted, showed that she was 'very fond of the company of men'. He reported that Wallis had many 'affairs' during her first marriage to Earl Winfield Spencer, a US navy pilot. The couple had lived in China and this fuelled speculation. Canning discovered that Wallis gambled heavily in the Peking gaming houses in 1925, and gossip suggested that she worked as a paid hostess in an exclusive Shanghai brothel or 'singing house'. Another rumour spread that her pilot husband had taken her to a brothel in Hong Kong, where she learnt ancient sexual practices such as Fang Yung, a form of massage. There was even talk that Wallis had conducted a passionate affair with a handsome Italian diplomat in Peking, Count Galeazzo Ciano, the fascist son-in-law of Mussolini. They also whispered that she suffered from 'gynaecological problems' following a secret visit to a women's hospital in China for an abortion.[24]

Canning was beginning to realise Wallis's powerful hold over the Prince. He came to share the King's view that the Simpsons were using the Prince of Wales to extract money. Canning described Mr Simpson as of 'the bounder type' who 'makes no secret of his association with POW and seems to enjoy some reflected glory because of this and to make what capital he can out of it'.[25]

Detectives also investigated the racy, promiscuous and pro-fascist 'Ritz Set' that encircled both Edward and the Simpsons. This list included Lady Emerald Cunard, Sir Oswald Mosley, Diana Mitford, Fruity Metcalfe, Lady Alexandra Curzon, Nazi Spy Princess Stephanie von Hohenlohe, and Alice 'Kiki' Preston (the Duke of Kent's former lover). During a high-spirited party at Bryanston Court, the Prince of Wales even donned a German army helmet and goose-stepped around the drawing room.[26] Privately, Edward started to speak about fascism being 'a good thing'.[27]

The German Embassy, London. 1935.
Wallis's new power over the future King had not gone unnoticed by the Germans, who became extremely anxious to court the Prince's influential

new mistress. Prince Otto von Bismarck, with his glamorous wife Princess Ann-Marie, was a rising diplomat attached to the German Embassy in London and hosted lavish parties attended by both Mrs Simpson and Leopold von Hoesch, the German ambassador. On many occasions, Wallis spent the night at the embassy.[28]

German intrigue, it seemed, engulfed Mrs Simpson. One of her neighbours at Bryanston Court was Hitler's secret agent Princess Stephanie von Hohenlohe, who had already struck up friendships with the Duke of Kent and Lady Cunard. The Nazi Princess was openly referred to in the press abroad as 'Europe's Number One Diplomat' and 'Hitler's mysterious courier'. The *New York Mirror* wrote: 'Her apartment has become the focus for those British aristocrats who have a friendly stance towards Nazi Germany. Her soirees are the talk of the town. Prominently displayed in her drawing room is a large picture of Hitler.'[29] A British intelligence report noted that Princess Stephanie became Hitler's 'talent spotter' in London and that she had been given the job of selecting from among the British Establishment 'possible future friends of Hitler and Nazi Germany'.[30]

Canning's detectives also noted that Joachim von Ribbentrop, Hitler's roaming envoy at large, who held the title Ambassador Extraordinary and Plenipotentiary on Special Mission, was a regular guest at the Simpsons' apartment in Bryanston Court. The mechanically charming Ribbentrop was determined to fulfil the role of intermediary between Hitler and the British Royal Family after his great success negotiating the Anglo-German naval agreement the previous year. He showered Wallis with gifts, sending her seventeen carnations every day from the florist shop of Mrs Simpson's great friend, Constance Spry.[31]

Soon, a rumour circulated in London that year that Ribbentrop and Wallis were lovers. According to the vehemently anti-Nazi Duke of Württemberg, another German cousin to the British royals, seventeen represented the number of occasions the two lovers had slept together. After the war, the German Duke became a Benedictine monk and called himself Father Odo. He briefed the FBI agents on the alleged Ribbentrop–Simpson matter. He repeated the allegation that the Prince of Wales was impotent until Mrs Simpson deployed skills learnt in a Chinese brothel to 'satisfactorily gratify the duke's sexual desires'.[32] Mary Raffray, Wallis's close American friend who stayed at Bryanston Court, sent letters to her sister Ann recalling the boxes of 'huge flowers' sent by Ribbentrop and also repeated the allegation about their affair.

Nuremberg. 12 September 1935.

By late 1935, only the wilfully blind could overlook the Nazi regime's sinister character. At Nuremberg, a leading German physician, Gerhard Wagner, announced the Nazi government's intention to strip Jews of their German citizenship. Predictably, this provoked a wave of anti-Semitism across the country as Nazis harassed Jews on the street and vandalised their property. Non-Jews stopped socialising with Jews or shopping in Jewish-owned shops. At public lidos, it was considered entirely appropriate to display a sign reading, *Juden ist der Zutritt utersagt* (Jewish entry is prohibited), to prevent Jews and non-Jews swimming together.[33] The Nuremberg Laws crippled the Jewish community, as Jews were no longer permitted to work in the civil service or professions such as teaching, architecture, law and medicine. Many middle-class professionals took menial work. Emigration was problematic; the Nazis required Jews to remit 90 per cent of their wealth as a tax if they left Germany, and by 1938 Jewish emigrants could not find a country willing to take them.

The pro-German lobby in Britain overlooked these stark facts, and there seemed a complete lack of urgency to deal with the more unpleasant aspects of Nazism. As far as the British aristocracy was concerned, Nazism provided a bulwark to communism and offered full employment to the German people. A general feeling prevailed that it was somewhat unfair to adopt a British standard on un-British conditions. Many people wanted to find some way of justifying the unfathomable evil of Nazi policies. Veron Bartlett MP used words like 'explanation' and 'understanding' when writing about Hitler. He penned, 'Brutality can never be excused, but it sometimes can be explained.'[34] Ernest Tennant regretted the fact that 'World opinion seems to be concentrated on discussing and exaggerating the bad in the Hitler movement, and ignoring the good'.[35] The Jewish problem was deplorable, admittedly, but 'our Press should pay more attention to the constructive side of the Hitler movement'.[36]

Sandringham, Norfolk. 15 January 1936.

On the evening of 15 January 1936, King George V took to his bedroom at his private Sandringham residence in Norfolk complaining of a cold; he never left that room again. Each day, he became gradually weaker, drifting in and out of consciousness. The King directed his last words to his nurse, Catherine Black, mumbling, 'God damn you!' when she gave him a sedative. His son, Edward, was at his bedside when he passed away on

20 January. The 41-year-old playboy pro-German Prince was now King-Emperor. Edward's intense grief at that moment was considered 'frantic and unreasonable' and 'it far exceeded that of his mother and three brothers'.[37] Chips Channon wrote in his diary: 'My heart goes out to him. He will mind so terribly being King. His loneliness, his seclusion, his isolation will be almost more than his highly strung and unimaginative nature can bear.'[38]

The day after, the new King Edward VIII sat down to have a fireside chat with his first cousin once removed, Charles Edward, Duke of Coburg. They smoked their pipes and then travelled back to London together. The Duke had been staying at Princess Alice's apartment inside Kensington Palace. Alice explained in her memoirs that Charles Edward had come to London to watch a friendly football match between England and Germany. However, in reality, Coburg knew that George V was dying and wanted to be on hand to influence Edward and push Hitler's agenda. Princess Alice was helping Charles Edward politically, inviting Anthony Eden, Neville Chamberlain, Lord Astor and Duff Cooper to dine with her Nazi brother at Kensington Palace.

The Duke of Coburg wrote a detailed report to Hitler about his conversation with the new King. He claimed that Edward VIII now felt that a German–British alliance was an urgent necessity and a guiding principle for British foreign policy. When Coburg asked about the possibility of a meeting between Hitler and Prime Minister Baldwin, Edward had replied: 'Who is King here? Baldwin or I? I wish myself to talk to Hitler, and will do so here, or in Germany.' Charles Edward concluded that:

> The King is resolved to concentrate the business of government on himself. For England, not too easy. The general political situation, especially the situation in England herself, will perhaps give him the chance. His sincere resolve to bring Germany and England together would be made more difficult if it were made public too early. For this reason … the peculiar mentality of the Englishman must be taken into account if we want to achieve success – which undoubtedly is attainable.
>
> The King asked me to visit him frequently so that confidential matters might be more speedily clarified in this way. I promised – subject to the Führer's approval – to fly to London at any time he wished.[39]

For a new monarch to show any sign of favour to Nazi Germany would be quite outrageous, since it would signal Britain's support for the despicable

internal policies of the Third Reich. Even as his father had lain dying at
Sandringham, Edward had summoned Leopold von Hoesch, the German
ambassador, and expressed sympathy with what was happening in Nazi
Germany. He informed Hoesch that he fully intended to visit the Berlin
Olympics that were due to take place in the summer of 1936.[40] By stepping
into politics, Edward VIII cast himself in the mould of his grandfather,
Edward VII, who frequently intruded into foreign affairs, particularly
with his two cousins Tsar Nicholas II and Kaiser Wilhelm II. However,
the world had moved on considerably since the intimate diplomacy of
Queen Victoria's family grapevine.

St James's Palace, London. 1936.

Edward VIII's first public act was to present himself before an Accession
Privy Council and 100 councillors assembled in the beautiful old ban-
queting hall of St James's Palace in London. Here, the new King promised
to work for 'the happiness and welfare of his subjects'.[41] Stanley Baldwin,
the Prime Minister, noticed Edward's hands were shaking so much that
he rested the paper copy of his speech on the table, and he expressed his
doubts to Clement Attlee, the Leader of the Opposition, whether or not
the new King would 'stay the course'.[42] That night, Edward dined with
Mrs Simpson, and the following day she watched the Garter King of Arms
proclaim his Accession outside St James's Palace. Mrs Simpson and the
new King stood together at an upstairs window, and a press photographer
caught them. For the first time, the British public glimpsed Mrs Simpson.
The following day, her picture appeared in the newspapers, a mysterious
woman talking to Edward VIII.[43] So far, Baldwin had suppressed coverage
of their relationship, and it remained known only to a tiny circle.

At George V's funeral at Windsor Castle on 28 January, the Duke of
Coburg caused a stir by wearing his SS uniform as he walked behind the
coffin and sat with King Edward at the funeral dinner. In Berlin, Hitler
held an elaborate memorial service for the late King, sitting alongside
Crown Princess Cecilie of Prussia, Heinrich Himmler, Joseph Goebbels
and Hermann Göring. The Führer was determined to win over the new
King, but he overestimated Edward VIII's political power and influence.

Lord Wigram, the late King's Private Secretary, sensed radical change
was about to happen within the royal household. Edward was careless
and the palace staff complained that his odd hours were inconsiderate.
His subservience to Mrs Simpson's wishes and extravagance offended
many courtiers. When the King's great-uncle, the Duke of Connaught,

visited Fort Belvedere for afternoon tea and walked in the grounds, Mrs Simpson commanded the King without warning, 'Take off my dirty shoes and bring me another pair!' To the astonishment of Connaught, his nephew 'knelt down and smilingly complied'.[44] One of the royal footmen at the Fort resigned and explained his reason to a prospective employer: 'Mr Osbourne, the butler, sent me down to the swimming pool with two drinks. When I got there, what did I see but His Majesty painting Mrs Simpson's toenails? My Sovereign painting a woman's toenails. It was a bit much ... I gave notice at once.'[45]

Wigram's most significant concern was security. Top-secret documents were carried in the famous red boxes from Downing Street to Buckingham Palace, where they were meant to stay for the King to read. However, Edward took the boxes to the Fort and often it was weeks before anyone returned them. Baldwin fretted that the bored young King left crucial documents scattered about in his rooms.[46] Sir Eric Phipps, the British ambassador to Germany, wrote:

> Berlin was filled with loose talk about Edward. It was said that he neglected his duties in the handling of official documents. Secret Ambassadorial reports were especially emphasised. At Fort Belvedere, the Foreign Office despatch bags were said to be left open, and it was possible that official secrets had leaked out ... these rumours cast an undesirable reflection upon their king.[47]

Wigram resigned in 1936, making it clear that the new King was unreasonable, and Major Alexander Hardinge, an arch-conservative, took over. Chips Channon described him as a 'dreary narrow-minded fogie' who should be sacked.[48] Hardinge quickly came to loathe Edward – and their relationship would soon break down.

Controversially, Prime Minister Baldwin kept up the police surveillance on Edward which George V had started. For years, the British government denied such activity could happen. Still, recently declassified documents reveal that back in the 1930s, British intelligence created a secret dossier unlike any in British history. This security operation was no longer the King's investigation into the Prince of Wales. It was now an investigation authorised by the Prime Minister against the ruling monarch. Sir Robert Vansittart, the Permanent Under-Secretary at the Foreign Office, unofficially headed up the British intelligence service. Tall, broad-shouldered and athletic, Vansittart radiated sound judgement. He was 'suspicious of

Germany, shocked by Nazi brutality, disdainful of Hitler and pessimistic about the future of European peace'.[49] He became convinced that Mrs Simpson was a German spy after a Russian agent, Anatoly Baykalov, claimed that she sent secret messages to the Nazis via her dressmaker Anna Wolkoff.[50]

Wolkoff was the daughter of Admiral Nicholas Wolkoff, a White Russian émigré who was the former aide-de-camp to the murdered Tsar Nicholas II, and the last Imperial naval attaché in London. Like many Russian exiles, Anna and her father had fled the Bolshevik Revolution in 1917, and both held extremely right-wing anti-Semitic views.[51] Together, they ran the Russian Tea Rooms in South Kensington. These premises became a meeting point for members of the so-called Right Club led by Captain Archibald Ramsay, a Jew-hating Conservative MP[52] who recruited the Duke of Wellington and Lord Redesdale, father of the Mitford sisters, as members.[53] Posing as a White Russian, Baykalov infiltrated this group and discovered their mission to rid the Conservative Party of Jewish influence. Their badge had the logo of an eagle killing a snake with the initials 'P.J.' (Perish Judah).

In 1935, Anna was placed under surveillance, and for many Wallis Simpson was guilty by association. The American ambassador Robert Worth Bingham reported to Roosevelt: 'Many people here suspect that Mrs Simpson was in German pay. I think this is unlikely.'[54] However, Vansittart had two spies inside the German Embassy who for years kept him well informed: Jona von Ustinov (father of the actor Peter Ustinov) and Wolfgang zu Putlitz, who reported on Edward's leakage of valuable security information.

The evidence that Edward VIII and Mrs Simpson were dangerously pro-German was accumulating.

ABDICATION

The Rhineland, Germany. 7 March 1936.
On 7 March 1938, three Wehrmacht battalions marched across the Rhineland bridges into Germany's demilitarised zone at dawn. This armed invasion was the first test of Edward VIII's new kingship and an open breach of the Locarno Treaty. Edward telephoned Leopold von Hoesch, the German ambassador to London. Fritz Hesse, the press attaché, was a witness to the conversation:

> I was with von Hoesch when the telephone rang. Von Hoesch whispered to me: 'The King!' and handed the second receiver to me, so that I could listen to the conversation.
>
> 'Hallo,' a voice called, 'Is that Leo? David [Edward VIII] speaking. Do you know who is speaking?'
>
> 'Of course, I do,' replied von Hoesch.
>
> 'I sent for the Prime Minister [Baldwin] and gave him a piece of my mind. I told the old-so-and-so that I would abdicate if he made war. There was a frightful scene. But you needn't worry. There won't be a war.'
>
> Von Hoesch put down the receiver. He jumped up and danced around the room. 'I've done it. I've outwitted them all, there won't be a war! Herr Hesse, we've done it! It's magnificent, I must inform Berlin immediately.'[1]

Joachim von Ribbentrop also reported to Hitler on 11 March that Edward had issued a directive to the government that 'complications of a serious nature are in no circumstances to be allowed to develop' with Germany.[2]

At the time, Hitler was travelling to Munich aboard his private train, the *Führersonderzug* (Leader's Special Train), while nervously waiting for the British reaction to his latest manoeuvre. The atmosphere was jittery. The strength of the German war machine was still a bluff, but the trick succeeded. When the train stopped, a waiting soldier on the platform handed him a message.[3] The Führer opened the cable and 'sighed with relief'. 'At last!' he declared in triumph. 'The King of England will not intervene. He is keeping his promise. This means it can all go well.'[4]

Hitler's bold gamble fortified his popularity at home; it proved to him that the British had no stomach for a new war. Had France and Britain acted, they might have triggered Hitler's political downfall before he had time to consolidate his power base. However, the King, Stanley Baldwin and the aristocracy all favoured appeasement. Lord Lothian remarked: 'The Germans, after all, are only going into their own back garden.'[5] Only Churchill fully understood Hitler's ruse and the dangerous shift in Europe's balance of power that had occurred.

Hitler immediately dispatched the Duke of Coburg to London. Nerves needed smoothing to help ensure that Britain remained neutral. Charles Edward told them what they wanted to hear – that Hitler wanted peace. The Duke stayed in London long enough to discover Edward VIII's state of mind towards Germany. He was greatly reassured when the King sent a birthday telegram to Hitler on 20 April, wishing him 'happiness and welfare'.[6]

When Leopold von Hoesch died, ostensibly of a heart attack on 10 April 1936, Hitler replaced him as ambassador in London with Mrs Simpson's admirer, Ribbentrop. Ribbentrop's task, along with other Nazis such as Princess Stephanie von Hohenlohe and the Duke of Coburg, was to marginalise British critics of Hitler's regime. Hitler wanted to emphasise the common bonds between the two Aryan nations in the face of the growing communist threat from the Soviet Union, and hoped to reach an understanding with England which would leave Germany free to declare war on Russia.[7] He intended to use Edward's far-right susceptibilities to accomplish this policy. George Messersmith, an American diplomat, observed: 'It is probably that his [Edward VIII's] personal influence did much to retard British policy' during this period.[8]

As Nazi overtures continued towards the new King, it was also inevitable that the spotlight would fall on Wallis Simpson. There were wild rumours that she was supplying the German government with British state secrets.[9] Sir Robert Vansittart, the Permanent-Under Secretary of State for Foreign

Affairs, claimed that Mrs Simpson 'was in the pocket of Ribbentrop'.[10] He informed civil servants that Mrs Simpson had compromised the secret codes used by British embassies abroad. Meanwhile, the wife of the King's new Private Secretary, Helen Hardinge, noted Mrs Simpson's 'partiality for the Germans'.

The Foreign Office was starting to become extremely anxious about Edward and Mrs Simpson. Anthony Eden, the Foreign Secretary, complained that while George V knew much and interfered little, Edward VIII knew little and interfered much.[11] Eden asserted that 'if the King went on like that, they were ways and means of making him abdicate'.[12] By the summer of 1936, the Foreign Secretary had started to withhold all confidential information from the new King.

York House, St James's Palace. March 1936.

While Europe was on the brink of war, Edward was obsessed with how to make his mistress 'Queen Wallis'. To those ends, Ernest Simpson, the long-suffering husband, was invited to dinner at York House while Wallis was on a shopping trip to Paris that Edward had paid for. Accompanying Ernest was Bernard Rickatson-Hatt, the editor-in-chief at Reuters. Speaking frankly, Ernest told the King that his wife needed to choose between them, and asked Edward what his proposed intentions were. Edward quickly responded: 'Do you really think I would be crowned without Wallis by my side?'[13] Realising this was an opportunity to avoid a substantial divorce settlement, Ernest struck a deal with Edward: if Ernest agreed to a divorce, Edward would take care of Wallis financially.[14]

News of this meeting swept through the King's courtiers, including Sir Maurice Gwyer, First Parliamentary Secretary to the Treasury, Sir Lionel Halsey, then a council member for the Duchy of Cornwall, and Walter Monckton. They all questioned if the King would have dared speak so frankly and predicted 'blackmail upon an extravagant basis'.[15]

Wallis, who was staying at the Hotel Meurice in Paris, was distraught and entirely taken by surprise when Ernest informed her of his pact with the King. Not only was she furious that the two men in her life would discuss this matter behind her back, but at this stage, she had no intention of divorcing Ernest. She stubbornly clung to the fantasy that everything would remain the same.[16]

Edward was becoming more impulsive and showered Wallis with more expensive gifts. He had the words 'Hold tight' engraved on the clasp of a beautiful ruby and diamond bracelet by Van Clef & Arpels.

Edward also transferred a large sum of money to her account. It made Wallis feel financially secure, no matter what happened.[17] Wallis returned his romantic and practical gestures with a gift – a gold memorandum case engraved in her handwriting with a children's poem by Eleanor Farjeon:

> King's Cross! What shall we do?
> His purple robe is rent in two.
> Out of his crown, he's torn the gems.
> He's thrown his spectre into the Thames.
> The Court is quaking in every shoe.
> King's Cross! What shall we do?
> Leave him alone for a minute or two.
> April 1935. WE.[18]

The *Nahlin*, Mediterranean Sea. Summer 1936.

Edward felt trapped in the loneliness and boredom of his new job. That summer, he and Wallis escaped together on a Mediterranean cruise abroad the *Nahlin*, a large 250-foot yacht owned by Lady Yule, crowned with two tall masts and a white funnel. Wallis's and Edward's bedrooms were in the forepart of the ship. The other guests – Lady Diana Cooper, Duff Cooper, Lord and Lady Brownlow, Lord Sefton, Helen Fitzgerald (Lord Beaverbrook's sister-in-law), Lady Cunard and two American friends of Mrs Simpson, Katherine and Herman Rogers, were in the aft. The King stood half-naked in shorts on the freshly painted deck, provoking hundreds of camera shots from the foreign paparazzi. Such lack of discretion allowed Albert Canning's police surveillance to get closer. One of the courtiers called the yacht a 'floating whorehouse' because of all the shenanigans going on on board, and during the boat's refit the library had been removed and turned into a bar.[19] Wallis was broadcasting her position as *maîtresse-en-titre* to London society, which the old guard considered vulgar. It was this display, rather than any immorality, that justified their criticism of her in their minds.

Lady Diana Cooper resented Wallis's presence and her grating wisecracks. 'It's impossible to enjoy antiquities with people who won't land for them and who call Delphi Delhi,' she caustically wrote. Continuing in this vein, she grumbled, 'Wallis is wearing very badly. Her commonness and Becky Sharpness irritate.'[20] She was comparing Mrs Simpson to the determined social climber in Thackeray's *Vanity Fair*. In Athens,

Edward and Wallis met the Greek King, George II of the Hellenes, and his English mistress, Rosemary Brittain-Jones. 'Wallis' opposite number', Lady Diana acerbically observed. 'Why doesn't he marry her?'[21] Wallis asked, and Diana delighted in explaining to her that it was impossible for a king to marry someone who was a commoner and already married. This statement put Edward into a bad mood, but as Diana penned in her diary, 'he refused to face the implications, and the pair continued their *folie à deux*.'[22]

Malcolm Muggeridge dubbed the voyage 'The good ship Swastika' as Edward and Wallis stopped off in Athens to meet the authoritarian Greek premier General Metaxas. Later, the *Nahlin* anchored close to the Dalma Bagtche Palace in Turkey and Edward met another dictator, Kemal Ataturk. The Turkish President staged a Venetian-style regatta complete with fireworks that floodlit the Hagia Sophia dome to entertain the unmarried couple.[23] From Turkey, Edward and Wallis travelled to Bulgaria, where pro-Hitlerite King Boris greeted them. They brazenly slept together in the private car as the Imperial train driven by the Bulgarian King headed towards Austria, and refused to get out of bed early to greet the waiting children who were holding flowers on the station platform.[24]

16 Cumberland Terrace, London. October 1936.

While Edward finally took up residence at Buckingham Palace on their return to London, Wallis moved into 16 Cumberland Terrace on 7 October 1936. The house was a large and sumptuously furnished property designed by John Nash, with a vast drawing room overlooking Regent's Park, and the King sent over various royal household possessions including china, sumptuous furnishings, mirrors, bed linen and silver.[25] It was questionable whether Edward had the right to remove these items from Buckingham Palace, and later these belongings went to his home in France.

Edward was full of reassurances, and Wallis had begun to believe them. Her solicitor, Theodore Goddard, had started divorce proceedings on her behalf in the Ipswich County Court, because the London courts had a backlog of cases. At first, it did not occur to anyone that Edward intended to marry her. Society expected that he would tire of 'the lady of the moment', as he had all the others. Thanks to the severe censorship imposed by Britain's two most powerful press barons, Lord Beaverbrook and Lord Rothermere, there was never any mention of Mrs Simpson in the press, and she remained unknown to the British public.

Fort Belvedere, Windsor. 20 October 1936.

A nervous Prime Minister, Stanley Baldwin, arrived at the Fort at 10 a.m. on 20 October and was immediately shown into the drawing room. Baldwin's mission was to stop the Simpson divorce.

Much to the King's surprise, Baldwin asked for a morning whisky and soda, and the King rang for a member of staff to bring the alcohol. As Baldwin mixed his drink, he turned to King Edward and asked if he would like one as well.

'No thank you, Mr Baldwin,' the King replied. 'I never take a drink before seven o'clock in the evening.'

Finally, Baldwin asked about Mrs Simpson's upcoming divorce. 'Must this go on?' he enquired.

'Mr Baldwin,' Edward replied disingenuously, 'I have no right to interfere with the affairs of an individual. It would be wrong were I to attempt to influence Mrs Simpson just because she happens to be a friend of the King's.'[26]

Baldwin had secretly hired an American lawyer, Raymond Neudecker, to investigate Wallis's divorce from her first husband, Earl Winfield Spencer, in 1927. If Baldwin could not stop Wallis's second divorce, he was determined to find irregularities with the first marriage breakup. However, Aubrey Weaver, Wallis's divorce lawyer, succeeded in having the judge, Peck Alexander, seal the files on the case and blocked Baldwin's interrogations.[27]

Ipswich Court, Suffolk. 27 October 1936.

At last, the time had arrived: 2.15 p.m. Mrs Simpson, exhausted with nerves, sat in the courtroom in a small navy blue felt hat and a matching double-breasted coat and skirt. She was accompanied by her barrister, Norman Birkett, in his shabby wig and large horn-rimmed spectacles. Ernest Simpson was not present, but his solicitor North Lewis represented him. The public gallery was also cleared, on the King's instructions.

Wallis's American accent struck an incongruous tone in the drab British courtroom. Under oath, she detailed her husband's adultery. Reluctantly, the judge, Mr Justice Hawke, resolved, 'I suppose I must come to the conclusion that there was adultery in this case. Very well decree nisi.'[28]

The courtroom ordeal lasted nineteen minutes, and an obedient British press scarcely made any mention of the divorce in their newspapers. Under the law, it would take a further six months before the courts would declare the decree absolute on 27 April 1937. Meanwhile, the Palace had set Edward's coronation date for 12 May.

That evening, Wallis and Edward met at Cumberland Terrace, where he reassured her all would be well. For the King, it was an evening of celebration. He pulled from his pocket a Cartier box and presented it to her. There was a massive Mogul emerald engagement ring inside. Cartier had undertaken a worldwide search to find the jewel and located this stone in Baghdad. Engraved on the back was: 'WE are ours now.'[29]

House of Lords, London. 3 November 1936.

A week later, Edward presided at the State Opening of Parliament, looking 'like a young, happy Prince Charming'. Westminster was humming with rumours, and in every seat in the House of Lords sat inquisitive peers and peeresses who looked upwards at the Distinguished Strangers' Gallery, where the audacious Mrs Simpson sat. 'She must be a brazen-faced woman to appear thus among the assembled aristocracy within a week of the divorce,' wrote Archbishop Lang's chaplain, Rev. Alan Don.[30]

After Wallis's appearance inside Parliament, events moved quickly; until this point, Mrs Simpson had only been a problem for palace courtiers rather than the government. With the support of senior government ministers, Alan Hardinge, the King's Private Secretary, composed a letter to the King marked 'Urgent and Confidential',[31] cautioning Edward that the British press would not stay silent for much longer and the outcome would be 'calamitous'. Hardinge warned that if the King proposed to marry Mrs Simpson, then Baldwin's Conservative government would resign and the King's unthinkable marriage to a twice-divorced woman would become the chief subject of any subsequent election. Edward was furious and cut Hardinge off. On Walter Monckton's advice, he did not sack him, wanting to avoid any negative publicity that such a move would attract. Wallis was horrified when she read Hardinge's letter; she realised it could only mean 'that the Government was preparing for a crisis'.[32] A confrontation between the King and Parliament was inevitable.

Buckingham Palace, London. 16 November 1936.

'I understand,' said Edward to Stanley Baldwin in the audience chamber of Buckingham Palace, 'that you and several members of the Cabinet have some fear of a constitutional crisis developing over my friendship with Mrs Simpson.'

'Yes sir, that is correct,' answered the Prime Minister.

The King asked if a marriage between him and Mrs Simpson would meet with his approval, and Baldwin warned him that it would be unlikely.

Reporting the conversation later to Parliament, Baldwin pointed out the stark reality of the situation:

> That marriage would have involved the lady [Wallis Simpson] becoming Queen. I did tell His Majesty that I might be a remnant of the old Victorians, but that my worst enemy would not say of me that I did now know what the reaction of the English people would be to any particular course of action ... I pointed out to him that the position of the King's wife was different from the position of the wife of any other citizen of the country. His wife becomes Queen; the Queen becomes the Queen of the country; and therefore, in the choice of a Queen the voice of the people must be heard.[33]

Privately, Baldwin emphasised to Edward that he could keep Wallis as his mistress because, 'There has always been a leniency regarding the private relations of the King just because they are the only people subjected to strict regulation with regards to their marriages and wives.'

The King protested indignantly, 'I am going to marry Mrs Simpson.'[34]

Merthyr Tydfil, South Wales. 19 November 1936.

Three days later, Edward made a scheduled visit to South Wales in order to inspect the deprived mining villages facing pit closures and layoffs. It was a gesture of sympathy, and the hardship he witnessed shook the King, and he muttered, 'Terrible, terrible, terrible.'[35] Exploring the impoverished neighbourhoods, seeing the hungry faces and eyes, he announced, 'Something must be done to find them work.'[36] Such an impromptu comment made worldwide headlines. The *News Chronicle* declared: 'The King is above and outside politics. What he has done is in the sole interest of truth and public service ... The man in the street feels that Whitehall stands condemned.'

Baldwin's embarrassed Conservative government had to act, as the King's popularity swelled during the visit. Neville Chamberlain, the Chancellor of the Exchequer, ordered a new study on mining conditions and proposed government funding to ease the miners' suffering. Labour MPs fiercely demanded new legislation to attract industrial investment to South Wales. There was gossip that Edward, the crowd-pleaser, had overstepped his constitutional boundaries and was trying to score points at his government's expense. Whereas he had previously discussed the possibility of abdicating to marry Wallis or the possibility of a morganatic marriage, he seemed determined, after the visit to Wales, to keep his throne and to make her queen.

On 20 November, Edward returned to London and met his brother George, Duke of Kent, telling him he planned to marry Wallis. Alarmed, Prince George asked, 'What will she call herself?'

'Call herself? What do you think – Queen of England of course.'

'She is going to be Queen?'

'Yes, and Empress of India, the whole bag of tricks.'[37]

Buckingham Palace, London. November 1936.

The King started to meet Walter Monckton in secret towards the end of November. Monckton liked and respected Wallis; she had persuaded Edward to stop drinking and cut down smoking. He also knew that the King had been miserable and tortured before meeting her. A daily routine became established where the donnish lawyer would park his car at the back of Buckingham Palace and enter by the Privy Purse entrance to avoid being seen by Hardinge, who was always spying for Baldwin and Vansittart. From this side entrance, he would take the lift to the first floor, walk across the entire building, and then take another lift to descend into the Belgian Suite on the ground floor which the King used as his private apartment. This deception was useless, as the palace staff reported Monckton's sleuth-like movements directly to the Private Secretary, and Hardinge disingenuously made a point one evening of inviting Monckton to his office for a drink.[38] Afterwards, Monckton used his 17-year-old daughter Valerie as a secret messenger; she drove around London and out to Fort Belvedere in her battered old Morris car. Once, she was stopped by the police for speeding but was not at liberty to explain the real cause of her rush.[39]

Monckton offered the King sage advice: do nothing until the decree absolute of the divorce in April 1936, after which the coronation would soon follow, and Edward's position would be more robust. Winston Churchill, also a close friend of Edward's, gave him similar advice.[40] Edward refused – he was not prepared to go through with the coronation under false pretences. Monckton, impressed by his honesty, wanted to strike a compromise between 10 Downing Street and the Palace.

However, on 1 December, the Right Reverend Dr Blunt, Bishop of Bradford, made a speech at the annual diocesan conference expressing the hope that the King was aware of his need for God's grace. The insinuation was clear. The British press reported the Bishop's attack on the King and broke the story of the King's 'close friend' Mrs Simpson. Wallis's picture suddenly appeared in every newspaper. Distraught, Edward burst into panic-stricken rages, denouncing Wallis's critics and professing his love for her. Churchill, casting himself as a cupid and 'romantic monarchist',[41] suggested a morganatic marriage whereby Wallis would be Edward's wife, but not queen. Wallis would become a non-royal Duchess of Cornwall and any children they had would not inherit the throne. However, legal morganatic marriages were an alien concept under British law, and it was unlikely that Parliament would pass the required legislation.[42]

In Germany, on the Führer's express instructions, Dr Goebbels issued a directive prohibiting the German media mentioning the British constitutional crisis.[43] Hitler watched the news with trepidation as he was counting on Edward's support to maintain the Anglo-German special relationship. In Berlin, Diana Mitford talked to Hitler and Goebbels about the looming disaster and the King's plight. Goebbels was disgusted by the news and complained, 'That an empire can sink so low.'[44]

One night, Wallis woke up screaming, roused by the sudden noise of a smashed window. Someone had pitched a brick through the window of her Cumberland Terrace home, and the King told her it was no longer safe to stay at the Fort.[45] Scotland Yard doubled the number of Wallis's protection officers on the King's instructions, but she decided to go to France. Before leaving, Wallis had scrawled one final note to the King, reading, 'Tell the country.'[46] However, the Home Secretary, Sir John Simon (nicknamed 'Snake'), declared it unconstitutional for a king to give a speech against the advice of his prime minister, and blocked any radio broadcast.

Perry Brownlow, a personal friend of the King's and his lord-in-waiting, accompanied Wallis with two Special Branch detectives. Travelling under the disguised name 'Mr and Mrs Harris',[47] they raced across France to Herman Rogers's villa near Cannes, hunted down by a press pack. Any hope that Wallis had for a safe refuge disappeared when news journalists and hundreds of spectators lay siege to the house. Endless long-distance phone calls took place between Wallis and Edward, which became emotionally draining. Wallis shouted down the phone with her 'harsh voice twang of a rich American invective'[48] telling Edward to hold firm and not to abdicate, but he started to realise his power as king was fast evaporating.[49]

Baldwin needed every shred of information to outmanoeuvre the King, and he went directly to British intelligence. The head of MI5, Sir Vernon Kell, was summoned to Downing Street and asked to investigate Edward and Mrs Simpson; he refused because this reconnaissance wasn't a security issue. Kell considered it a party political or social matter, and he referred it to the board at MI5; they advised Kell to do what the Prime Minister asked. The Home Secretary and Baldwin's closest official advisor, Sir Horace Wilson, ordered the security forces to start tapping the phones of the King, Mrs Simpson and the Duke of York. Edward thought his calls were safe, protected through the Royal Exchange at Windsor. However, Kell had put his best recruit on the job, Tar Robertson. From a junction box in Green Park, he listened to their private conversations.[50] In December, Edward VIII made a telephone call to his brother the Duke of York, and Robertson found himself eavesdropping on earth-shattering news: the King was willing to abdicate and hand over the throne to his younger brother. Edward was finally accepting the inevitable: he could not be King and marry Mrs Simpson. Baldwin was quickly informed.[51]

Newspapers such as the *Daily Mail* and *Express* – as well as the British Union of Fascists (BUF) led by Sir Oswald Mosley – attempted to rally support for the King. The BUF distributed pro-Edward leaflets, chalked the walls with pro-Edward graffiti, and a specially printed newspaper, *Crisis*, sold 37,000 copies. One Blackshirt headline read: 'LET KING MARRY WOMAN OF HIS CHOICE.' A picture of the King landing at an airport, with the sub-headline 'A Symbol of the Modern Age which the old men hate', appeared on the front page of the fascist newspaper *Action*.[52]

The country became bitterly divided, and the Establishment feared revolution; some worried that Edward might dismiss the government and launch a right-wing takeover. A poster showed Edward against a Union Jack backdrop, with the caption, 'England's Sore Need – A Benevolent Dictator.' Ribbentrop described Edward as 'kind of English National Socialist' and Goebbels declared that 'the King is to be pitied. The men in England have no guts.'[53]

Mosley announced:

> The King has been loyal and true to us. My simple demand is that we be loyal and true to him … The recompense of his country for twenty-five years' faithful service is the denial of every man's right to live in private happiness with the woman he loves. Let the man and woman who has never loved cast the first stone …[54]

During a visit to Liverpool, Mosley even claimed he was in communication with the King. Within the BUF, there was a feeling that 'something was going on'. They believed that they were 'about to achieve power'. However, on 4 December, the King had 'a night of soul searching' about overtly supporting Mosley, but he wrote, 'In the end, I put out of my mind the thought of challenging the Prime Minister. By making a stand, I would have left the scars of civil war.'[55] Beaverbrook told Churchill, 'Our cock won't fight. No dice.'[56]

The following day, the King decided to abdicate, and he summoned Baldwin, who called a Cabinet meeting for 6 December. The King sent Mosley 'a polite thanks for his offer of support', of which he had 'felt unable to take advantage'.[57] On 7 December, during Prime Minister's Questions in the House of Commons, Churchill pleaded with Baldwin to give the King more time. However, MPs shouted him down with roars of 'Twister' and 'Drop it!'[58] They hounded Churchill out of the chamber, but before he left he turned to the Prime Minister: 'You won't be satisfied until you've broken him, will you?'[59] Fear had spread that the King might dismiss Baldwin and attempt a fascist coup d'etat, inviting either Churchill or Mosley to form a government. MI5 continued to monitor the situation closely.[60] Churchill's ill-judged intervention severely damaged his career prospects: within three minutes, it seemed he had destroyed any chance of returning to power.[61]

On the eve of the abdication, a crowd of 5,000 including 500 fascists assembled outside Buckingham Palace. They shouted, 'One two three four five, we want Baldwin, dead or alive!' BUF youths led 800 protestors to Downing Street, and other marchers besieged Parliament with posters and billboards reading, 'Sack Baldwin. Stand by the King!' Scotland Yard flooded central London with extra police officers, and Special Branch feared a public uprising instigated by Mosley's Blackshirts.[62] A band of women marched from Marble Arch to Buckingham Palace with huge banners which read: 'After South Wales you cannot let him down. Come to the Palace and cheer him. Let the King know we are with him.'[63] In the East End, 3,000 people attended a meeting in Stepney where Mosley demanded a people's referendum on the abdication issue. His Blackshirts smashed windows, and there was a street battle with anti-fascists. In the end, the police made only five arrests that night, quashing Ribbentrop's alarming prediction that 'there would be shooting in the streets'.[64]

While many working-class people were happy for their King to marry Mrs Simpson, the Establishment was united in opposition, including Queen Mary, the Prime Minister, the Dominion premiers, the Archbishop of Canterbury and Geoffrey Dawson, the influential editor of *The Times*.

The middle classes mostly considered Mrs Simpson an affront to their petit bourgeois sensibilities.

The King had to vacate his throne.

Fort Belvedere, Windsor. 10 December 1936.

On the morning of 10 December at Fort Belvedere, Edward VIII signed six copies of the Instrument of Abdication brought by Monckton. That afternoon, Stanley Baldwin made a speech in the House of Commons, famously exclaiming, 'What an opportunity wasted!'

The following day, Britain woke up to fog. Churchill had lunch with Edward and helped him finalise his speech which was to be broadcast that evening on the BBC.[65] When he left, Churchill became overcome with grief. 'Winston got into my car with tears flowing,' said his chauffeur, 'and silently, we drove home to Chartwell.'[66] At 10 p.m., from Windsor Castle, Edward finally told his people via the radio: 'You must believe me when I tell you that I have found it impossible to carry the heavy burden of responsibility and to discharge my duty as King I would wish to do, without the support of the woman I love.'[67]

The ex-king then drove to Royal Lodge in Windsor Great Park, for a final dinner with his mother Queen Mary, his sister and brothers, and his aunt, Princess Alice, Countess of Athlone. The new King, George VI, announced that he would make his brother the 'Duke of Windsor' with the style of His Royal Highness. That night, Edward's car sped him to Portsmouth accompanied by Walter Monckton, and he left Britain.

Tea with Hitler

Berghof, Bavaria. 11 December 1936.
Hitler was staying at Berghof, his private mountain retreat near Berchtesgaden on the Austrian–German border, when he received an urgent call from Ribbentrop informing him of Edward VIII's abdication. The Führer was seated having a vegetarian lunch in his jade green dining room, lined with cembra pine.[1] During the two-hour meal, Hitler went to the phone ten times. After each conversation, he returned to the dinner table looking more downcast.[2] Ribbentrop explained to Hitler that the abdication was 'the result of the machinations of dark Bolsheviks powers against the Führer-will of the young King'. Hitler stated Baldwin pushed Edward because he wanted Anglo-German rapprochement and there was 'no other person in England who is ready to play with us'.[3]

Château de Candé, Tours. 3 June 1937.
Edward finally married Wallis Simpson at 11.47 a.m. at the Château de Candé outside Tours, six months after the abdication. During that waiting period, Wallis stayed in France, while Edward passed the time at Enzesfeld Castle, a Rothschild estate outside Vienna, in a state of frustration. Finally, in May, Wallis telephoned Edward to announce her divorce was absolute, and he left Austria the same day to join his bride-to-be.

The Château de Candé was the lavish home of the industrial-systems tycoon and big game hunter Charles Bedaux, who had offered the Duke use of his estate via Wallis's close friend Herman Rogers. Bedaux was a manic character, short and stocky, with the look of a prize fighter – and he was solely devoted to his self-interest. He was particularly anxious to keep in the good books of the Nazis after they had closed his German management consultancy business, which he wanted reopening.[4]

Wallis had arrived at the château during a horrendous thunderstorm a week before. She entered the estate from a side entrance to avoid the press and was escorted by two French detectives who followed behind in a second car. She watched from her car with Herman and Katherine Rogers, as the turrets and grey stone walls of the castle appeared through the pouring rain at dusk. Charles's wife, the elegant Fern Bedaux, met Wallis at the massive wooden door.

Everything at the château was perfect, from the Bedauxs' monogrammed silver cutlery to their pure silk bedsheets. The extravagance of the 1,000-acre estate made even Wallis gasp with its twenty-four liveried staff and marble bathrooms.[5] However, that night, Herman slept in the room next to Wallis with a gun underneath his pillow, to guard her against possible attack.[6]

The wedding itself was low-key and private. George VI would not permit any member of the British Royal Family to attend the service. The only blood relation present was Wallis's Aunt Bessie, who worried that her niece looked rather thin. The bride wore a close-fitting powder-blue crêpe dress made by Mainbocher in Paris. A brooch of clustered sapphires and diamond was at her throat and a crucifix dangled from a bracelet of gold and sapphires. She carried no flowers, but the florist Constance Spry had arranged hundreds of white, yellow and pink peonies and lilies throughout the château – which was almost devoid of wedding guests. Edward dressed in a black morning coat and striped trousers, with a grey tie and white carnation. In the absence of his three brothers, Metcalfe supported the ex-king as his best man, and Handel's 'Wedding March' played as Wallis walked up the aisle, escorted by Herman Rogers.

Telegrams and letters of congratulations, as well as threats and hate mail, arrived along with boxes of gifts and flowers. Adolf Hitler sent the couple an inscribed gold box. Helena Normanton, a distant cousin of Wallis, reported the story for the *New York Times*. During an interview, she boldly asked Wallis about her Nazi connections. Wallis disingenuously replied that she could only recall meeting Ribbentrop twice, 'once at a party at Lady Cunard's before he became Ambassador, and once at a big reception. I was never had more than a few words of conversation with him, simply the usual small talk, that is all. I took no interest in politics.'[7]

The newly knighted Sir Walter Monckton arrived with more bad news from Buckingham Palace. On no account was the new Duchess of Windsor to be called 'Her Royal Highness', nor should she be curtsied to, or enjoy any of the traditions of respect accorded to a member of the Royal Family. This humiliation and rejection struck the Duke like 'a wound in battle. It struck his deepest emotions, and it altered him as a gunshot might have altered him.'[8] It was illegal under British common law to deny the status of a husband to a wife, as it reduced the Windsors' marriage to a mere morganatic one. 'I have taken you into a void,' said the Duke to his wife.[9] He burst into tears and buried his head on the shoulder of Dudley Forwood, his equerry.[10] There was no chance now of 'Queen Wallis'. The Duchess of Windsor had lost the throne to her sister-in-law Elizabeth, who loathed her as a brash American upstart. British cinemas did not even show newsreels of their semi-royal wedding.

That evening, the Duke and Duchess of Windsor said their goodbyes to their wedding guests and put on a brave face. They climbed into a Buick and drove off on their three-month honeymoon. Their destination was another loaned castle – Wasserleonberg in Carthinia – the home of Count Paul Munster, an Austrian aristocrat who was under British intelligence surveillance for financially backing Sir Oswald Mosley's British Union of Fascists.[11] The couple cushioned themselves against exigencies of their new exile and travelled with 266 pieces of baggage, including 186 trunks, loaded on a train to arrive ahead of them. This habit of 'travelling much and travelling heavy' became a characteristic that they adopted for the rest of their lives.[12]

More disenchantment would follow. While the Windsors were staying at Wasserleonberg Castle, the Duke and Duchess of Kent went on holiday nearby with Prince Paul of Yugoslavia at Brdo in Slovenia. However, Kent's wife, Princess Marina, refused to meet the American Duchess. Edward was incensed by this slight and returned the Kents' wedding gift – an elegant Fabergé box. Edward wrote angrily to his mother:

> I unfortunately know … that you and Elizabeth instigated the somewhat sordid and much publicised episode of the failure of the Kents to visit us … I am at a loss to know how to write to you, and further to see how any form of correspondence can give pleasure to either of us under these circumstances … It is a great sorrow and disappointment to me to have my mother thus cast out her eldest son.[13]

Amongst this family bitterness and disappointment, Charles Bedaux arrived at Wasserleonberg in his polished Rolls-Royce full of ideas for the Duke's re-emergence as a public figure. Bedaux was keen to cash in on his new royal connections and now proposed the Duke tour Nazi Germany to make a study of German labour. Edward grasped onto this suggestion as salvation and Bedaux secretly met Hitler's adjutant, Captain Fritz Wiedemann, at a health spa in Bad Reichenhall, a few miles from Berchtesgaden.[14]

Wiedemann had just started an affair with Princess Stephanie von Hohenlohe, the Nazi spy who had been the Duchess of Windsor's neighbour at Bryanston Court in London. He was a cunning Nazi fanatic, and he arranged for Bedaux to meet Dr Robert Ley, the notorious head of the Nazi *Arbeitsfront* (Labour Front). Critics described Wiedemann as 'an uncultivated, primitive mind with the shrewdness and cunning of an animal,'[15] but Ley was worse – an absolute thug. The Nazi leader had suffered a traumatic brain injury during a plane crash in the First World War and for the rest of his life spoke with a stammer. His behaviour was frequently erratic, a trait aggravated by heavy drinking. By 1937, Ley was also editing the viciously anti-Semitic newspaper *Westdeutscher Beobachter* (West German Observer). His unswerving loyalty to Hitler meant the Führer overlooked his egotism, incompetence and drunkenness.[16] As Bedaux and Ley immediately started drawing up plans for the royal visit, the German branch of Bedaux's business was returned for services rendered.[17]

Hotel Meurice, Paris. September 1937.

Back in Paris, Wallis and Edward settled down in their luxurious nine-room hotel suite overlooking the Tuileries Gardens at the Hotel Meurice. While the Duke started to fret about money, the Duchess spent lavishly on clothes by Chanel and Schiaparelli, as well as furs and jewels. Wallis and Edward replayed, again and again, the events of the past few months, wondering what they could have done differently.[18] This pattern spoiled the newlyweds' marital bliss. The Duchess wrote: 'After the first burst of joy in rediscovering each other and being together we found our minds turning back in interminable post-mortems concerning the events surround the Abdication … This endless re-hashing of the lost past became almost an obsession.' Finally, the Duke said despairingly to his new wife, 'Darling, if we keep this up, we are never going to agree, so let's drop it for good.'[19]

Concurrently, Bedaux and Ley finalised preparations for the German tour, and the Windsors were about to swim into the Nazi cesspool. The Duke viewed the trip as a chance to get back at his family and provide his new wife with the royal status denied in England. For Wallis, the visit broke up the monotony of exile. She was bored post-abdication, life seemed empty, and she couldn't 'reconcile herself to the fact that by marrying her, he [Edward] had become a less important person'.[20] Cabin fever had firmly set in, and to cure this disease, they searched for the celebrity spotlight in Hitler's Germany. Forwood explained that the Duke wanted 'his beloved wife to experience a State visit. He wanted to prove to her that he had lost nothing by abdicating.'[21]

Churchill was dismayed when he heard about their plans; he thought it amounted to crass stupidity, as Hitler's thuggish anti-Semitic regime had fast become the bullyboy of Europe. However, he did not attempt to stop the Duke. Lord Rothermere, by contrast, travelled to Paris and pleaded with the Windsors not to go to Germany, but he failed.[22] Hitler's adjutant met the Duke at the Paris Ritz to seal the deal.

Bedaux's plan was not just for the Windsors to tour Germany. Following the visit to the Reich, he planned for the Windsors to tour the United States. Inside the Foreign Office in London, Sir Robert Vansittart had amassed a sizable security file on the Duke and Duchess detailing their leaks, dubious meetings and casual indiscretions, and he called Sir Ronald Lindsay, the British ambassador in Washington. Lindsay was amazed at the blatant hostility at court towards the Windsors, as the Palace secretaries viewed both trips with unmitigated horror.[23] During a visit to Balmoral, he found George VI and Queen Elizabeth in a state of near hysteria, and utterly paranoid about the Duke making a success of either trip or outshining them.[24] George VI insisted that if either tour went ahead, the Windsors would receive zero official recognition – nor any cooperation – from any British embassy in Germany or America.[25] The Nazis, however, were going to optimise any visit by the world's most famous couple, and as the German government were funding their stay, they would inevitably stage-manage the tour.

Berlin, Germany. 11 October 1937.

The *Nord Express* drew into Berlin's Friedrichstrasse railway station for the start of a twelve-day ducal visit on the morning of 11 October. Strings of Union Jacks decorated the platform, interspersed with Nazi swastikas, which flapped in the crisp wind. The SS band played 'God Save the King' while the crowd cried, 'Heil Edward!' ('Hail Edward!').[26] The British ambassador, Sir Nevile Henderson, absented himself, but the Nazis were out in full force. Dr Robert Ley headed the welcoming German delegation. He was, for once, not drunk.

Edward wore a light-grey suit with a red carnation in his lapel and Wallis, looking chic as usual, sported a tailored suit in navy blue wool with a matching cape, hat and shoes.[27] She appreciated the gesture of being handed a box of chocolates with a card bearing the inscription '*Königliche Highness*' ('Royal Highness').[28] For the Duchess, these things mattered. The Nazis had realised that the best method of gratifying the Duke was through his wife. They ensured that well-rehearsed crowds chanted, 'We want the Duchess!' along the route as their sleek black Mercedes made its way to the Kaiserhof Hotel. SS guards stood on the car's running boards, and three vehicles crammed with detectives followed.[29] This acclaim was what it felt like to be a queen. For the Duchess, it was a spectacular 'what might have been'.

The following day, the obsequious Joachim von Ribbentrop hosted the Windsors at Horcher's, a gourmet restaurant. The guests included Heinrich Himmler, Rudolf Hess and his wife Isle, and Josef Goebbels and his famous wife Magda. Goebbels failed to make a good impression, and the Duchess described him as 'a tiny, wispy gnome with an enormous skull. His wife was the prettiest woman I saw in Germany.' The pair reminded her of 'Beauty and the Beast'.[30] The coarse Dr Ley was described as a 'particularly odious Nazi thug'.[31] On one occasion, he was sufficiently drunk at the wheel of the Windsors' Mercedes that he crashed it through closed factory gates.[32]

The tour was something of a family affair. Among their entourage was the Duke's cousin, Prince Philipp of Hesse, while his brother Prince Christoph of Hesse bugged their telephones for the duration of the visit.[33] Charles Edward of Coburg had also written to Edward before his arrival in Germany:

> Dear David [the name family members called Edward],
>
> I hear that you are coming to Germany ... I naturally would be delighted if you could take this opportunity to see me; perhaps I could introduce you to a couple of interesting personalities whom you otherwise wouldn't meet.[34]

On 19 October, Coburg hosted the Windsors' first formal reception at the Grand Hotel in Nuremberg, with over 100 guests 'including many of the [German] aristocrats with whom the Duke [of Windsor] had hob-nobbed during his father's funeral and the jubilee'.[35] Wallis noted that everyone she had met curtsied or bowed to her, while in England they had snubbed her.[36] The Nazi Duke of Coburg was the only member of the family to afford Wallis such royal recognition.

Edward and Wallis saw only what the Nazis wanted them to see as they toured various factories and coal mines inspecting Germany's excellent working conditions. While giving a speech declaring the economic model of the Third Reich to be a 'miracle', Edward delivered a Nazi salute. At Crossensee, the Duke visited the training school of the Death's Head Division of the Elite Squad of the SS. After the band played 'God Save the King', Edward toured the medieval castle and then boarded a plane for an aerial inspection of the Hitler Youth camps along the Baltic Sea, while the Duchess visited the Kaiser's former palace in Potsdam. Throughout the visit, the Duke and Duchess purposefully ignored the realities of the Nazi regime and did little to investigate the menacing existence of the concentration camps and gangster violence. Instead, Edward swallowed the never-ending propaganda pageant of handsome Aryan youth and happy workers.

Towards the end of the tour, they also stayed with Hermann Göring and his wife Emmy at their magnificent hunting lodge. Karinhall was now filled with Rembrandts and priceless art treasures looted from Jewish families.[37] In the library, a large map showed Austria as part of Germany, an ominous sign of the coming *Anschluss*. As he left Karinhall, the Duke turned to Göring and said, 'This was the nicest visit of all those we have made in Germany.'[38]

However, the highlight of the visit came on 22 October, when the Duke and Duchess accepted an invitation from Hitler to join him for tea at Berghof. Accompanied by Rudolf Hess, they were driven up the mountain into the very heart of the Nazi cult. By 1937, Berghof had taken on a semi-mythical quality; Hitler spent half his time here, and it was from this sanctuary that the most critical strategic decisions were made. Other prominent Nazis, including Albert Speer, Hermann Göring, and Martin Bormann, had built homes in the vicinity, creating a small colony. Nearby barracks could accommodate 10,000, and there was even a hotel for special guests. The entire area was designated a high-security zone surrounded by a fence, the *Führergebiet'* ('Leader area').[39]

The police cleared traffic from the roads, so the motorcade arrived at the house one hour ahead of schedule. However, Hitler was taking an afternoon nap – and no one dared wake him up. The only person who would have roused the sleeping Führer was his mistress, Eva Braun, but she had been sent away, under loud protest, to avoid potential royal embarrassment – for Wallis was no longer a paramour, but a wife.[40] For an hour, Hess took the Duke and Duchess to local tourist sites; eventually, Hitler, dressed in a brown Nazi jacket, black trousers and black shoes, was ready to greet them at the front door. He shook the Duchess's hand, and then turned to the Duke and gave the Nazi salute. The Duke answered: 'Heil Hitler.'[41]

Wallis recalled:

His face had a pasty pallor, and under his moustache, his lips fixed in a kind of mirthless grimace. Yet at close quarters, he gave the feeling of great inner force. His hands were long and slim, a musician's hands, and his eyes were truly extraordinary – intense, unblinking, magnetic, burning with the same peculiar fire.[42]

Inside the vast, sprawling house, a large portrait of Chancellor Bismarck dominated the reception hall. Tall, well-built men stepped forward to take the couple's coats as they walked down three steps into the sizable oak-panelled drawing room with views of the snow-capped Alps.[43] From the windows, you could see the dramatic mountains which straddled Germany and Austria. There was an enormous marble fireplace with heaps of logs on both sides. Both the marble and the carpet were a matching cherry red, while the furniture covers displayed stitched swastika motifs and Nazi mottos. Tapestries of Frederick the Great mounted on different horses hung from the walls, and Richard Wagner's bust stood atop the grand piano,[44] which was covered by an antimacassar.[45] Everywhere there were white and yellow flowers, hydrangeas, roses, carnations and zinnias filling the air with their vibrant, sweet tang.[46]

Hitler ordered tea. He loved to copy the genteel traditions of the British upper classes, including tea, cucumber sandwiches and reading *The Tatler*. The gentle tinkle of fine bone china, with swastikas on the teacups, accompanied their polite conversation. White-coated lackeys offered both Indian and China tea, with their woody and flowery smells, and four different types of sandwiches were served on tiered plates. The Führer had a sweet tooth; there were also three large cakes – walnut, fruit and Victoria sponge.[47]

The Führer and the Duke retreated to a private room.[48] Only two men witnessed the interview itself: Hitler's translator, Paul Schmidt, and Dudley Forwood. Hitler made every effort to be as amicable as possible towards the Duke, whom he regarded as Germany's friend.[49] However, the Duke was annoyed at the presence of the translator because he spoke perfect

German, and occasionally would observe that Schmidt had misinterpreted something. Every few minutes, the Duke would say, irritably, to Schmidt, 'That is not what I said to the Führer,' or, 'That is not what the Führer said to me.'[50]

Misunderstandings aside, the Duke bonded with Hitler, saying: 'The Germans and the British races are one. They should always be one. They are of Hun origin.'[51] The two men agreed upon the issue of Russia, with Edward encouraging Hitler to strike east and smash communism forever. Edward's plan had always been to remain neutral, while the Nazis and the Reds slogged it out. He turned a blind eye to the Nazis' anti-Semitism, going so far at the meeting as to suggest the mass emigration of Jews from Germany.[52]

Outside, Wallis waited in the drawing room with Rudolf Hess, and together they did their best to discuss music.[53] Hess's taste was for German composers, preferably Beethoven, while Wallis preferred jazz.[54] Finally, the Duke and Hitler returned to join Wallis for more tea, talking together energetically.[55] The Duchess listened attentively, but only joined in when the subject held a specific interest for women.[56] Hitler even called her 'Royal Highness'.[57] However, when Wallis complimented Hitler on Germany's impressive new architecture, he responded with a chilling prophecy, that the buildings would 'make more magnificent ruins than the Greeks'.[58]

After the Windsors left, Hitler turned to Schmidt and announced, 'She would have made a good queen.'[59] Of the Duke, Hitler later concluded, 'His abdication was a severe loss for us … if he had stayed, everything would have been different.'[60]

When Pathé showed footage of the German tour in British theatres, Churchill wrote to the Duke: 'When scenes of it (your tour) were produced in the newsreels in the cinema here your Royal Highness' pictures were always loudly cheered.'

Edward's popularity in Germany did not go unnoticed at Buckingham Palace. At the time of the tour, George VI and Queen Elizabeth were less concerned by the Duke of Windsor's far-right sympathies than his potential to upstage them: the shallow ex-king was a charismatic crowd-pleaser. Faced with the potential of a rival court, Edward and Wallis had to be denigrated and marginalised. So repeated were the humiliating blows dealt out by the palace that an exasperated Duchess of Windsor wrote to the Conservative MP Victor Cazalet, 'Why not whisper to your Government to "ease up" a little on the anti-Windsor propaganda? We are really too harmless to be worth such efforts.'[61]

In reality, Soviet Russia, not Nazi Germany, was viewed as the real threat. Like his father George V, George VI adopted an extreme pro-appeasement attitude towards Germany, which permeated his whole family. Prince George, Duke of Kent, still made frequent private visits to Germany, staying with his two cousins Prince Philipp and Prince Christoph of Hesse at Friedrichshof Castle, or with his sister-in-law Countess Törring-Jettenbach in Munich. The Royal Family reflected public opinion. Pacifist sentiments were common following the carnage of the First World War and Vera Brittain's book *Testament of Youth*, a passionate record of a lost generation, became a bestseller. The British public was almost universally behind the appeasement policy of the new Prime Minister, Neville Chamberlain. Jewish persecution and the gangster-like behaviour of the Nazis was viewed by many as an unpleasant internal problem. The British Establishment, like the displaced German one, saw the Nazis as a force that needed to be civilised, not overthrown.

9

HITLER'S PEACE

London. December 1937.

If George VI and Queen Elizabeth felt annoyed that the Duke of Coburg hosted the Windsors in Nazi Germany, they forgave 'Cousin Charlie' quickly. Within the month, Charles Edward was drinking tea with Queen Mary at Windsor Castle and visiting King George VI at Sandringham.[1] After returning from Norfolk, he reported back to the German Embassy in London – attending five meetings over three days.[2] Officially, the Duke was in Britain on behalf of the Anglo-German Fellowship promoting industrial and financial interests between the two countries.

Meanwhile, Soviet spies had infiltrated the Anglo-German Fellowship. Two young Russia moles, Kim Philby and Guy Burgess (who were later infamous as members of a Cambridge spy ring called the 'Apostles'), won the Fellowship's trust 'by the simple trick of acting like a Nazi sympathiser'. The pair attended swastika-bedecked dinners in Mayfair hotels and Philby even edited the Fellowship's newsletter. The first information that Philby passed on to his Russian handlers was the names of pro-Nazi sympathisers within the British aristocracy.[3]

Most Germans involved with the AGF were 'chosen with great sensitivity to English psychology'.[4] As a member of the Royal Family, the Duke of Coburg exerted power in business circles, and AGF members included Lord Rothermere, Lord Lothian, Lord Mount Temple, Lord Londonderry, Lord Brocket, Lord Duncan-Sandys (Churchill's son-in-law), Francis Cooper (President of Unilever), Samuel Hoare (a banker), Sir Arnold Wilson MP and so on, right into the heart of the British Establishment. Wilson enthusiastically wrote: 'Herr Hitler himself impressed me profoundly ... a man who is nationalist by temperament, socialist in method, but, like our best conservatives, desirous of change in particular directions.'[5]

Although Mount Temple did raise the issues of the Nazi treatment of Jews, Prince Otto von Bismarck warned all British members not to believe 'bias press reports but instead visit Germany and see what was going on for themselves'.[6] However, Heinrich Müller, the head of the secret Gestapo police, demanded a list of all British Jews from the German Embassy in London who had either been knighted or were members of the aristocracy. In 1937, embassy officials sent him a detailed study divided into several sections, including a category for 'mixed blood' and 'half-breeds in the making'. The latter included people who might soon have children, such as the pro-German Marquess of Londonderry, whose daughter had married a Jew. Hitler became convinced that the majority of his British critics were Jewish, and the Führer ordered an investigation into the racial purity of all the leading politicians' wives, including Clementine Churchill and Beatrice Eden, to see if any had Jewish roots. Sir Oswald Mosley's 'racial background' was scrutinised, as the Germans believed he was too liberal towards Jews because he socialised with members of the wealthy Rothschild and Sassoon families.[7] Hitler was never fully convinced by Mosley. However, his wife, Diana Mitford, and her sister Unity enchanted him.

Hitler's great hope was Neville Chamberlain, the new Prime Minister, who, with his umbrella and droopy moustache, came to epitomise British upper-class complacency towards Nazi Germany with its policy of persistent moral nullity. Charles Edward was increasingly visible in London society, dining with Conservative politicians in London – including Chamberlain and attending country house parties set up by his sister at her Sussex home, Brantridge Park. After his dinner with the Prime Minister, Charles Edward reported his conversation with Chamberlain back to the authorities in Berlin: 'Chaimberlain [sic] hates Russia. His son studied in Germany and has heard Adolf Hitler speak in Munich. His accounts are so enthusiastic that Chaimberlain [sic] would very much like to see the Führer himself one day.'[8]

Shortly after the coronation on 12 May 1937, Chamberlain stayed with the King and Queen at Balmoral, where he enjoyed fishing on the River Dee. Although he didn't catch any fish, he did 'hook the King'.[9]

George VI was even chummier with Lord Halifax, whom Chamberlain appointed Foreign Secretary on 21 February 1938. The aristocratic and stately Halifax had the King's trust, and George VI was 'far closer to him than to any other senior politician of the day'.[10] Lady Halifax was the Queen's lady-in-waiting, and the King honoured Halifax by giving him a key to the gardens at Buckingham Palace so that he could take a scenic shortcut between his home in Eaton Square and the Foreign Office in Whitehall.[11]

Halifax also paid a visit to Hitler at Berchtesgaden in November 1937, where he almost created a diplomatic incident. He mistook Hitler for the footman because he wore black trousers, black silk socks and patent leather shoes. Fortunately, German diplomat Baron von Neurath hissed into Halifax's ear, '*Der Führer, Der Führer*,' before Lord Halifax offered him his coat. The meeting achieved little. Hitler remained peeved until he drank a large cup of hot chocolate with a 'floating iceberg of whipped cream' on top.[12] Halifax found Hitler 'sincere' but with 'a different set of values'.[13] He also managed to send out the unfortunate pro-appeasement message that 'England was ready to consider any solution, provided that it was not based on force', which amounted to acquiescence to German territorial ambitions in Eastern Europe.[14] Hitler contemptuously called Halifax the 'English Parson'.[15]

Chamberlain and Halifax became the architects of Appeasement, a policy which would allow Hitler to guzzle up the small countries of Europe until the German frontier reached the Soviet Union. Like most members of the upper classes, Chamberlain and Halifax viewed communism – rather than Nazism – as the threatening 'virus' that could infect the working classes. Both politicians seemed to accept that the *Anschluss* (Germany's annexation of Austria) was inevitable. The Foreign Office transferred the anti-Nazi British ambassador, Sir Eric Phipps, from Berlin to Paris for failing to make enough progress with Hitler's regime. His replacement was the pro-Nazi Sir Nevile Henderson, who had a more fatalistic streak – accepting the *Anschluss* and German hegemony in Eastern Europe. He viewed the Nazis as a 'great social experiment' – a view that alarmed anti-appeasers including Churchill, Eden and Vansittart – and was able to get on with dictators generally. Vansittart called him a 'complete Nazi',[16] and he was a friend of the Duke of Coburg – as the two men were at Eton together.[17] This quintessential Etonian Englishman looked like a parody of a facetious and suave diplomat. He went shooting with Göring and enjoyed baffling the Nazis by responding to their '*Heil Hitler!*' with 'Rule Britannia!'[18]

The German Embassy, London. 10 March 1938.
That evening, a farewell party was held at German Embassy for Ambassador von Ribbentrop while the German army was massing on the Austrian

border. In the room decorated with red, black and white swastikas, the entire British government and diplomatic corps, as well as the usual right-wing aristocrats like Lord Londonderry, came to pay their respects. Outside, demonstrators shouted, 'Ribbentrop get out!'[19] Inside, Chamberlain asked Ribbentrop to convey to Hitler that he earnestly wanted an understanding with Germany. However, Ribbentrop was rapidly becoming resentful of his lack of success in London, and told Fritz Hess, the embassy press attaché, that he had 'written England off forever'.[20] Ribbentrop had now transformed from 'chief Anglophile to leading Anglophobe'. He spent his last months in London writing a mammoth report explaining why his mission to London had failed and that Germany should consider Britain 'among her most implacable enemies': Hitler's dream of an Anglo-German alliance was over.[21]

Mr and Mrs Chamberlain gave a farewell luncheon in Ribbentrop's honour at 10 Downing Street the following day. The atmosphere was 'grim',[22] and the guest list included all the arch-appeasers such as Halifax, Hoare, Simon and Londonderry. Churchill was also present. He remarked to Ribbentrop's wife, Anna, 'I hope England and Germany will preserve their friendship.' She retorted, 'Be careful you don't spoil it.'[23] After that exchange, Frau von Ribbentrop left, and Chamberlain escorted Ribbentrop, who was oblivious to the atmosphere in the room, to his study and read him two telegrams: one from the Austrian Chancellor Kurt Schuschnigg, appealing for British advice; and a second from Hitler, commanding his immediate resignation.[24] Ribbentrop was completely unmoved, and Chamberlain despaired. In a letter to his sister Hilda, the Prime Minister wrote disparagingly of the exiting German ambassador: 'He is so stupid, so shallow, so self-centred and self-satisfied, so totally devoid of intellectual capacity that he never seems to take in what is said to him.'[25]

Vienna, Austria. 11 March 1938.

In Vienna, the hopes for a referendum allowing Austria to remain independent from Germany were high. The crowds in the street shouted their support for Chancellor Schuschnigg – '*Heil Schuschnigg! Heil Liberty!*'[26] The city's Jews raised over 500,000 schillings ($80,000), realising this referendum was their last bastion of freedom. However, that morning the Austrian chief of police woke Schuschnigg to inform him of troop movements on the German border.

By 7 p.m., Radio Vienna revealed the cancellation of the plebiscite, and the resignation of the entire Austrian Cabinet, except for the

Nazi-supporting Arthur Seyss-Inquart, who ominously stayed on as the Minister of the Interior. Seyss-Inquart was a devotee of Heinrich Himmler's concepts of Aryan racial purity.[27]

At 7.50 p.m., Schuschnigg broadcast Hitler's ultimatum to the nation and he explained that the Nazis had demanded he resign and appoint 'a candidate chosen by the Reich Government to the office of Chancellor … or … German troops would begin to cross our frontiers this very hour'.

The Nazis in Austria erupted with joy. Floods of Brownshirts swarmed into the street as car horns blasted and the police appeared wearing swastika armbands. Trucks in the street suddenly had swastikas on them, and men shouted: '*Ein Volk, ein Riech, ein Führer,*' and, '*Heil Hitler, Sieg Heil!*'

At 11.15 p.m., Nazi flags were hanging from all government buildings as Vienna's mayor, Major Klauser, declared that 'Austria is National Socialist'.

Squadrons of Luftwaffe planes flew low over the city the following day, and the first German troops crossed the border. That evening, Nazis marched in a torchlit procession through Vienna. There was terror; people were picked off the street and bundled into cars or trucks. Activists, Jews and troublemakers were arrested and sent to Dachau. The guards placed Schuschnigg in solitary confinement. Men in uniform appeared everywhere. Nazi thugs broke the first Jewish shop windows and the word '*Jude*' – painted in yellow – appeared on a door. Uniformed soldiers beat people up, and ordinary German citizens screamed: '*Juden verrecken!*' 'Death to the Jews!'[28]

As disaster engulfed Austria, the Duke of Coburg paid a timely visit of reassurance to his British cousins at Sandringham, and Hitler also dispatched Prince Philipp of Hesse to Rome to deliver a comforting letter to Mussolini, stating that the invasion of Austria was not a threat to Italy. Later that day, the Prince received an enthusiastic call from Hitler with news of the Italian leader's compliance.

On 13 March, Hitler signed the Law for the Reunion of Austria with the German Reich – although no such union had previously existed. Although Prime Minister Chamberlain denounced Germany's use of violence to annex Austria, it was a feeble protest. By contrast, Churchill called the *Anschluss* the 'rape of Austria' and stated there could be no relaxation while 'the boa constrictor' digested its victim. He demanded a military alliance with France, a commitment to defend Czechoslovakia and rapid rearmament.[29]

Over the following weeks, the Nazis dismissed Jewish teachers and lawyers from their jobs and banished all 200,000 Austrian Jews from the economic, cultural and social life of their country. Jewish businesses were 'Aryanised', which meant they were seized outright, looted or sold for a fraction of their value. Laughing Nazi mobs forced Jewish citizens to perform humiliating menial tasks, such as scrubbing pro-Schuschnigg graffiti off the streets or washing cars, without respect of age, class or gender. Tragically, 160 suicides of Jews occurred within the early months of Nazi occupation, and American journalist William Shirer described an 'orgy of sadism' worse than anything he had seen in Germany.[30]

Amongst this chaos in Vienna, a Jewish relative of British Royal Family was now at risk.

Schomberg House, London. July 1938.

Inside Schomberg House, on the south side of Pall Mall, two old royal ladies, Princess Marie Louise (nicknamed 'Thora') and Princess Helena Victoria (dubbed 'Snipe'), were frantic with worry. Both were grand-daughters of Queen Victoria, and they turned to the Royals' favourite lawyer, Sir Walter Monckton, for help. Their niece Valerie Marie was trapped in Vienna and needed their help, but her existence was a family secret – she was a Jew.

Snipe and Thora's parents were the late Princess Helena (Queen Victoria's fifth child) and Prince Christian of Schleswig-Holstein. In Victoria's eyes, their father, a rather dull prince, had the advantage of being penniless and therefore amenable to her constant demands – so she allowed the marriage provided they lived at Cumberland Lodge in Windsor. Like their Anglo-German Saxe-Coburg cousins, the Schleswig-Holsteins were a family divided by the First World War. While Marie Louise and Helena Victoria lived in Britain all their lives, their brother Prince Albert served in the Prussian army after being educated at Charterhouse. During the First World War, the two sisters relinquished their German titles in 1917, while their brother inherited his cousin's German dukedom in 1921.[31]

By 1938, the two princesses lived the quiet life of minor British royals. Always bejewelled and perfectly dressed, they lived in 'refined eccentricity … being slightly removed from everyday reality'.[32] Neither the two sisters nor their brother ever successfully married. Kaiser Wilhelm had arranged a wedding between Princess Marie Louise and Prince Aribert of Anhalt. However, the groom was homosexual, and the marriage was never con-summated. After the Prince's indiscretion with a male attendant, the courts quickly dissolved their union, coming so soon after the Oscar Wilde trial.[33]

At the time, King Edward VII summed up the situation sardonically: 'Ach, poor Louise, she has returned as she went – a virgin.'[34]

Valerie Marie was their only direct descendant, but she was illegitimate, the product of their brother's affair with an attractive Hungarian aristocrat. Being a single mother with an illegitimate child would have been a significant scandal, so the young woman handed the baby girl over to Anna Rosenthal and her husband, Rubin Schwalb, to raise. During her childhood, Valerie grew up in the Jewish community. She also went to a Jewish school with her foster brother Alfred, who was one year younger. Valerie used the Schwalb surname until her first marriage in 1925 to a Viennese lawyer called Ernst Johann Wagner. She knew nothing of her parentage until she received a letter from Duke Albert of Schleswig-Holstein in 1931, on the eve of his death: 'I am not sure whether it was not cruel that I wrote you all that. Please, forgive the dead. I wish you all the best from my heart. God bless you. Your father.'[35]

By 1938, Valerie of Schleswig-Holstein, as she now called herself, had divorced her middle-class husband and was planning a grand second marriage to Prince Engelbert Charles, the Duke of Arenberg. Prince Engelbert owned Nordkirchen Castle, an imposing family seat at Lüdinghausen in Westphalia. However, there were obstacles as far as the authorities in Nazi Germany were concerned. While the prospective groom had impeccable racial credentials, all the documents about Valerie showed that she was undeniably Jewish. The Nuremberg laws forbade Aryan–Jewish marriages and persons convicted of violating these laws suffered prison sentences. Valerie appealed to her two aunts in London and to Hermann Göring, who proudly declared: 'It is I who decides who is royal and who is not.'[36]

Snipe and Thora sent Sir Walter Monckton to meet Valerie and Prince Engelbert at the Hotel Bristol in Paris, to give them his personal reassurance that all would be well. In July 1938, Valerie's two aunts co-signed a letter acknowledging their niece and attesting to the fact that although her foster parents were Jewish, Valerie Marie was a Roman Catholic:

We hereby acknowledge and declare that Valerie Wagner is the illegitimate daughter of our brother His Highness Duke Albert of Schleswig-Holstein, who died on the 27th April 1931. We are entirely ignorant of the names and identity of a Valerie Wagner's mother, but we understand that she was a lady of very high rank. Our brother in order to shield this lady's honour never divulged her name to anyone. Valerie Wagner's foster parents, in whose name she was registered, were of Jewish descent, but we desire to emphasize the fact the Valerie Wagner herself is not of Jewish birth. Our brother, the Duke of Schleswig-Holstein, in a personal letter to Valerie Wagner, deplored the fact that she had been entrusted to the care of a family of a different race and faith to her own.[37]

Valerie and Engelbert married discreetly in Berlin on 15 June 1939. Sir Nevile Henderson, the British ambassador to Germany, was present and the bride was given away by her cousin Prince Frederick Leopold of Prussia. Afterwards, Princess Helena Victoria wrote to Monckton thanking him for all the work he had done 'to bring the happy event about for the young couple'.[38]

Tragically, Valerie's entire Jewish foster family was arrested by the Nazis and died in concentration camps during the war. Valerie would die childless in an apparent suicide on 14 August 1953 at Mont Boron in the South of France after the war. Her only surviving aunt, Princess Marie Louise, attended her funeral in Belgium, where the Arenbergs had large estates. Valerie remains a footnote in history, but an intriguing story.

Berchtesgaden, Germany. 15 September 1938.

Six weeks after the *Anschluss*, there would be another crisis: the Sudetenland in Czechoslovakia. This area which bordered Germany and Austria was home to 3 million Germans. As German troops gathered on the frontier, the mood was critical. Hitler wanted to unite all Germans under his leadership and falsely claimed that the Czechs had killed 300 Sudeten Germans. Europe was on the verge of war, and in London, the government started to dig trenches and distribute gas masks.

On 15 September, Chamberlain flew to Munich. The Germans were somewhat taken aback by 'this funny little man with an umbrella';[39] as the British Prime Minister emerged from his plane, he was welcomed by cheering crowds and a 'strident band' as he inspected the guard of honour.[40] Chamberlain then boarded Hitler's private train for a three-hour journey to Berchtesgaden. In his Cabinet report, he would describe the Führer as 'the commonest little dog he had ever seen', though it was 'impossible not to be impressed with the power of the man' who greeted him on the steps of the Berghof.[41] The guileless Chamberlain believed that Hitler's ambitions were limited and that he was 'telling the truth' when he said he didn't want to absorb Czechoslovakia into the Reich.[42] Then, within the week, Hitler was demanding the full occupation of Czechoslovakia when he met Chamberlain a second time at Bad Godesberg near Bonn on 22 September 1938. Hitler read out a memorandum demanding the Czechs evacuate the Sudetenland within three days.

Back in London, a group of anti-appeasers met in Churchill's flat in Morpeth Mansions in Westminster. They drank whisky and soda and Churchill declared that 'Chamberlain will return tonight, and we shall have war'. Outside, over 10,000 protestors marched through Whitehall, angry at the government's betrayal of the Czechs. Even Halifax was furious: 'Hitler has given us nothing ... he had won a war but without having had to fight.'[43] In a staggering transformation, the Foreign Secretary led a Cabinet revolt against Chamberlain's compromise. A political stalemate followed. There was no appetite for war, and the country's leaders were defeatist.

George VI wrote to his mother, Queen Mary, on 27 September. He explained that Chamberlain had agreed to give in to Hitler's demands for the Sudetenland in return for peace: 'if Hitler refuses to do this then we shall know, once and for all, that he is a *madman*.'[44] The following day the House of Commons was packed, and Queen Mary sat solemnly in the visitors' gallery ready to report back to the King the mood on the floor of the House. Next to her sat the former Prime Minister, Stanley Baldwin, and Lord Halifax. Both the air force and the navy were preparing for war. Chamberlain talked for an hour in meticulous – and often irrelevant – detail, outlining his negotiations with Hitler as the atmosphere tightened:

> On 15th September I made my first flight to Munich. Then I travelled by train to Herr Hitler's mountain home at Berchtesgaden ...
>
> On the 22nd I went back to Germany to Godesburg on the Rhine, where the Chancellor had appointed a meeting place as being more convenient for me than the remote Berchtesgaden. Once again, I had a very warm welcome in the streets and village through which I passed ...

As he was speaking, a note was passed to him – it was an invitation from Hitler and Mussolini to come again to Munich. The House erupted in jubilation: Conservative, Liberal and Labour MPs jumped to their feet applauding and waving their order papers. Even Churchill eventually stood up – although he sulked.

'We are all patriots,' declared the Prime Minister, 'and there can be no Honourable Member of this House who did not feel his heart leap that the crisis has been once more postponed to give us an opportunity to try what reason and goodwill and discussion will do to settle a problem ...'[45]

Queen Mary quickly left to inform the King: there was the hope of peace.

German Embassy, London. 22 September 1938.

While Chamberlain met Hitler at Godesburg, the Duke of Coburg arrived in London on 22 September, where diplomats briefed him at the German Embassy. The following day, he saw 'Bertie and Elizabeth' (George VI and Queen Elizabeth) and then reported back to the embassy again. He then left for Europe on a series of goodwill visits to King Victor Emmanuel of Italy and Prime Minister Mussolini in Rome, as well as President Moscicki in Warsaw. These meetings were an adroit display of royalty's soft power, and the Duke was received as a senior politician, 'making sure that the façade was kept up while war plans were finalised in Berlin'.[46]

Munich, Germany. 28 September 1938.

Chamberlain boarded a plane on 28 September for a third time, heading for Munich, and Lord Hugh Cecil commented that the Prime Minister's policy was akin to 'scratching a crocodile's head in the hope of making it purr'.[47] The infamous Munich conference took place at the *Führerburg*, Hitler's stark Nazi Neo-classical headquarters, complete with Doric columns and draped in swastikas. Visitors walked across a red carpet through a vast hall of lurid marble and up stairs swathed with flowers, until they eventually reached the Führer's private study.

At 12.30 p.m., the politicians sat down together around a low table surrounded by armchairs – Chamberlain, Hitler, Göring, Mussolini and Édouard Daladier, the French Prime Minister. Over the mantelpiece, a picture of Bismarck gazed down at them.[48] Here SS officers clicked their heels and asked the delegates if they needed anything. Despite all the garish totalitarian splendour and flummery, the organisation broke down as vexed delegates were not provided with pens and notepads. They took notes on any odd pieces of paper they could find.[49]

Two days later, on 30 September, all the parties signed the Munich Agreement. This allowed the German army to complete the Sudetenland occupation by 10 October. An international commission would decide the future of Czechoslovakia's disputed areas.

Later that day, Chamberlain stepped out of his plane at Heston Aerodrome in West London, returning from Germany in triumph. Wearing an Edwardian collar and waving a piece of paper, he walked up to the waiting microphone and delivered his infamous 'Peace for our time' speech. The crowds roared their approval, delaying his exit from the airport as people engulfed his car, trying to shake his hand.[50] The next day Hitler took the Sudetenland, promising he would demand no more territory, but over 150,000 German and Czech refugees fled the Nazi occupation. The peace wasn't for everyone.

Ignoring the plight of the Jews and Czechs, George VI and Queen Elizabeth invited Chamberlain to their private apartments at Buckingham Palace to offer the Prime Minister royal congratulations. Mr and Mrs Chamberlain then appeared on the balcony that evening 'under the beam of the searchlight' as the King 'motioned Mr Chamberlain forward, and he stood alone at the front, acknowledging the acclamation'.[51] Critics later accused the King of political bias[52] – such an invitation was partisan, and unconstitutional, setting a dangerous precedent as the Prime Minister was planning to use the Munich euphoria to call a snap general election.[53] Chamberlain ruthlessly marked rebel anti-Munich Tory MPs down for deselection.

The Munich Agreement catapulted Chamberlain's popularity as 20,000 telegrams of support poured into Downing Street. In the euphoria, 'Chamberlain dolls' were sold in shops wearing either a suit or fishing garb, and *The Times* offered its readers the chance to buy a special Christmas card with an exclusive souvenir photo of the King and Queen standing next to the Chamberlains, waving from the balcony at Buckingham Palace.[54] You could even buy a souvenir plate embossed with the Prime Minister's face.[55]

Chamberlain's return was not universally acclaimed: 15,000 protestors assembled in Trafalgar Square, three times more than those who welcomed him home at 10 Downing Street. Due to Chamberlain's power to manipulate the BBC, this news was largely suppressed.[56] Churchill denounced the Munich Agreement and the appeasement route as the first taste 'of a bitter cup which will be proffered to us year by year',[57] while the Labour Party divided on the issue, believing Chamberlain failed to achieve the best terms for the Czechs. Hugh Dalton, an economist and Labour MP, suggested that the piece of paper Chamberlain waved was 'torn from the pages of *Mein Kampf*.[58] Isolated in the Cabinet, Duff Cooper resigned as First Lord of the Admiralty.

Nevertheless, a bewildered Queen Mary wholeheartedly agreed with the Prime Minister's pro-appeasement position, writing to the King: 'I am sure you feel as angry as I do at people croaking at the Prime Minister's action. He brought home peace, why can't they be grateful?'[59]

Germany. 9 November 1938.

In Paris, on the morning of 7 November, a young 17-year-old Jew called Herchel Grynszpan shot dead German diplomat Ernst vom Rath – avenging the anti-Semitic treatment of his parents. Hitler now decided it was time for the Jews in Germany 'to feel the anger of the people'.[60]

Within two days a wave of anti-Semitic violence erupted across Germany as members of the SA paramilitary and ordinary German citizens launched a nationwide pogrom against the Jews. On *Kristallnacht* (Night of the Broken Glass) the Nazis burned 250 synagogues, destroyed 7,000 Jewish businesses, sent 30,000 Jews to concentration camps, and murdered 91 Jews.

Tens of thousands of Jews fled Germany, abandoning their former lives. Still, the British people, their government and the King continued to support appeasement and turn a blind eye to the plight of German Jews stripped of their citizenship rights. Jewish immigrants to London were classified 'prosperous, arrogant and ungrateful'[61] and anti-Semitism was shared amongst the British upper classes. The right-wing Lord Brocket, a friend of the Duke of Coburg and his sister Princess Alice, continued with his hunting trip with Göring and returned claiming neither his host nor Hitler had any hand in *Kristallnacht*.[62] Lord Halifax admitted he had 'always been rather anti-Semitic',[63] and Chamberlain's close friend Sir Joseph Ball and former director of the Conservative Research Office ran the grossly anti-Semitic *Truth* magazine which portrayed Jews as criminals, feeding into the myth that the Jews controlled the black market: 'the Hebrew flock numbers more black sheep than prize winners.'[64]

Not everyone shared this prejudice. Harold Macmillan, a future Prime Minister, gave refuge to forty Jewish refugees in his Sussex home.[65] A former one, Stanley Baldwin, raised £522,651 to help Jewish exiles.[66] Even Lord Londonderry, the pro-Nazi who fraternised with Ribbentrop, registered his disgust at Hitler's 'medieval' behaviour, and Lord Mount Temple resigned from the Anglo-German Fellowship.[67]

The Prime Minister was shocked by the Nazi barbarities, but the question was: 'What price were Chamberlain and the British establishment willing to pay to avert war?' Churchill thought he knew the answer: 'The Government had to choose between war and shame. They chose shame. They will get war, too.' Churchill launched an attack on the government, arguing that Chamberlain's policy assumed that he was dealing with rational men – a notion crushed by *Kristallnacht*. In response, German propaganda targeted Churchill and even attempted to connect him to the Paris murder, claiming there was 'a straight line from Churchill to Grynszpan'.[68]

By February 1939, thousands of Jewish refugees were attempting to enter Palestine, which was becoming an acute problem for the government as it was a British Mandate. George VI wrote that 'he is glad to think that steps are being taken to prevent these people leaving their country of origin'.[69] Given that most of the refugees were fleeing Nazi Germany, this was a remarkably callous observation. The King's primary concern was that war would destroy the Monarchy and Empire – protecting those interests was his priority. The culture of human rights that exists today was still in its 'infancy'.[70]

On 20 April 1939, George VI sent a congratulatory telegram on Hitler's birthday; although arguably these were no more than the conventional courtesies between two heads of state, it nevertheless reflected the Establishment's desire for friendship with Germany on almost any terms. Meanwhile, Hitler remained intractable, in his haste for territorial gains and in his abuse of German Jews.

Hitler and Mussolini (who was now firmly in the Nazi camp) both thought that Britain was weak, with no appetite for war. When Chamberlain met Il Duce in Venice on 18 January 1939, he hoped to persuade 'Musso', as he called him, to restrain Hitler from any 'mad dog' acts.[71] However, Mussolini was uninspired, and following dinner at the Palazzo Venezia he turned to Count Ciano, his Foreign Minister, made fun of Chamberlain's umbrella, and declared that the British Prime Minister and Lord Halifax were not cast in the same mould 'as the Francis Drakes and other magnificent adventures who created the Empire' but were 'the tired sons of a long line of rich men and they will lose their Empire'.[72]

Prague, Czechoslovakia. 15 March 1939.

Vansittart's spy network started to warn of a looming invasion of Czechoslovakia in mid February, so when German troops crossed over the Sudetenland border on 15 March to seize what remained of Czechoslovakia this new crisis was entirely predictable.

At 6 a.m., seven German Army corps crossed into Bohemia, and after encountering no resistance reached Prague within three hours. As the motorbike columns descended on the city, they drove through deserted streets – the Czechoslovak President, Emil Hácha, warned his people not to resist the might of Hitler's army, so the Czechs watched silently as the Nazis drove into their city. That evening, a triumphant Hitler arrived in

Prague to view his new conquest with Prince Philipp of Hesse in his touring party. They spent the night in Hradčany Castle, and the Czech people woke up in a new country. Swastika flags now hung from government buildings and SS guards, ominously dressed in black, surveyed the streets. Signs asserted that shops were now for Aryans only. The populace was trapped as it was forbidden to leave the country without a visa. In contrast to the subdued mood in Prague, the crowds back home in Germany were euphoric. Hitler had conquered Austria and Czechoslovakia in the space of six short months – adding millions of inhabitants to the Nazi Empire.

This invasion reversed everything that Hitler had agreed at Munich and the policy of appeasement capsized utterly. That image of hope, Chamberlain's white sheet of paper which fluttered in the wind only a few weeks earlier, became a symbol of gullibility.[73] The King knew his Prime Minister was broken-hearted, and he yearned to intervene.[74] Still, the Foreign Office quashed his proposal to appeal personally to Hitler as 'one ex-Serviceman to another'.[75]

Not to be outdone by Hitler, Mussolini invaded the Kingdom of Albania on 7 April 1939, and Chamberlain, who cancelled his fishing holiday, was fuming. Although British appeasers were now on a 'backfoot',[76] Chamberlain and Halifax still obstinately believed they could negotiate a deal with Hitler – despite considerable evidence to contradict this notion. The House of Commons, rather than rising to the crisis, almost unbelievably debated about adjourning until October. A politically frustrated Churchill observed, 'dictators help themselves to a country' while the Commons is on recess.[77]

A small minority of aristocrats thought that a war between Britain and Germany was something that only the socialist Jews wanted. The Duke of Buccleuch, the King's Lord Steward, was such a keen supporter of the Munich Agreement that he and Lord Brocket visited Berlin just before Hitler's fiftieth birthday celebrations on 20 April 1939, frustrating the British Foreign Office's determination to look unyielding. Sir Alexander Cadogan, the Permanent Under-Secretary, dubbed them 'those two lunatics', and cried, 'Ye Gods and little fishes! Is the world upside down?'[78]

Chamberlain could have sent a defiant signal to Germany by including Churchill in his Cabinet. However, the Prime Minister allowed him to languish in the wilderness, ostracised by his party for being a warmonger. Count Gerhard von Schwerin, an officer on the German General Staff, attempted to persuade members of the British government to recall Churchill. He explained that Churchill was 'the only Englishman Hitler is afraid of', and 'the mere fact of giving him a leading ministerial post would convince Hitler that we really mean to stand up to him'.[79] Despite the risk that Schwein had taken, risking the capital charge of high treason, Chamberlain ignored his powerful analyses.

On 24 July 1949, a large advertising poster appeared on the Strand, asking: 'What Price Churchill?' It was part of a campaign for his inclusion in Chamberlain's ministry by the *Daily Telegraph*. Still, Chamberlain ignored these demands and gloated to his sister: 'As for the Churchill episode … it has in [US ambassador] Joe Kennedy's picturesque phrase "fallen out of bed" … I hear that Winston himself is very depressed and he certainly looked it at the dinner at Buckingham Palace on Monday.'[80]

During that dinner, held in honour of Prince Paul of Yugoslavia, Chamberlain sat between Queen Elizabeth and the Duchess of Kent (who was Prince Paul's sister-in-law). He wrote, 'neither of them left me in any doubt about their sentiments.' These two royal women encouraged the Prime Minister not to take Churchill back into the government. Not only was he against appeasement, but he was far also too close to the exiled Duke of Windsor, Queen Elizabeth's bête noire.[81]

Verdun, France. 9 May 1939.

While Britain was preparing for war, the Duke of Windsor made a notorious anti-war speech from the Hotel Coq Hardie in Verdun, famous as a First World War battlefield. His message, a plea for peace, was broadcast on NBC radio in America, while the BBC refused to transmit it:

> I speak simply as a soldier of the last war, whose most earnest prayer is that such a cruel and destructive madness shall never again overtake mankind. The grave anxieties of the time compel me to raise my voice in expression of the universal longing to be delivered from the fears that beset us.[82]

As his brother George VI was travelling to the United States and Canada for a goodwill tour, Edward's speech proved ill-timed and played to the Queen's fears of that the Duke of Windsor could upstage her husband. On the day of the broadcast, Ambassador Bullitt, who was on amicable terms with the Windsors, reported to President Roosevelt not to raise the subject of his brother with the King:

> About a month ago the Duke of Windsor wrote to Queen Mary that Bertie [George VI] had behaved toward him in such an ungentlemanly

manner because of 'the influence of that common little woman' the Queen [Elizabeth], that he could have no further relations with Bertie ...[83]

The Queen and the Duchess of Kent loathed Wallis Simpson, who they dismissed as 'That Woman' or 'Mrs S', and along with Queen Mary, these three royal ladies still refused to receive the American Duchess.

Florence, Italy. 2 July 1939.

Even though Europe was on the verge of war, the people of Florence decked the streets with flags and bunting in anticipation of a royal wedding. The bride and groom were Princess Irene of Greece and Prince Aimone Roberto di Savoia-Aosta, the Duke of Spoleto. The event provided cover for some secret royal diplomacy, as the guest list included both Prince George, Duke of Kent and Prince Philipp of Hesse. The two cousins met at least twice in July, first in Florence and then in Rome. The Duke of Kent was representing the British Royal Family, and he was given a detailed diplomatic brief, even down to the language he would use when he met King Victor Emmanuel III in Florence. Although war was seeming inevitable, the British government wanted to keep Italy out of the conflict for as long as possible.[84]

George VI also wanted his younger brother to invite Prince Philipp to London. He planned to ask Philipp to arrange a direct 'face-to-face' meeting with Hitler.[85] However, both Chamberlain and Halifax disagreed, fearing that the situation was far too complex for royal negotiation. In truth, they considered both the King and the Duke of Kent as well-meaning amateurs.[86] While the King did not press the issue, he had a mind of his own and was determined to avoid war. When Kent met Philipp, he cautioned the Nazi Prince that Britain would regard the invasion of Poland as an act of war, and that Germany should be under no illusions about the probable outcome.

After his discussion with the Duke, Hesse returned immediately to Berlin and tried to speak to the Führer. Hitler kept him waiting until late August, a sign that his influence was diminishing – at least temporarily. When Prince Philipp finally passed on the warning from Buckingham Palace, Hitler ignored it. In front of Philipp, Hitler picked up the phone to take a call from Ribbentrop, his new favourite, who was in Moscow negotiating with the Soviets. Hitler no longer cared about Britain's opinion, as Germany and Russia were about to sign the Molotov–Ribbentrop pact. Both Hitler and Ribbentrop wrongly assumed that Britain was too reluctant to fight.[87]

According to Henry Winterbottom, the head of British air intelligence, the Duke of Kent also regularly met with Baron William de Ropp, a secretive figure described as one of the most 'mysterious and influential clandestine operators' of the era.[88] Kent and Ropp were both in a position to act as go-betweens for high-ranking Nazis and the Royal Family.[89] Although a British agent, Ropp was Hitler's confidant on British affairs and very close to Alfred Rosenburg, the author of many Nazi racial theories.

Dartmouth, Devon. 22 July 1939.

With the war approaching, Lord Mountbatten – now the King's aide-de-camp – arranged for George VI and Queen Elizabeth to visit the Royal Naval College at Dartmouth. Coincidentally, his young 17-year-old nephew, Prince Philip of Greece, was a naval cadet at the college after leaving Gordonstoun that summer. The entire family sailed into the harbour in the gleaming white and gold Royal Yacht, *Victoria and Albert.*

Princess Elizabeth was still a shy 13-year-old girl who liked ginger biscuits and lemonade. Her governess, Marion Crawford, recalled that Philip made an entrance, 'a fair-haired boy, rather like a Viking, with a sharp face and piercing blue eyes,' and came over and said, 'How do you do?' While outside, he started to show off, first demonstrating his tennis skills, including leaping over the net, and later at a game of croquet. Princess Elizabeth was suitably impressed: 'How good he is, Crawfie. How high he can jump.'[90] The following day Lord Mountbatten procured Philip an invitation to tea on the Royal Yacht, where the cook served shrimps, followed by banana splits and some trifle. Philipp spent a lot of time teasing plump little Margaret, but Elizabeth 'never took her eyes off him the whole time'.[91]

As *Victoria and Albert* sailed away, Philip was the leader of a group of cadets who commandeered a flotilla of small craft to escort the Royal Yacht out of the harbour. Gradually the boats fell back, until one solitary oarsman was left rowing in the yacht's wake. Philip was showing off again while Elizabeth watched through binoculars. When the King saw him, he snapped, 'Damned young fool! Signal him to go back!'[92]

Within a year of the encounter, some of Philip's closest relatives, including Lord Mountbatten and the Duchess of Kent, began mooting Philip's chances that he would become Prince Consort to the future Queen.[93]

Château de la Croë, South of France. August 1939.

Banned from London, Edward and Wallis were busy creating a new life for themselves on the French Riviera. They celebrated their first anniversary on board the luxury yacht *Gulzar* with their friends Herman and Katherine Rogers as they cruised the Amalfi coastline. They were relaxed, happy and affectionate with each other. Fit and tanned, the Duke looked like a man finally at peace with himself.

The Windsors established a magnificent court-in-exile, with two opulent homes at 24 Boulevard Suchet in Paris and the Château de la Croë in Cap d'Antibes. They travelled between these two properties on the famous overnight Blue Train. The château was a gleaming white villa surrounded by 12 acres of green lawns and shaded by fir, pine, yew, eucalyptus and cypress trees with a swimming pool at the edge of the sea and tennis courts. Wallis had spent lavishly here, filling the house with antiques shipped from their homes in England, including the large mahogany desk on which Edward signed the Instrument of Abdication. There was no mistaking its royal atmosphere; luxury pervaded every room, from the family portraits to the gold-plated bathtub. As the new Duchess of Windsor always entertained, there were sixteen servants, including liveried footmen wearing scarlet coats with gold collars, cuffs and buttons.[94]

Churchill was a frequent guest; he first visited the Château de la Croë in January 1938 and concluded that 'The Ws are very pathetic, but also very happy ... She made an excellent impression on me, and it looks as if it would be a most happy marriage.'[95] He was back again the following year. Over dinner one evening, the Duke and Churchill argued viciously over a series of newspaper articles that Churchill had written which were critical of Spain's General Franco and in favour of negotiating an alliance with Soviet Russia. Vincent Sheean, a guest at the dinner party, witnessed: 'Mr Churchill frowning with intentness at the floor in front of him, mincing no words ... declaring flatly that the nation stood in the gravest danger of its long history.' Meanwhile, the Duke was 'eagerly interrupting whenever he could, contesting every point, but receiving – in terms of the utmost politeness so far as the words went – an object lesson in political wisdom.' 'There was something dramatically final, irrevocable about this dispute,'[96] as Churchill had discovered how 'unsound the ex-King was about the Nazis'.[97]

Six months later, after staying at Ritz Hotel in Paris in August 1939, Churchill toured French defences along the Maginot Line and then accepted a third invitation from the Duke to visit the Riviera for a holiday.

When Churchill arrived in Cap d'Antibes, he received a warning from French intelligence about a possible assassination attempt by undercover Nazi agents. He immediately sent a telegram on 22 August to his former bodyguard, Walter Thompson, asking him to join him in France: he considered that there was a serious threat to his life.

Churchill was the one man in British politics whom Hitler feared. In the Reichstag, the Führer called Churchill an 'apostle of war'.[98] How the Germans knew about his impending visit remains unknown, but the Duke and Duchess of Windsor were known for their indiscreet gossiping, and the château had a large staff, so the news could easily have leaked.[99] However, Churchill's visit was cut short by the announcement of the Nazi–Soviet pact on 23 August, and he immediately returned to London. Soviet Russia's alliance with Germany meant that war was now only a matter of weeks away.

The German invasion of Poland started on 1 September, with their attack from the north, south and west. On 3 September, from the Cabinet Room at 10 Downing Street, Chamberlain announced on BBC radio that Britain was at war with Germany. Hitler was astonished at Britain's declaration of war. 'It was plain to see how stunned he was,' wrote his press chief, Otto Dietrich.[100] The Nazi leadership, including Göring and Goebbels, was furious with Ribbentrop's encouraging Hitler's delusion that Britain would not fight for Poland and that he 'could invade Poland with impunity'.[101] Sixteen days later, on 17 September, Russia invaded from the east.

Meanwhile, at Château de la Croë on 3 September, the Duke of Windsor took a phone call from the British ambassador in Paris, Sir Ronald Hugh Campbell. He then walked out to the swimming pool where Wallis and Fruity Metcalfe were sunbathing. Shrugging his shoulders as he sauntered past, he quietly told them, 'Great Britain has just declared war on Germany. I'm afraid in the end, this may open the way for world Communism.' He then walked to the edge of the pool and dived into the water with a splash.[102]

Prince Charles Edward in 1906. He was Duke of Saxe-Coburg and Gotha in Germany, and Duke of Albany in Great Britain. However, in 1917 he was declared a traitor peer for supporting Kaiser Wilhelm II in the First World War, and lost his British title.

Princess Alice of Albany (also Princess of Saxe-Coburg and Gotha) in 1911. Alice was Charles Edward's sister. During the First World War, she gave up her German title and became known as Princess Alice, Countess of Athlone.

Charles Edward, Duke of Saxe–Coburg and Gotha. He was the first German royal to support Adolf Hitler and the Nazi Party in 1922. Charles Edward was cousin to King George VI and grandfather of King Carl XVI Gustaf of Sweden.

Princess Alice, Countess of Athlone, in 1947. She entertained visiting Nazis at her Sussex home and attempted to whitewash her brother's criminal record at the denazification trials after the Second World War.

Edward VIII and Wallis Simpson just before the abdication. Prime Minister Baldwin had their telephones bugged and placed Mrs Simpson under police surveillance.

After the abdication in 1937.
Adolf Hitler welcomes Edward
and Wallis, now Duke and
Duchess of Windsor, to Germany.
During the visit, Hitler treated
Wallis with the full royal
deference denied to her in Britain.
(© Popperphoto/Getty Images)

The Duke and Duchess of
Windsor with Adolf Hitler
at Berchtesgaden in the
Bavarian Alps. This meeting
destroyed their reputation.

King George VI. After the Second World War, the King, with Winston Churchill's help, covered up the pro-Nazi activities of members of his family.

Winston Churchill, cigar in mouth, gives his famous 'V for victory' sign during a visit to Bradford on 4 December 1942.

Prince George, Duke of Kent, and his wife Princess Marina, Duchess of Kent. George had numerous affairs with men and women, but Marina never publicly complained. (© The Print Collector/Getty Images)

Princess Olga of Yugoslavia, Princess Marina's sister. People joked that while Marina brought high fashion to London, Olga introduced the Nazi Party to Belgrade.

Prince Philipp of Hesse and Princess Mafalda of Savoy on their wedding day at the Racconigi Palace outside Turin, 25 September 1925. Mussolini was guest of honour. Philipp became a Nazi diplomat and Hitler's art agent.

Siegfried Sassoon, the famous war poet and Prince Philipp of Hesse's lover.

Benito Mussolini and Adolf Hitler. As son-in-law to King Victor Emmanuel III of Italy, Prince Philipp of Hesse acted as a messenger and diplomatic intermediary between Hitler and Mussolini.

Prince Josias of Waldeck and Pyrmont. He was the Duke of Coburg's protégé and oversaw Princess Mafalda's imprisonment in Buchenwald concentration camp.

Prince Christoph of Hesse and Princess Sophie of Greece and Denmark on their wedding day. Christoph was head of the Nazi wiretapping unit, a Luftwaffe officer and a close friend of Hermann Göring, his mentor. (© Ullstein bild/Getty Images)

The bombastic Hermann Göring at a Nazi Party rally. Göring played a critical role in wooing the German royals to lend the Nazis an aura of credibility. (© Library of Congress/Getty Images)

Princess Sophie of Hesse. She supported the Nazi Party and named her eldest son Adolf. Sophie was Prince Philip's youngest sister and was banned from his wedding to Princess Elizabeth in 1947. (© Ullstein bild/Getty Images)

Prince Philip of Greece and Princess Elizabeth in 1947, the year of their wedding.

Winston Churchill stands on the balcony of Buckingham Palace with George VI, Queen Elizabeth and Princess Elizabeth on VE Day, 8 May 1945.

To Catch a King

Admiralty House, London. 3 September 1939.
Winston Churchill had been right about Hitler. Right about the evil brutality of the Nazi regime. Right that Chamberlain's policy of appeasement would fail, and right about the British army's current weakness to confront her enemies. Churchill called for more ships. More expenditure. More preparation. When the government declared war on 3 September, Chamberlain at last allowed Churchill to returned to the Cabinet as First Lord of the Admiralty. 'Winston is back' was the signal flashed to the fleet as he sat back at the same desk he had used between 1911 and 1915.[1] No other political leader perceived the situation with his clarity of vision, but the challenge was now to do something about it. He was part of a small minority – everyone else persisted with a pacifist delusion.

For the first eight months of the war, nothing happened except for intense preparation and a naval blockade. During this period – dubbed 'The Phoney War' – everyone still hoped that Chamberlain would negotiate a peaceful solution. All members of the Royal Family were 'staunchly behind Chamberlain'[2] and 100 per cent pro-Munich. Privately, George VI and Queen Elizabeth considered Churchill a terrible warmonger and the entire royal household viewed him as old, irreverent, unpredictable and inconsiderate. Sir Alan 'Tommy' Lascelles, the King's Private Secretary, called him 'repugnant'. Hence, the First Lord of the Admiralty sarcastically returned the favour by calling him Alan – never Tommy, which he preferred.[3] George VI even told President Roosevelt 'that in only very exceptional circumstances would he consent to Churchill being made Prime Minister'.[4] It was also personal, because Churchill had keenly championed Edward and Wallis over the abdication.

Portsmouth Harbour. 13 September 1939.

When the Duke and Duchess of Windsor arrived back in Portsmouth on 13 September, local officials hurriedly produced a length of red carpet, but no family member or royal car was there to welcome the ex-king home. It was left to Walter Monckton to explain to the Duke the brutal reality of the situation – neither his mother, Queen Mary, nor his sister-in-law Queen Elizabeth would receive the Duchess. Their bitterness ran deep. The Duke was even denied accommodation at the Palace. 'He might not even exist,' wrote Lady Alexandra Metcalfe in her diary.[5] With no royal lodgings on offer, the Windsors stayed with the Metcalfes in Sussex, where they posed for newspaper photographers in the garden.[6] When the Duke was cheered in the streets, 'the news caused consternation at the Palace'.[7]

Edward visited the King at Buckingham Palace and Chamberlain at 10 Downing Street on 14 September 1939. Both George VI and Queen Elizabeth wanted Edward out of Britain as quickly as possible and fully intended to quash any comeback plans. The Queen complained to Prince Paul of Yugoslavia: 'What a curse black sheep are in a family! I think he at last realises that there is no niche for him here – the mass of the people do not forgive quickly the sort of thing that he did to this country, and they HATE her!'[8]

Paris, France. October 1939.

The ex-king was quickly sent back to Paris with the rank of Major General and assigned to the British Military Mission in Vincennes. The Duke's nemesis, Sir Robert Vansittart, reinforced the King's view that the Duke must stay out of Britain. Vansittart remained convinced the Duchess was still in touch with the Germans. He suspected that the Duke was overfamiliar with various 'peace' factions operating in Britain that were in reality Nazi fronts.[9] Edward met secretly with Lord Beaverbrook and Sir Walter Monckton to discuss creating an international peace movement. City donors and private individuals such as Charles Bedaux would provide private funds to cover operating costs. Beaverbrook promised to support him as the 'peace candidate', until Monckton explained that such a proposition was high treason and that if the Duke returned to England, he would become liable for income tax. The Duke's zeal quickly disappeared.[10]

The Royal Family's paranoia over the Duke of Windsor increased when, on 11 October 1939, Sir Stewart Menzies of the Secret Intelligence Service (SIS), in co-operation with the BBC, decided to test the Duke of

Windsor's popularity in Nazi Germany. His SIS team arranged for a fake BBC radio broadcast to transmit throughout Germany that there had been a coup d'état in London forcing George VI's abdication, Chamberlain's resignation as Prime Minister and the restoration of the Duke of Windsor to the British throne. The Minister of Propaganda, Joseph Goebbels, received reports of spontaneous celebrations in the street as strangers hugged each other and people were 'on fire with excitement' at the news.[11] Goebbels immediately saw through Menzies' fake news scheme. It proved that the Duke of Windsor was a hazard to the British Establishment and popular with the German people. Goebbels instructed every newspaper in Germany to run the headline: 'FURTHER INSOLENCE FROM THE BRITISH MINISTRY OF LIES.'[12]

In Paris, the Duke was infuriated by this 'back-door intrigue', and sent a letter of complaint to Sir Walter Monckton, while Goebbels dismissed the hoax as something to 'frighten spinsters ... in the London suburbs'.[13] Irritated, the Duchess of Windsor dropped loud asides about the 'big' Phoney War and the 'little' war with the Palace. While playing cards one night and listening to the radio with Clare Boothe Luce, the famous playwright, the BBC news reported German fighter planes shelling English coastal towns. Luce said how awful she felt for the English, but the Duchess just looked up from her cards and sarcastically answered, 'After what they did to me, I can't say I feel sorry for them – a whole nation against one lone woman.'[14] Lady Diana Cooper was equally outraged when she visited the Windsors, and the Duke announced that the English must be mad not to see they were doomed. 'Well, maybe we are, but I'd rather be mad than turn slave by fear or reason,' Lady Diana responded.[15]

When the Duke was finally driven to Vincennes by his chauffeur Ladbroke, he started the made-up task of surveying the French defence forces. There was already a detailed report, for Churchill had made a complete tour of the line in mid August. Military leaders ignored any recommendations he made – this was a pure vanity project.[16]

On 27 January 1940, the German ambassador in The Hague, Count Julius von Zech-Burkersroda, wrote to Baron von Weizsäcker, the Secretary of State in Berlin. He noted that the Duke was dissatisfied about his current position and had gone to London in September to seek 'a field of activity ... that would permit him a more active role'. Zech realised that Windsor was being frozen out and noted that the Duke 'achieved nothing and is supposed to be disgruntled about it'. Weizsäcker passed the ambassador's report to Ribbentrop, who in turn took it to Hitler. Less than a month later, on 19 February, Zech was able to inform Ribbentrop that the Duke had leaked the Allied war plan for the defence of Belgium. The Duke of Windsor, according to Zech, had attended an Allied War Council meeting to discuss potential military strategies should Germany invade Belgium. In order to protect her neutrality and not provoke Nazi Germany, Belgium had barred Allied troops from entering the country. At the meeting, military commanders argued that the defence line should hold at the Belgium–France border, 'even at the risk that Belgium should be occupied'. Political leaders had 'at first opposed this plan', but the consensus had finally swung behind the military view.[17]

There was either a spy in the Windsor household, or Edward and Wallis were being indiscreet at dinner parties, or they were deliberately leaking information.[18] A likely conduit for their secrets was their old friend Charles Bedaux. He was making frequent trips to The Hague at the time, and it is possible that 'an intelligence leak leading back to the Duke of Windsor may well have played a significant part in prompting Hitler to order his generals to change their battle plan'.[19]

London. April 1940.

Hostilities arrived with a vengeance in the spring. On 9 April, the Germans took Denmark and attacked Norway. On 10 May, Hitler's ground and air forces invaded the Netherlands, Belgium and Luxembourg in a determined onslaught stretching from the Moselle to the North Sea. That afternoon, Chamberlain offered his resignation to the King. The collapse of the Munich Agreement had shattered the Prime Minister's confidence, and a negotiated peace with fair terms for Britain no longer looked viable. The Germans seemed unstoppable.

Queen Elizabeth was horrified by Chamberlain's resignation: 'I must write you one line to say how deeply I regretted your ceasing to be our Prime Minister. I can never tell you in words how much we owe you. During these last desperate & unhappy years, you have been our great support & comfort ...' Chamberlain's farewell, broadcast on the evening of 11 May, reduced Princess Elizabeth to tears. 'My eldest daughter told me, that she and Margaret Rose had listened to it with real emotion – In fact she said, "I cried, mummy."'[20]

There were only two candidates to replace him as Prime Minister: Winston Churchill or Lord Halifax. Both the King and Queen quickly transferred their affections from Chamberlain to their old friend Halifax. George VI and Lord Halifax were both quiet, moral, family men whom the Establishment considered sound. Both suffered from speech impediments, which perhaps made them distrust Churchill's enthusiastic eloquence, which often targeted his opponents. 'Halifax's virtues have done more harm in the world than the vices of hundreds of other people,' was one of Churchill's disdainful putdowns.[21] Halifax, however, recognised that Churchill, who loved and understood military strategy, would make a better wartime leader. It may have been self-sacrifice – or the fact that Halifax was unwilling to surrender his peerage and return to the Commons to face the 'bear-pit' of scrutiny – but he refused the premiership.[22] Faced with no alternative, the King invited Churchill to Buckingham Palace and asked him to become Prime Minister on 10 May. When he met Halifax the following day in the palace gardens, George VI told his Foreign Secretary that he 'was sorry not to have him as PM',[23] and Halifax noted in his diary that the King was 'apprehensive about Winston's administrative methods'.[24]

One of Churchill's first acts as Prime Minister was to arrest potential traitors. He interned Sir Oswald Mosley on 22 May under Defence Regulation 18B, and during his stay in Brixton Prison his cell was bugged by MI5. Police arrested British fascists Archibald Ramsay MP and Admiral Sir Barry Domvile. Mosley's wife, Diana Mitford, was incarcerated inside Holloway Prison, and by the end of December, there were over 1,000 detainees in custody. Churchill was taking no chances should there be any counter-activity from pro-Hitler groups in Britain. The changes swept through Buckingham Palace as well: the Duke of Buccleuch, the King's pro-German Lord Steward, resigned from his office before being sacked.

The day Winston Churchill became Prime Minister, Hitler unleashed his Blitzkrieg on the West by attacking Belgium and Holland, outflanking the Maginot Line and invading France. As Paris was on the brink, the Duke and Duchess fled to the South of France, arriving at the Château de la Croë on 29 May. During a War Cabinet meeting in Downing Street, Halifax argued for negotiation and compromise with Nazi Germany. Unbowed by the pressure, Churchill used his 'stirring rhetorical gifts'[25] to outmanoeuvre Halifax, asserting that conciliation at this point would diminish Britain's status to that of 'a slave state'.[26] Churchill ordered the massive evacuation of British and Allied forces trapped in France, which began from Dunkirk, with 330,000 men being rescued from the beaches by the historic flotilla of small boats. Despite the 'miracle of Dunkirk', most of the British army's best equipment was abandoned in France, and negotiation seemed Britain's best option.

France tumbled into chaos as the Germans quickly arrived at Dijon, while the Italians threatened to cross the border at Menton. On 17 June, three days after the fall of Paris, a defeated French government under Marshal Pétain contacted their new Nazi rulers for armistice terms. Meanwhile, the Duke and Duchess of Windsor were escaping the country on busy roads jammed with other refugees fleeing into Francoist Spain. They stayed first at Biarritz, only for a German commercial station to broadcast news of their arrival. Details publicised included their room number: Suite 104E. FBI agent Edward Tamm reported to Hoover that the British Secret Service felt that the Duchess was keeping Ribbentrop informed of their location and schedule. Finally, the Windsors crossed the border at Perpignan and drove towards Madrid, arriving at the luxurious Ritz Hotel on 23 June. Spain was a hotbed of pro-Nazi diplomatic and espionage activity, and its fascist government under General Franco was on the brink of entering the war on the side of Hitler and Mussolini, as throughout the Spanish Civil War these two dictators had been sending aid to Franco.

Ritz Hotel, Madrid. June 1940.

At the Ritz, the Windsors now became the centre of attention. The Italian newspaper *Il Messaggero* and the Spanish fascist newspaper *Arriba* claimed a mutiny of British troops had restored the Duke of Windsor to the throne, and that he had flown to Berlin to negotiate peace terms with Hitler. Such stories were outrageous propaganda, but Ribbentrop became excited by the opportunities the Windsors' presence in Madrid offered the Nazis. At this moment, the Germans truly believed they were about to conquer Britain.

Lord Halifax certainly thought so; his political ally Rab Butler contacted Swedish diplomat Dr Björn Pryzt to tell him that politicians should formulate British policy with 'common sense not bravado'. Pryzt claimed Butler had assured him 'that no opportunity for reaching a compromise [peace] would be neglected if the possibility were offered on reasonable conditions'.[27] Churchill was furious when he found out, probably through intelligence intercepts of Swedish diplomatic cables. He wrote to Halifax on 26 June, complaining of Butler's 'odd language', which hinted at a defeatist attitude. Butler was lucky not to be sacked, and Halifax quickly delivered a speech rejecting Hitler's public 'peace offer' of 19 July.[28]

Meanwhile, the Duke of Windsor was trying to establish contact with the Germans, via his friend Don Javier 'Tiger' Bermejillo – a Spanish diplomat in Madrid. Edward and Wallis were deeply (and venally) concerned that their Paris house, crammed with rich treasures, would need protection during any occupation. Ribbentrop was delighted to help old friends. A teletype survives of his ordering 'unofficially and confidentially an unobtrusive observation on the duke's residence'. He instructed the German ambassador to Spain, Dr Eberhard von Stohrer, 'to inform the Duke confidentially through a Spanish intermediary that the Foreign Minister [Ribbentrop] is looking out for its protection'.[29]

Wallis became obsessed about losing her possessions. She insisted that the Duke make arrangements through their new Spanish intermediaries for her maid, Jeanne-Marguerite Moulichon, to go into German-occupied France and retrieve items. Moulichon's mission was to extract the Duchess's prize possessions and the contents of their locked safe from their Paris house. Some of the goods were put in cars, while the more valuable possessions rode in limousines. The 'desire of the Germans to please the Duke and Duchess of Windsor was absolutely marked and evident …'[30] A similar request was sent by the Duke to the Italian government to protect the Château de la Croë should the Italians occupy Antibes.[31] Further evidence that the Duchess had lost all sense of reality was her agitation that she had left her favourite Nile-green swimming costume behind at the château, so she enlisted the American consul in Nice 'to repatriate the garment'. The mission was dubbed 'Operation Cleopatra Whim' by the Americans.[32]

The British government wanted the troublesome and self-centred Windsors out of Spain quickly and had arranged for a boat to picked them up in neutral Portugal, while Ribbentrop wanted to explore whether the Duke of Windsor would be willing to become the head of state of a Nazi puppet government in Britain, providing a role similar to that of Marshal Philippe Pétain in Vichy France.[33] He immediately telegraphed Stohrer:

> Is it possible to detain the Duke and Duchess in Spain for a couple of weeks to begin with before they are granted an exit visa? It would be necessary to ensure … all events that it did not appear in any way that the suggestion came from Germany.

Just as the Windsors were about to move to Portugal, British paranoia caused a dangerous delay. The Duke of Kent was coincidently making a goodwill mission to Portugal on 26 June, to prevent their government allying with the Axis powers. George VI and Churchill didn't want the two troublesome brothers meeting, so the Windsors stayed on in Madrid. Kent was capable of making mischief by himself and rumours persisted that the Duke of Kent met his German cousin Prince Philipp of Hesse in Lisbon – although there is no hard evidence of a reunion.[34]

Forced to wait in Madrid, the Duke and Duchess of Windsor started to exploit the situation to their advantage. The British ambassador to Spain, Sir Samuel Hoare, distilled their demands down to one fundamental request: that they meet the King and Queen briefly, and for the Court Circular to publish that meeting. This request seemed petty, but the Windsors wanted official recognition of their relationship from the Royal Family. Hoare feared the ex-king might never leave Europe, and he wanted them out of Spain.[35]

All over Madrid, the Windsors were broadcasting their defeatist attitude to pro-fascist Spanish aristocrats and neutral diplomats. Wallis blabbed first to Alexander Weddell, the American ambassador in Madrid, that France had lost because their country was 'internally diseased'. 'A country which was not in a condition to fight a war should not have declared a war,' she announced.[36] Weddell concluded, 'Wally herself gives every suggestion of extreme acuteness and unlimited ambition; her exterior suggests heavy armoured plate or some substance slightly harder than a diamond. But very pleasant, very genial, and very witty.'[37]

The Duke was equally undiplomatic and disclosed to the Spanish Foreign Minister, Colonel Juan Beigbeder y Atienza, that he would not return to Britain without getting what he wanted. Bermejillo reported to his superiors that the Duke of Windsor was loudly blaming 'the Jews, the Reds and the Foreign Office for the war' and that the Duke had announced that he would like to put Anthony Eden and other British politicians 'up against a wall'. In another conversation on 25 June 1940, Bermejillo described that the Duke observed that if Germany bombed England successfully, this could force peace. He concluded that the Duke wanted this to happen: 'He wants peace at any price.'[38] Meanwhile, on 10 July, the bombing of Britain began.

Beigbeder, who was in regular contact with Ribbentrop, immediately offered to place a lavish Moorish palace in Andalusia at the Windsors' indefinite disposal if they remained.[39] It was a tempting proposition. However, the Duke's military rank as a serving officer would become a problem if Franco joined Germany in the war. The Duke finally left Madrid for Lisbon on 3 July, feeling it would be an expedient place to wait while Churchill and George VI pondered his terms.

When Ribbentrop heard the news, he flew into a rage, but he was not about to surrender the chase. Walter Schellenberg, who headed German foreign counterintelligence organisation the *Sicherheitsdienst* (SD), arrived in Lisbon with a plan. Under Operation Willi, Schellenberg was tasked by both Hitler and Ribbentrop with bringing the Duke and Duchess back to Spain. As an inducement, Hitler authorised him to offer the Duke up to 50 million Swiss francs (about $200 million today) if Edward agreed to break with Britain and move to a neutral state such as Switzerland. Hitler even decided to use force if necessary, and personally telephoned Schellenberg and advised him to win over the Duchess: 'she has great influence over the Duke.'[40] Schellenberg quickly assembled a team of eighteen agents who started working for him in the vicinity of the Windsors' temporary home in Portugal.

Ricardo Espirito Santo Silva's Villa, Lisbon. July 1940.

In Portugal, the Duke and Duchess of Windsor were not only surrounded by German agents, but were staying in a house belonging to one, Ricardo Espirito Santo Silva. To frighten them, Nazi agents threw stones at their borrowed villa's windows, shattering the glass, and flowers containing an ominous warning were delivered. One of the Portuguese guards warned the Duke of a British intelligence plot to assassinate him.[41] Don Ángel Alcázar de Velasco, a Spanish fascist who worked for Schellenberg, approached the Duke in person and repeated this warning, stoking the Duke's paranoia about the British government. Velasco even suggested that the Duke should return to Spain for protection.[42]

Schellenberg hoped that if the Windsors could be coaxed back to Spain, they could be 'persuaded' to support the Germans; and if not, the Duke was to be kidnapped during a hunting party and smuggled over the border by force into Spain. An old friend, Don Miguel Primo de Rivera, the Marqués de Estella, arrived at the villa and presented a detailed travel plan for the Windsors to return discreetly to Spain. During their meeting, the Duke made critical remarks about Churchill's government, calling the King 'stupid' and observing that the Queen was a 'clever intriguer' – but surrounded by German agents, the Duke did not know who to trust and asked for forty-eight hours to reflect.[43]

Frustrated about what to do with the errant ex-king, Churchill offered the Duke of Windsor the governorship of the Bahamas, hoping to keep his troublesome presence out of Europe. In reality, the Duke realised this was a sentence of banishment, but the position was resentfully accepted. It's 'the St Helena of 1940' and 'a pathetic little job in a ghastly backwater' Wallis bitterly quipped. When the Duke started to haggle again that his family should receive and recognise Wallis, Churchill then sent a curtly worded telegram:

> Your Royal Highness has taken active military rank and refusal to obey direct orders of competent military authority would create a serious situation. I hope it will not be necessary for such orders to be sent. I most strongly urge compliance with the wishes of the Government.'[44]

To reinforce his message, Churchill dispatched Sir Walter Monckton, who 'was not the usual action hero', to Lisbon on 28 July. He arrived in a flying boat exuding 'an air of Britishness; the bowler hat, briefcase and quality overcoat' as Churchill had ordered him to stiffen the Duke's wavering upper lip and to get him on a boat to the Bahamas.[45]

Santo Silva spoke to the Duke again on 1 August, the day of his departure to the Bahamas. Edward once again hedged his options, stating that 'he should not now be in negotiations carried on contrary to the orders of the Government' as these 'might bring about a scandal and deprive him of all prestige at the period when he might possibly take action'. He was fully prepared for 'any personal sacrifice' when the time was right and would remain in contact. He 'could, if the occasion arose, take action from the Bahamas'. The Duke even agreed on a code word that would recall him to Europe. He was saying that he was going along with Churchill's wishes, but he could still change his mind later if the bombing of London forced the British government into talks with the Nazis.[46]

Lord Lloyd, the Colonial Secretary, was so concerned that he wrote the first draft of a telegram, justifying the Duke's appointment, to all the Dominion Prime Ministers. It read: 'The activities of the Duke of Windsor on the Continent in recent months have been causing HM and myself grave uneasiness as his inclinations are well known to be pro-Nazi and he may become a centre of intrigue.' To protect the Duke's reputation, Churchill vetoed Lloyd's wording and toned it down.[47]

The failure of Operation Willi was a blow to Hitler's Anglo-German fantasies. Edward, the ex-king turned political pawn, was off the chessboard.

WORLD ON FIRE

Rideau Hall in Ottawa, Canada. June 1940.

After an erratic voyage across the Atlantic, where their boat had to zigzag to avoid German U-boats, Princess Alice and her husband Lord Athlone arrived in Canada. Athlone, now 65 years old and too old to serve in the military, had accepted the appointment of Governor-General of Canada. On 21 June, Lord Athlone and Princess Alice were installed in Rideau Hall, their new official home, and applauding Canadians crowded around the railway station entrance to welcome them. The pair look rather stiff and glum in photographs. 'The whole proceedings, accompanied by torrents of rain, was quite mournful,' wrote the Princess, 'as we were all oppressed by the Fall of France and our own serious predicament.'[1]

Princess Alice spent her first day at Rideau Hall reorganising the furniture and hanging the portrait of herself by Philip de László over the fireplace in the main drawing room. Here, they would entertain President Roosevelt, Winston Churchill, Charles de Gaulle, Anthony Eden and even the formidable Madame Chiang Kai-shek, the First Lady of the Chinese Republic. One evening at dinner, Lord Athlone asked James, the English butler, the name of the wine he was serving. It was Liebfraumilch, but James, horrified to use a German word in wartime, did a rapid literal translation and unblinkingly replied: 'Milk of the virgin, Your Excellency.'[2]

Times were desperate, and the house was often full of royal refugees fleeing Nazi-occupied Europe, including King George II of the Hellenes, Empress Zita of Austria and Queen Wilhelmina of the Netherlands – who was Alice's aunt. There was even a German royal prisoner of war: Princess Alice's godson, Prince Frederick of Prussia, who would occasionally be allowed out of Camp L, a Quebec internment camp, to have tea with his godmother. After the war, he would renounce his German citizenship, despite the fact he was the Kaiser's grandson, and marry an Englishwoman, Lady Brigid Guinness. If Princess Alice and Lord Athlone ever discussed the Duke of Coburg, they did so privately.

Alice spent most of her time in Canada wearing a uniform. 'Our chief preoccupation,' she wrote, was inspecting 'endless, endless war factories'. However, watching the entire Canadian nation throw itself into the war effort made it 'very inspiring to be there at that time'.[3] Alice and her husband repeatedly visited hospitals, Red Cross centres and all societies dedicated to the war effort in an exhausting and often tedious daily schedule. Every evening they would ask, 'What are we doing tomorrow?' and, 'When do we start?'

The Villa Coburg, Berlin. July 1940.

While the Duke of Windsor had turned down Hitler's money, his cousin Charles Edward, Duke of Coburg, received 4,000 Reichsmarks monthly from a special fund called the '*Dipositionsfunds*' used for the elite Nazi staff.[4] Charles Edward was too old to serve in the military but he occupied two significant roles in the Third Reich: Secretary of the Kaiser Wilhelm Society for the Advancement of Science, and President of the German Red Cross.

During the First World War, the Kaiser Wilhelm Society had broken international law by using poison gas as a weapon. By the Second World War, its fatal weapons research, experimentation and production used living test subjects in concentration camps.[5] Dr Josef Mengele sent the Society preserved Jewish bodies from Auschwitz for study and display in their anthropological department.[6]

The Duke of Coburg also played a critical role in transforming the German Red Cross from a humanitarian organisation into a branch of Hitler's killing machine. Charles Edward was not a mere figurehead, and he was fully aware of the Reich's plans to sterilise and remove the 'genetically unfit' from German society.[7] Under his leadership, the German Red Cross became the prototype for an 'efficient racial hygiene programme' to be unleashed once the war had started. Their ambition was to free the *Volk* from 'useless eaters' and increase the resources needed for military operations.[8] The headquarters at Tiergarten 4 in Berlin (hence its name, T4) co-ordinated various government agencies involved in this mass murder, such as the Charitable Foundation for the Transport of Patients, which provided motor transport for the victims to their final destinations. Their first killing centre opened in the old Brandenburg prison, close to Berlin, and other 'hospitals' opened in Grafeneck, Hartheim, Bernberg and Hadamar.[9] The estimated number of victims murdered in the T4 programme range from 100,000 to 180,000.[10]

The horrors of the T4 endeavour trapped a member of Charles Edward's family. In July 1941, the Duke received notification that his 'niece', Princess Marie Karoline of Saxe-Coburg and Gotha, had died of natural causes at the Hartheim sanatorium near Linz in Austria. Charles Edward and Marie Karoline were third cousins once removed and shared a common great-grandfather. The Princess was mentally disabled and had lived at home for many years until September 1938, when her widowed mother, the Archduchess Karoline Marie of Austria, admitted her to the Salzburg Hospital, which specialised in neurological diseases. Marie Karoline's father, Prince August Leopold of Saxe-Coburg and Gotha, had died in 1922.

Unfortunately, one of the doctors at the Salzburg Hospital, Dr Heinrich Wolfer, was a vigorous supporter of Nazi racial eugenic policies.[11] On 6 June 1941, the Princess was one of eighty-six patients taken to Hartheim. The process at the hospital was supervised with cruel efficiently by Dr Rudolf Lonauer and Dr Georg Renno.[12] 'Patients' were met at the reception and told to remove all their clothes. At the same time, they were measured, weighed and underwent a physical examination in an attempt to legitimise the procedure and give it the illusion of a medical routine. Doctors photographed the 'patients' to record any physical defects for 'scientific reasons' and then escorted the 'patients' into the gas chambers which the hospital authorities had disguised to look like shower rooms. During the years 1940–41, the Nazis killed over 18,000 people at Hartheim. Today, the whitewashed basement rooms where the killings occurred are a museum and memorial.[13]

The Duke of Coburg was reportedly shocked by the news of his niece's death. The 'hospital' sent the urn with her ashes to Coburg, where a memorial service was held on 16 July 1941. The programme for the service showed that many family members attended, with 'one notably absent figure' – Charles Edward.[14] He was probably in Coburg at the time of the memorial service, as three days later he celebrated his 57th birthday at Coburg Castle with his family.[15]

Despite this tragedy, Charles Edward associated himself with the cruellest elements of the Nazi regime. He shared his Berlin home, Villa Coburg, with his maternal cousin Prince Josias of Waldeck-Pyrmont.

Josias was twelve years younger than Charles Edward and the Duke of Coburg willingly became his mentor, clearly feeling the young Prince's character 'had showed great "promise" for future brutalities' and opening doors to 'the "right" people'.[16] As a cruel teenager, Josias had set one of his teachers on fire. As a sadistic young Stormtrooper recruited during the Röhm purge in June 1934, he oversaw an execution unit at Stadelheim prison near Munich.[17] Such murderous deeds proved his worth to the Nazi regime. In April 1941, Hitler appointed him Higher SS and Police Leader for Weimar, a status giving him supervisory authority over Buchenwald concentration camp and a significant leadership role in the Holocaust.[18] Josias was blond and stereotypically Aryan looking, and the Nazi Party publicised him as a poster boy for their movement. Prince Josias competed in international horse-riding competitions – a sport associated with race and breeding – with other aristocratic athletes like Prince Christoph of Hesse. They were both considered by the regime to be genetic superstars.

Kassel, Hesse. August 1940.

In 1940, Prince Philipp of Hesse stated the T4 euthanasia project was an 'open secret'.[19] He was aware of events, as on 27 September 1938 the *Erbgesundheitsgericht* (Hereditary Health Court) ordered his cousin, Prince Alexis of Hesse-Philippsthal-Barchfeld, to be sterilised. Members of the unfortunate Prince's family claimed that a childhood riding accident had caused Alexis's epilepsy and that it was not a hereditary problem. However, the operation went ahead at the hospital in Hadamar and Alexis died the following year in Berlin on 22 October, although the remaining files fail to give the cause of death.[20]

Only later was Hadamar transformed into one of the T4 killing centres, and Prince Philipp, as *Oberpräsisdent* (Governor) of Hesse-Kassel, signed a contract placing the sanatorium at the disposal of the Reich Interior Ministry under Fritz Bernotat, who then ushered in a programme of systematic murder. Prince Philipp later claimed that he went to Berlin and complained about the 'repurposing' of Hadamar and met with Reichsleiter Philipp Bouhler, the chief of the Führer's Chancellery and Head of the T4 project. Philipp expressed his fear that, as the regional governor, he would 'later have to bear the responsibility'. Nonchalantly, Bouhler informed the Prince that he 'bore no responsibility for incidents in Hadamar and that there were good reasons for the measures in question'.[21] Dissatisfied, Philipp went straight to Hitler and asked for his immediate intervention because local people were angry, and it was 'troubling his conscience'.[22] Hitler insisted that 'the programme was definitely necessary ... the war forced him to do it', and 'he made it clear that he felt the measures were justified – or at least, he would not intervene to stop them'.

'My dear Prince,' said Hitler. 'What you say here is quite correct, and I can understand your point of view. But in this case, you must trust me more than you trust yourself. I have already determined that you do not have enough toughness for war. Prince, you must be tougher.'[23]

Hitler found a better use for Philipp, who as the King of Italy's son-in-law became messenger and diplomatic intermediary between the Führer and Mussolini. Philipp's international contacts were also useful as an art agent, and Philipp diligently located art treasures for the Führer, who planned to build the world's largest museum in his hometown of Linz. Both Hitler and Philipp shared a passion for art; it was the foundation of their friendship, and the Prince helped Hitler buy at least ninety works of art by Canaletto, Rubens, Titian, Lotto, Pannini, Da Vinci and Tiepolo. Philipp's illustrious social connections opened many Italian collectors' doors, and records show he spent over 1,650,000 Reichsmarks acquiring artworks.[24]

However, Hitler also stole much of the art he acquired, and many of his victims were Jewish. Prince Philipp fell 'into a grey area of complicity in the Nazis' art plundering'.[25] However, he seemed to stay clear of the nastiest pillages which occurred in France, where the Nazis stole one-third of the art in private ownership. Philipp's sister-in-law Princess Sophie of Hesse recalled:

> During the war, we met once in Kronberg, and there he expressed anger about the 'transporting' of artworks from outside Germany to Reich territory and declared that the Party people had 'sticky fingers,' a fact that would come back to [haunt] Germany and would be regarded as a black mark.[26]

Throughout the war, Philipp's brother, Prince Christoph of Hesse, remained as the Head of *Forschungsamt* (Research Office), Göring's intelligence agency, which dramatically grew after the *Anschluss*. By 1939, its 6,000 employees were intercepting on average 43,000 telegrams each year, making it 'the most capable and precise information collecting agency in the world'.[27] As the war progressed, this 'coldly efficient operation' established branches in Paris, Amsterdam, Brussels, Sofia and Copenhagen, eavesdropping on journalists, diplomats, trade unionists and all potential enemies of the Third Reich, including other government agencies.[28]

Princess Sophie joined the *NS Frauenschaft* (Nazi Women's Auxiliary) but recorded that her husband had warned her that:

> I must be extremely cautious and discreet about my opinions and views, as all foreign wives [she was born a Princess of Greece and Denmark] were being watched and shadowed. He even advised me only to talk about politics with my sisters and cousins, if we were out of doors and out of ear-shot of other people.[29]

There was always a possibility that the vast spy machine Christoph had built could trap members of his own family.

The power of the *Forschungsamt*, with its access to secrets, gave Göring a noticeable advantage over enemies in Hitler's backstabbing court. In 1939, Göring was elevated to the grandiose position of *Reichsmarschall*. He was named the Führer's official successor, as well as remaining Supreme Commander of the Luftwaffe and Prime Minister of Prussia.

Prince Christoph attached himself to Göring's rising star, and was so rigidly devoted to his new career that he and Sophie even called their first-born son 'Adolf'. Christoph, like Prince Josias, had proved himself during the Röhm purge in 1934. Although documents that detail Christoph's precise role in the Night of the Long Knives have disappeared, by remaining at Göring's side, he demonstrated his cold callousness. Christoph advanced rapidly within the Nazi hierarchy, being promoted six times until he received his final rank as *Oberführer* (Colonel) in June 1939.

Christoph was also a true believer, and he fervently believed in the Nazi ideology. He was even a member of the Lebensborn Association devised in 1935, which promoted the birth of 'racially pure' Aryan children. The Lebensborn programme paired up genetically superior SS officers with women, usually unmarried, to breed a 'master race' of super babies for Germany.[30] In theory, there was no social stigma attached to the women, but the births of 'racially pure' blond blue-eyed children took place discreetly at anonymous maternity homes.[31] Most of the unknown fathers were married members of the SS with their own families, who were following Hitler's instructions to spread their superior Aryan seed. Approximately 8,000 German soldiers were members of Lebensborn, and around 8,000 children were born in Germany.[32] The Nazis baptised the babies in ritualistic ceremonies with an SS dagger, where their adoptive parents, usually SS members, promised the child's loyalty to the Nazi cause. Christoph made monthly payments to the Lebensborn Association, suggesting 'a special commitment to the SS and its goals'.[33]

In September 1940, Prince Christoph asked Göring to join the Luftwaffe. Combat was an important undertaking under the tenets of Nazi ideology and, surprisingly, Göring agreed, although he insisted Christoph remained head of the *Forschungsamt*. As the Nazi army swept through Western Europe, Christoph wrote again to his wife, Princess Sophie: 'What do you say to our success? Isn't it marvellous! I wonder what will happen next?'[34] He enthused about his role: 'It is really interesting work and independent, which I like. To know how everything is planned and then to wait until you hear the success is thrilling ...'[35]

Christoph's successes were lethal. He helped the Luftwaffe prepare for the bombing of Rotterdam on 13 May 1940, where 900 Dutch people died, and 78,000 were left homeless. The obliteration of the city led to the capitulation of the Netherlands two days later. Prince Christoph was awarded an Iron Cross (second class) by General Bruno Loerzer – one of Germany's leading flying aces. It was a medal previously reserved for acts of bravery.

After the Rotterdam Blitz, Christoph regularly visited Berlin and the *Forschungsamt*'s offices. He also enjoyed a trip to occupied Paris in June. The French city was now a recreation destination for German soldiers, and under the slogan '*Jeder einmal in Paris*' ('everyone once in Paris') every soldier was promised one visit. The best hotels, movie theatres and restaurants were reserved exclusively for Nazis who wandered down the Champs-Élysées, and with an exchange rate fixed in their favour. The famous Rex Cinema became *Deutschen Soldatenkino* (cinema for German soldiers). The Nazis renamed French brasseries in German and redubbed street signs. Swastika flags and propaganda posters appeared everywhere, while newspapers were offered news pre-approved by Dr Joseph Goebbels, the sardonic and unscrupulous Minister of Propaganda. As the occupiers indulged themselves, Parisians endured rations, misery and humiliation. Another new sight in the Paris streets was the French Jews being forced to wear the yellow Star of David badge. Christoph described the city as:

> Empty ... Only German military cars en masse. The people are very depressed but polite and correct ... Paris is certainly a beautiful town. We live in the Grand Hotel at the expense of the Armed Forces, but

there is no breakfast. So, we had breakfast in a café and lunch and dinner at the Ritz where of course all the bigwigs live.[36]

During the summer of 1940, Christoph returned to work. Based in a small requisitioned château outside Ghent, his work intensified as the Battle of Britain approached. He complained of fatigue, but he was vague about his work in a letter home: 'I'm afraid there is no leave to be expected just now because the air force is just very much engaged as you know.'[37]

The conflict officially started on 10 July, when the Germans led mass airstrikes against British industrial targets in a struggle for air supremacy with the Royal Air Force. However, the Luftwaffe failed to batter Britain into submission – so Göring ordered his air fleets to concentrate their attacks on the capital and personally took over direction of the London Blitz on 7 September, determined to break the nation's spirit by obliterating the capital.[38]

London. 13 September 1940.

Friday, 13 September went down in history as the day the Luftwaffe came close to killing George VI and Queen Elizabeth by dropping a bomb on Buckingham Palace. The King recorded in his diary:

> We heard an aircraft making a zooming noise above us, saw 2 bombs falling past the opposite side of the Palace, & then heard 2 resounding crashes as the bombs fell into the quadrangle about 30 yds away. We looked at each other … Two great craters had appeared in the courtyard. The one nearest the Palace had burst a hydrant & water was pouring through the broken windows in the passage. 6 bombs had been dropped. The aircraft were seen coming down the Mall below the clouds having dived through the clouds and had dropped 2 bombs in the forecourt, 2 in the quadrangle, 1 in the chapel & the other in the garden. There is no doubt it was a direct attack on the palace.[39]

In a letter to Queen Mary, Queen Elizabeth described how she heard the 'unmistakable whirr-whirr of a German plane' and the 'scream of a bomb'. In a poignant statement, she also said, 'I am glad we have been bombed. It makes me feel I can look the East-End in the face.'[40] Until then, only the most impoverished nearest the London docks had been devastated.

The Queen confided in a second letter: 'It does affect me, seeing this terrible and senseless destruction – I think that really I mind it much more than being bombed myself. The people are marvellous, and full of fight. One could not imagine that life could become so terrible.'[41]

It could have been worse but for Raymond Holmes, a Royal Air Force pilot. He boldly rammed his Hawker Hurricane into an attacking Luftwaffe Dornier Do 17 – at the loss of his aircraft and almost his life. After stopping the Luftwaffe, he parachuted out of his plane and calmly landed in a Chelsea garden, where two young women kissed him. He was feted in the press as a war hero and appointed a King's Messenger, delivering the mail for Winston Churchill.

George VI was traumatised by such a narrow escape: 'I quite dislike sitting in my room … I found myself unable to read, always in a hurry, & glancing out of the window …'[42] He felt privately that whoever planned the attack had detailed knowledge about the layout at the Palace and he suspected his German relatives. British secret intelligence knew that the Nazis wanted to replace George VI and return the Duke of Windsor to the throne. The bombing of the Palace may have been part of a much larger plot. Several historians have suggested that Prince Christoph could have been one of the pilots, pointing to the fact the Prince was intent on revenging the death of his elder brother Prince Maximilian in the First World War.[43] However, in 1940 the Prince did not have the training to partake in such a mission – either as a pilot or a navigator – although he could have helped plan the mission to target Buckingham Palace.[44]

This bombing incident, and the King's refusal to take Foreign Office advice and leave Britain, won the Royal Family enormous approval across the country. The Queen declared: 'The children will not leave unless I do. I shall not leave unless their father does, and the king will not leave the country in any circumstances, whatever … We must win in the end.'[45]

This defiance in the face of the German Blitz gave the country a boost in the war efforts, forging a sense of unity throughout the United Kingdom. In many ways, the war defined George VI and Queen Elizabeth – finally exorcising the ghost of Edward VIII. The Queen guided her husband through the difficulties of the war. Elizabeth was much more than just the King's wife; she became de facto co-monarch and she even learnt to shoot a pistol, in case of a sudden invasion. The couple toured hospitals, factories, and all parts of Britain targeted by the Luftwaffe. Hitler called her 'the most dangerous woman in Europe', viewing her popularity as a threat to German interests.[46]

Coppins, Buckinghamshire. December 1940.

The King expected every member of the family to do their duty, and the House of Windsor closed ranks to support George and Elizabeth. There could be no more scandals or bad publicity.

Prince George, Duke of Kent, started a post with the intelligence division of the Admiralty in Scotland, and later became a staff officer in the Welfare Section of the RAF. He wore the dashing uniform of an RAF group captain and Pathé newsreels show him touring RAF bases inspecting aircraft, talking to mechanics and posing with the fighter pilots. The position was an innovation as there had been no previous welfare division within Training Command, and George threw himself into the role.[47] When he had lunch with the King at Buckingham Palace, shortly after starting work, it was clear that the former playboy Prince had found a useful role in the war effort.[48] Based mostly in Scotland, he rented Pitlever House in Rosyth, north of Edinburgh, and Marina came to stay whenever her duties allowed her the time.[49]

Churchill also put Princess Marina to work as Commandant of the Women's Royal Naval Service (known as the Wrens). Although the Duchess of Kent disliked wearing a uniform, she accessorised it discreetly with heels, jewellery and a low-cut collar. When deciding the Wrens' attire, she tried on several prototypes herself and made the point: 'No woman wants to wear a hat which makes her look unattractive war or no war.'[50] Marina also worked as a volunteer at the Iver and Denham Cottage Hospital, and national newspapers featured stories about the Duchess visiting cabbage fields and chatting to her fellow Wrens about the 'Dig for Victory' campaign.[51] Despite exhibiting a fetching inability to salute correctly, she had a talent for recruiting.

The Kents also offered to open up their country house Coppins in Buckinghamshire, which was close to RAF Northolt and RAF Uxbridge, to pilots and crews as a retreat where they could enjoy a meal, play a gramophone and relax.[52] As the Battle of Britain intensified, the Duke witnessed first-hand the RAF bases pitted with craters and 'inexorably he was drawn into this new, intense world where warm friendships made in the morning were lost in the fury of an afternoon air raid'.[53]

Apart from her young cousin Prince Philip of Greece, who was down at Dartmouth, all Marina's family living on the Continent were now enemy aliens – or about to become such. Her sister, Princess Olga, was married to Prince Paul of Yugoslavia. As Prince-Regent for his young nephew King Peter, Paul was being wooed by Nazi Germany, anxious for Yugoslavia to side with the Axis powers. Everyone felt Yugoslavia would remain a loyal ally as Paul was an anglophile, educated at Oxford, and was close friends with the entire British Royal Family.

Marina had last seen Paul and Olga on their state visit to London in 1938 when they stayed at Buckingham Palace. They hardly had time to unpack from this trip when Hitler invited them to Berlin. Feted by the Third Reich, the Nazis did everything possible to entertain them. A ballet on the lawn, a display of fireworks, special tours of the royal palaces in Potsdam, an SS guard of honour, a private visit to Göring's country estate Karinhall, and for seven nights in a row, Princess Olga sat next to the Führer at dinner. The Nazis did not forget the smaller details either. When the couple had arrived in Berlin, Olga's entire German family, including her sister Elizabeth and her three cousins – Sophie, Theodora and Margarita – were waiting to welcome her to Berlin.[54]

Before Paul and Olga left Germany, Hitler told Göring to give the visiting couple an aircraft display, and some of the Luftwaffe's best planes thundered above their heads. This demonstration of power was a clear threat, and now that the war had started, Hitler became more aggressive in his pursuit of an alliance with Yugoslavia. Prince Paul privately appealed to George VI in London for armaments, and the King replied to his friend, 'I only wish it were possible for us to supply you with them at once,' but British industry was still 'making up fast for our losses'.[55] Trapped in Belgrade, Prince Paul became a nervous wreck as he found himself stuck between the British request to help save Greece and Hitler's threatening stance. Not one of the Balkan countries was strong enough to withstand Germany, and British aid was remote. George VI knew Hitler was wooing Paul and wrote to him that the Nazis' word was 'never, and least of all now, to be trusted. We count on you.'[56] However, it was only words, and Paul attempted to appease Hitler by stepping up deliveries of copper.[57]

Belgrade, Yugoslavia. 25 March 1941.

With Hitler demanding his allegiance, Prince Paul of Yugoslavia finally caved in and signed the Tripartite Pact with the Nazis on 25 March. In his sympathies, he preferred that France and Britain win the war, but he was markedly afraid of the German armed forces. Protests swept across Belgrade, and Yugoslav tanks took positions outside the palace and forced Paul from office. Paul fled the capital with Olga, leaving his 17-year-old nephew, King Peter, frightened and alone as a puppet monarch.

Britain had supported this military coup d'état against Paul, but it triggered Hitler's revenge. The might of the German Luftwaffe bore down on Belgrade for three consecutive days in Operation Retribution. As many as 17,000 civilians died, and even the zoo was bombed, sending frightened animals running through the streets.[58]

The young King Peter fled to British-ruled Jerusalem, and then to Cairo, before arriving in London in June 1941 where he established a government-in-exile. Marina hoped Paul and Olga could also come to England, but over lunch at Chequers, Churchill dispelled this fantasy and made his position clear: 'Of course, Prince Paul could not possibly come here.' His actions had made him a traitor and outcast. Churchill explained that officials were seeking a location where the Prince-Regent could become a 'sort of semi-prisoner-of-state'.[59] They finally settled on a remote house in Kenya, and both Marina's sisters were now enemies of the Allied cause.

INTO THE ABYSS

Athens. January 1940.

The outbreak of war put Prince Philip of Greece in a catch-22 situation. He wanted to serve in the British navy. Still, as a Greek citizen (with three German sisters) he was barred from serving in a theatre of war, and the British government froze his citizenship application. Lord Mountbatten, 'Uncle Dickie', pulled strings which allowed him to continue his naval career, and Philip finally joined HMS *Ramilies* – a slow, old battleship escorting convoys of Australian and New Zealand troopships bound for Egypt – as a midshipman.

In January 1940, Philip enjoyed a pleasant five-week shore leave with friends and relations in Athens, dividing his time between his mother, Princess Alice, and his uncle, King George II of Greece, at the Tatoï Summer Palace. Henry 'Chips' Channon was also a guest at the Palace, and he described Philip as 'extraordinarily handsome' in his diary and the King as a 'mild bore'. Indiscreetly, he told Philip's aunt, Princess Nicholas of Greece, that 'He is to be our Prince Consort … and that is why he is serving in our Navy'.[1] This prediction seemed decidedly speculative, as Philip and Elizabeth hardly knew each other, and during his holiday Philip partied with his attractive cousin Princess Alexandra of Greece. She recalled him bounding up to their house 'ready for gramophone records and fun, and dancing with a whole new group of friends'.[2] Alexandra was in love with Philip, but Philip did not reciprocate her affection. When Italy entered the war in October, Philip joined the newly modernised battleship HMS *Valiant*, a critical vessel in the Mediterranean Fleet. Temporarily, Alexandra was broken-hearted, but she later met and married King Peter of Yugoslavia during his exile in London in 1944.

With each new German advance in the north, Mussolini's ego became more bruised. Keen to keep pace with his ally and rival Adolf Hitler, Il Duce surprised everyone with this move against Greece, even catching Hitler off guard. The Führer thought the entire Greek invasion to be a strategic blunder and wanted Mussolini to focus on North Africa, before advancing into Egypt. After just one week, the Greeks succeeded in pushing the Italian invaders back into Albania, and Hitler saw the potential risk of British intervention in the area, which would threaten Germany's rear. He was forced to come to Italy's aid.

During the Battle of Greece the following year, Greek and British forces were overwhelmed. The Nazi army invaded the country on 6 April, and Greece surrendered to German troops on 20 April 1941. The Axis powers divided Greece into three occupations zones: the Italian, German and Bulgarian. The red and black Nazi colours of the swastika flag were raised over the Acropolis, casting a dark shadow over Athens. Most of the Greek Royal Family fled into exile, but the Duchess of Kent's mother Ellen (Princess Nicholas of Greece) and Prince Philip's mother Alice (Princess Andrew of Greece) stubbornly refused to leave the city.

When a German officer came to requisition Princess Nicholas's home, he found an old lady sitting bolt upright in her chair. Very much the Edwardian *grande dame*, Princess Nicholas greeted him without a smile, her piercing eyes 'dark and lustrous'.[3] The officer decided it was best to leave her alone, and she was even granted the freedom to visit her husband's grave in the gardens of the Tatoï Palace. Ellen lived out the rest of occupation in relative comfort with four servants and was even allowed to keep her radio. Like many aristocrats, she was more concerned about the communists than the Germans.[4]

All Princess Alice's letters to her family give the impression of her life being mostly routine and uneventful. She complained about having 'little occupation',[5] and wrote 'my life in this house is always the same',[6] but this was an immense understatement. As the Athenians became permanently hungry under German occupation, Princess Alice worked tirelessly setting up soup kitchens and two shelters for orphan children, one for girls and one for boys. In some of the poorer districts, Alice organised nurses, who acted as district visitors, caring for the destitute sick in their homes. At one time, she became so exhausted that she went to stay with friends at a small farm outside Kephissia, writing to Philip in October:'I am quite my usual self again except for the 26 kilos I lost ... which happily have not returned.You will be quite surprised to see me with a decent figure again, only my face is more wrinkled.'[7]

When the Germans invaded Salonika in 1941, they exterminated the entire Jewish community of 60,000 people, and Alice decided to shelter a Jewish family. Rachel Cohen and her daughter Tilde were smuggled into Alice's home under cover of darkness and lived discreetly in two rooms at the top of the house. The Princess told staff that Mrs Cohen was a former Swiss governess to her children, and a month later Rachel's son Michel joined his mother and sister in hiding. Alice enjoyed visiting them upstairs and often discussed Judaism with the Cohen family. Sometimes the Germans became suspicious, but when the Gestapo interrogated her, she made use of her deafness, feigning not to understand their questions and pretending to be simpleminded.[8]

Château de Candé, Tours. October 1940.

After meeting Marshal Pétain in the small French town of Montoire, Hitler, Göring and Ribbentrop drove 33 miles to Charles Bedaux's home at Château de Candé, where the Duke of Windsor had married Wallis Simpson.Three Nazis gravely stood in front of the Duke and Duchess's portrait in the library. They gave the picture a Nazi salute.[9] Hitler still hoped that Edward would help Germany ally with Britain, and that the Duke was holding 'himself in readiness'.[10]

Palm Beach, Florida. April 1941.

Bored of their life in the Bahamas after nine months of tropical heat and humidity, the Duke and Duchess of Windsor cruised into Palm Beach, Florida, on the SS *Berkshire* from Nassau on 18 April 1941. A week of relaxation playing golf, drinking and gossiping with the Palm Beach set lay ahead of them. The Duchess loathed the Bahamas and resented the enforced exile. During dreary receptions at Government House in Nassau her jaw would clench in apparent boredom, and she wrote to her Aunt Bessie, 'I do wish we could move somewhere inhabited by people of our class. These awful people day in and day out ... it is as though you are associated with shop owners.'[11]

The Duke and Duchess did not know that President Roosevelt had instructed FBI Chief J. Edgar Hoover to spy on them, and an agent called Edward Tamm tracked their every move.[12] The President had two good

reasons for ordering this level of scrutiny. The first was that the Duke and
Duchess were socialising with Swedish multimillionaire Axel Wenner-
Gren, who owned the Bank of the Bahamas. Edward and Wallis partied
at his vast estate Shangri-La on Hog Island, and on board his large private
yacht the *Southern Cross*.

Wenner-Gren was friends with Hermann Göring, and both British and
American authorities suspected Axel Wenner-Gren of using his bank to
fund the Nazis.[13] Naval Intelligence Officer Commander C.A. Perkins
wrote that there was reason to believe 'considerable Nazi funds have,
during the past year, been cleared through the Bahamas to Mexico' and
that the Duke of Windsor may be an 'important Nazi agent'.[14] The Duke
came under pressure to cut his ties with Wenner-Gren for appearance's
sake, and the Americans placed the extravagant Swedish millionaire on a
pro-Nazi blacklist. When the government confiscated his bank, he fled the
Bahamas and spent the rest of the war in exile in Mexico.[15]

The second reason was a telling interview that Edward gave to Fulton
Oursler of *Liberty* magazine at Government House in Nassau. Oursler
was a well-connected journalist with access to the White House, and he
asked the Duke if a German revolution could remove Hitler. Edward
confidently replied: 'There will be no revolution in Germany, and it
would be a tragic thing for the world if Hitler were to be overthrown.
Hitler is the right and logical leader of the German people.' The Duke
argued that it was time to end this war between 'two stubborn peoples'
and 'the time was coming when someone has got to say, you boys have
fought long enough, and now you have to kiss and make up.' He even
warned that if the United States entered the war, it would continue for
another thirty years, and suggested to Oursler, 'Do you suppose that your
President [Roosevelt] would consider intervening as a mediator when, as,
and if the proper time arrives?'

Oursler left Government House shocked by the Duke of Windsor's
attitude to Nazi Germany: 'For the first time in my life, it was literally true
that I did not believe my ears.' The Duke's aide-de-camp, Captain Vyvyan
Drury, explained that the ex-king was subjected to 'cruel persecutions',
but wanted to be of service to both America and Britain. The following
morning Drury arrived at Oursler's hotel, and he asked Oursler to enter a
'Machiavellian conspiracy' and ask President Roosevelt to make an 'intervention for peace'. Then, 'before anyone in England can oppose it, the
Duke of Windsor will instantly issue a statement supporting it, and that
will start a revolution in England and force peace'.[16]

Roosevelt met Oursler on 23 December, but the President interrupted the journalist before he could finish his story:

Fulton, nothing can surprise me these days. Nothing will seem too fantastic. Why, do you know that I am amazed to find some of the greatest people in the British Empire, men of the so-called upper classes, men of the highest rank, secretly want to appease Hitler and stop the war? I call these people ignorant and uneducated.

The President dismissed the Duke as 'little Windsor', but Oursler observed how agitated Roosevelt became: his hands trembled in 'an unparalleled exhibition'. The President vented about Edward's carelessness with the red boxes at Fort Belvedere and Mrs Simpson's dalliance with Ribbentrop. Roosevelt was angry about the Duke's friendship with Germans, his dubious approach to soldiering as a liaison officer in France, and the fact what while in Paris he may have sent secrets to the German invaders. At the President's command, Oursler immediately wrote a letter to Drury:

Dear Captain Drury,
  On my way home to Florida, I stopped off in Washington and had a talk with a friend. His answer to my conversation was that in Washington today, everything is on a twenty-four-hour basis, and no man has the gift of being able to read the future. If you have anything else in mind, let me know.[17]

This message was a presidential dismissal. Edward's blindspot was that he saw himself as an honest go-between looking to promote a peace deal – much like all the royal princes on both sides of the war, including the Duke of Kent, Prince Philipp of Hesse and the Duke of Coburg. Britain had barely just survived Dunkirk, and now London was suffering from the devastating Blitz bombardments. When a toned-down version of the interview was published on 22 March 1941, the Duke claimed he had been misquoted and misinterpreted.

The Duke's views now made him the poster-boy for right-wing isolationists in the United States. Many American businessmen, such as Joseph Kennedy, Henry Ford, James Mooney, Robert Young and Ben Smith, wanted to avoid war with Nazi Germany, as it would be bad for business. The Duke said, 'America will help Britain more by not engaging in actual fighting but remaining a keystone for the new world which must be created when the war is over. There will be a new order in Europe, whether imposed by Germany or Britain.'[18]

In April 1941, the FBI sent a report to Roosevelt detailing their worries about the Duke and Duchess. This eighteen-page document described the Duchess of Windsor as 'exceeding pro-German in her sympathies and connections, and there is strong reason to believe this is the reason why she was considered so obnoxious to the British government that they refused to permit Edward to marry her and maintain the throne'. On 2 May, an FBI agent wrote to Hoover, claiming that their informant had definite proof that Hermann Göring and the Duke of Windsor had reached a deal. 'After Germany won the war, Göring, through control of the army, was going to overthrow Hitler and then he would install the duke as king of England.' The informant also stated that there was no doubt that 'the Duchess of Windsor had had an affair with Ribbentrop, and that, of course, she had an intense hatred for the English since they had kicked them out of England'.[19]

The Windsors were back in North America in November, first visiting the Duke's ranch in Alberta, Canada, and then visiting Washington DC, New York and Maryland. They travelled in a private train provided by railway tycoon Robert Young, and larger crowds greeted them than those for George VI and Queen Elizabeth in 1939 – with 250,000 people turning up in Baltimore, Wallis's home town.

The couple's extravagance during wartime was astonishing. They stayed in the grandest suite on the twenty-eighth floor of the Waldorf Towers, travelled with 118 trunks each with a numbered lid, and spent lavishly in the New York shops.[20] There was outrage in London. Labour MP Alexander Sloan asked for the Duke and Duchess's recall, complaining about their 'ostentatious display of jewellery and finery abroad when people at home are facing severe hardship'.[21] The *Daily Mirror*, which had previously supported the couple, turned against them, saying: 'Would it be considered unkind to suggest the Duke and Duchess should stay in the Bahamas for the rest of the war?'[22]

Churchill started to fear that Hitler might concoct another outlandish plot to kidnap the Windsors. German U-boats were causing havoc on British supply lines, and one would have little difficulty landing on their virtually unprotected island in the Bahamas. The Prime Minister dispatched a unit of Canadian Highlanders, all Dunkirk veterans, to protect the Duke, and had barbed-wire fences built around Government House. The Highlanders trained the Duke's staff against any possible German attack with mock raids, which the Windsors condescendingly found 'rather amusing'.[23]

On 7 December 1941, one month after the Duke and Duchess returned to Nassau, the Japanese bombed Pearl Harbor, the American naval base in Hawaii. In a two-hour attack, Japanese warplanes sank or damaged 18 warships and destroyed 164 aircraft. Over 2,400 servicemen and civilians lost their lives. The following day, a stunned President Roosevelt declared war on Japan, Germany and Italy. Borrowing from Churchill's style of oratory, he announced: 'No matter how long it may take us to overcome this premeditated invasion, the American people in their righteous might will win through to absolute victory.'[24] This moment was a turning point in the war as America became the production hub for the Allies, and by January 1942 the first American troops had started to arrive in Britain.

Eagle's Rock, Scotland. 25 September 1942.

On 25 September, Prince George was enjoying lunch in the officers' mess with Group Captain Geoffrey Francis at RAF Invergordon before taking off in his plane at 1.10 p.m. for a hastily planned, morale-boosting visit to the British troops stationed in Reykjavik, Iceland. Michael Strutt, his equerry, and John Hales, his valet, accompanied the Prince on the mission. Flight Lieutenant Frank Goyen led the plane's highly experienced crew, who were the best Coastal Control could find to travel to what George jokingly called 'the frozen North'.[25]

Launching its vast silver-grey bulk from the calm waters of Cromarty Firth on Scotland's east coast, the S.25 Sunderland Mark III flying boat measured over 85 feet long and had a wingspan of 113 feet. The Prince travelled in considerable comfort as the plane boasted well-equipped sleeping quarters and cooking facilities. That day, the sea was exceptionally tranquil, and it took a remarkably long 3-mile run-up to get airborne. Sunderlands were always more efficient taking off in choppy waters because the waves helped bump them into the air.

The plane's flight orders were to remain over the water, and only to cross land when it was unavoidable. The usual route was to follow the coastline northwards towards Duncansby Head, the northernmost tip of Scotland near John O'Groats, and then turn north-west over the Pentland Firth towards Iceland. The entire journey – had it been completed – would take seven hours, well within the Sunderland's twelve-hour range.

At 1.42 p.m., Flight W4026 smashed into a remote hill known as Eagle's Rock, 3 miles outside the Scottish town of Dunbeath.[26] Despite its craggy name, the terrain was not particularly rocky, although the scenery was bleak, covered in a peat bog and wild heather.

Moments before the collision, the S.25 Sunderland flying boat cleared the nearby 2,000-foot summit of Donald's Mount. Unexpectedly, the plane then sharply dropped to an altitude of 700 feet and thundered straight into a 650-foot hill, somersaulting on its nose to land violently on its back where it disintegrated on impact. Two thousand five hundred gallons of fuel carried in the wings of the plane exploded and scattered the wreckage. Bodies were flung from the plane and escaped the fireball, but those trapped in the cockpit received horrific burns which made the identification of their corpses difficult.[27] Of the fifteen men on board, only Flight Sergeant Andrew Jack, the rear gunner, survived. Jack received severe burns pulling bodies away from the plane; then he passed out before being taken to the hospital.

Nobody witnessed the crash because a dense sea mist known in Scotland as 'haar' blocked vision.[28] Two sheep farmers rounding up strays, Hugh Morrison and his son David, were the first to hear two explosions in quick succession: probably the impact itself followed by the fuel tank ignition. Hugh jumped onto his motorbike and sped off to find help. Local special constables Will Bethune and James Sunderland, and an elderly doctor called John Kennedy, cobbled together a search-and-rescue party from the village and within an hour and a half of the crash they had found the burning wreck.[29]

Bethune discovered an identity bracelet on the dead body wearing a flying suit which read: 'HRH, The Duke of Kent'. Dr Kennedy also read the inscription on the Duke's wristwatch and found his monogrammed cigarette case. Despite a deep gash to his head, the Duke's face was recognisable. Later, during a radio interview in 1985, the elderly Bethune stated that he saw an attaché case handcuffed to his wrist which had burst open scattering a large number of hundred-krona notes over the hillside: the krona was and still is Iceland's currency.[30] Since Hitler had invaded nearby Norway, the island had assumed enormous strategic importance as a defence base against German U-boats for transatlantic convoys.

Before nightfall at the crash site, a military team from RAF Wick arrived to support the early rescuers. The bodies were quickly removed in ambulances and taken to Wick. The rescuers placed the remains of the 39-year-old Prince George in an oak coffin draped with the blue flag of the Royal Navy and took his body to Dunrobin Castle. This curious

Victorian-styled château belonged to the Duke of Sunderland. When it became too dark, the rescuers postponed their mission and posted a guard to watch over the wreck.

That evening at Coppins, the phone rang. Princess Marina, the Duchess of Kent, had gone to bed intending to have an early night, but Kate Fox, who had nursed the Duchess as a baby and had recently come out of retirement to look after the 7-week-old Prince Michael, took the call. Shocked by the news, Nanny Fox anxiously climbed the stairs. Hearing her, Marina sensed disaster and opened the door. 'It's George, isn't it?' For days the Duchess wept and just stared numbly at the wall.[31]

At Balmoral, King George VI and Queen Elizabeth were having dinner with the Duke and Duchess of Gloucester and several other guests. A steward entered the dining room to explain that Sir Archibald Stewart Sinclair, the Secretary of State for Air, was on the telephone. While the King took the call, the Queen and the dinner guests waited in silence. The Duchess said in her memoirs:

> The King came back and sat in silence. I could feel he was in deep distress and soon the Queen caught my eye, signalling me to rise with her and lead the ladies from the room. In the drawing room, we all assumed the news must be of Queen Mary's death ... The Queen then left us and came back with the King who told us that it was the Duke of Kent who had been killed.[32]

Queen Mary was staying with her niece at Badminton when she was told the news over dinner. Prince George had been her favourite son, and later she mourned, 'He often used to say I looked nice. Nobody else ever did.'[33]

The Duke of Windsor organised a memorial service for his beloved younger brother in the Bahamas on 29 August 1942, the day of his funeral, which took place at St George's Chapel in Windsor. The Duke 'broke down and wept like a child'.[34] Later, both the Duke and Duchess of Windsor wrote of their feelings of loss, despite, as the Duchess put it, his having been a 'turncoat towards us'.[35] Yet his widow, Marina, received not a word from her brother- and sister-in-law. The family feud endured.

In Parliament, Churchill spoke with emotion and eloquence about the tragedy in the House of Commons:

> The loss of this gallant and handsome Prince in the prime of his life has been a shock to all the people of the British Empire ... I knew the late

Duke of Kent … his overpowering desire to render useful service to his King and Country during this period when we are all of us on trial … There is something about death on active service which makes it different from common or ordinary death in the normal course. It is accepted without question by fighting men. Those they leave behind them are also conscious of the light of sacrifice and honour which plays around the grave, or tomb of the warrior … Nothing can fill the awful gap, nothing assuages or comforts the loneliness and deprivations that fall on the wife and children when the prop and centre of their home life is suddenly snatched away. Only faith in a life after death, in a brighter world where dear ones can meet again – only that and the measured tramp of time can give consolation.[36]

Although imaginative conspiracy theories have flourished around the Duke's death, the Court of Inquiry concluded that the accident was 'due to the aircraft being on the wrong track at too low altitude to clear rising ground'; the captain of the plane changed the flight-plan for 'reasons unknown and descended through the cloud without making sure he was over water and crashed'.[37] Sir Archibald Sinclair gave a statement of findings to the House of Commons on 7 October 1942 which delivered a devasting blow to one grieving pilot's family: 'the responsibility for this serious mistake in airmanship lies with the captain of the aircraft [Goyen].'[38]

Bellevue Palace, Kassel. 1942.

Prince Philipp of Hesse privately mourned the news of his British cousin's death. Before the outbreak of war, Hitler viewed Philipp's close relationship with Prince George, Duke of Kent, as a useful asset in his secret diplomatic game plan. The Duke of Kent's death closed the opportunity the Kent–Hesse channel might have provided Hitler to foster direct communications with the British Royal Family, and Philipp became less critical to Hitler's plans.

The Nazis had helped the aristocracy to recover the status they had lost after the First World War, and at first, they were always keen to employ noble officers. In return, Hitler fully exploited the German princes' status to achieve and maintain power. When it suited him, he had even flirted with restoring the monarchy. Many princes had consequently become Nazi Party members, including fourteen Hesses and nine Coburgs.

By the summer of 1942, Germany had started to lose the war, and Hitler became increasingly paranoid about the German princes. He was deeply suspicious of these 'internationally minded' persons whose multiple foreign connections seemed to undercut their German nationalism. Had anyone dared to scrutinise the relationship between the Nazis and the princes, they would have realised their alliance was superficial.

CAPTIVES

Rome. 19 July 1942.

The Allied invasion of Italy was imminent, but it would prove bloodier than anyone foresaw. Between 11 a.m. and 12 noon in the clear skies above the Eternal City, 690 aircraft from United States Army Air Force dropped 9,125 bombs on San Lorenzo, a working-class district of Rome. They killed 1,500 civilians, targeting the freight yard and steel factory.

For Mussolini, the air raids were a shock. He had kept his headquarters in Rome, confident that the Allies would never attack the Holy City. Pope Pius XII even asked President Roosevelt not to bomb Rome because of the city's value to the whole of humanity, but the Americans ignored the request. In the spirit of solidarity with the Roman people, the Pope visited San Lorenzo to distribute money and received tumultuous applause: a sign that Fascism was losing its hold over the country.[1]

While the Americans bombed Rome, Hitler summoned Mussolini to meet him at the Villa Gaggia in San Fermo, a location in Northern Italy selected for its beauty and isolation. Here, Hitler tried to 'reinflate the Italian balloon'.[2] For three hours, the Führer lectured Mussolini, venting his anger about Italian ineptitude while peacocks screeched in the elaborate gardens outside. 'The resurrection of Germany took thirty years. Rome never rose again,' raged Hitler.[3] Il Duce was so shaken from the stress he could no longer stand Hitler's boasting, and he barely opened his mouth except to announce the air attack.

Although Mussolini had purported to be spending his time putting his nation's defences in order, in reality the burnt-out leader did nothing. The first piece of Italian territory to fall was the Sicilian island of Pantelleria, which Mussolini had deluded himself into thinking was impregnable. Hitler instructed him that he must hold onto Southern Italy so that 'Sicily becomes for the Allies what Stalingrad was for us'.[4]

For months, the Italian people's anger towards Mussolini had been building as his ubiquitous propaganda machine finally lost its grip. Carlo Scroza, the founder of the Italian Blackshirts, was appointed the new party secretary, but it was an act of desperation to bolster morale and discipline. Scroza's fascist goons reappeared in the streets, but these thugs were sometimes murdered in the night by members of the Italian resistance as labour unrest and strikes broke out across the country.

Villa Savoia, Rome. 26 July 1943.

Mussolini was sick, tired and overwhelmed. On the afternoon of 26 July, his driver – the former racing champion Ercole Boratto – drove him to San Lorenzo in his Alfa Romeo to inspect the damage, a tardy week after the Pope and King had visited. Boratto then chauffeured him across the city for his regular weekly audience with the King.

In the Villa Savoia's elegant drawing room, Benito Mussolini, fascist dictator of Italy, stood before Victor Emmanuel III, the King of Italy. Mussolini wore civilian clothes – a blue suit and soft brown felt hat – as was customary when he attended the King. By contrast, Victor Emmanuel had donned an elaborate uniform of a First Marshal of the Empire.

Unshaven and weary, Mussolini's appointment with the King took twenty minutes. The jittery King told him softly that Italy was a broken country, and that he was required to quit his office. The new President of the Council of Ministers would be Marshal Pietro Badoglio.

Mussolini, visibly shaken, asked: 'Then it is over? It is over; it is over. However, what will happen to me, to my family?'[5]

'I am sorry, I am sorry,' said the King. 'But there is no other solution … Things are no longer working. Italy is on its knees … the army's morale is rock bottom, and the soldiers don't want to fight anymore.'[6]

Victor Emmanuel was a weak man, but he was strategically important. He was the Head of State – something Mussolini had frequently forgotten – and this gave him influence during a political crisis, as he could appoint the government. The night before, the twenty-eight members of the Grand Council had met in the Palace Venezia. Here they debated into the early hours of the morning. Count Gino Grandi argued that Fascism had brought Italy to the brink of disaster, elevated incompetents to positions of power and alienated large portions of the population. After Grandi's passionate speech, the council voted to remove Mussolini from power, and this forced Victor Emmanuel to act. The King was so nervous and badly shaken by the whole affair he was unable to hold back his tears: the man did not match his position.

For years, Mussolini had continuously sidelined the King. Now the power had shifted in their relationship: 'At this moment you are the most hated man in Italy,' the King informed Mussolini. 'You cannot count on any more than one friend. Only one has remained with you, me.'[7] Victor Emmanuel's first instinct was to offer some comfort to the fallen dictator, and he assured Mussolini that he would personally take care of his security and that of his family. He then escorted Mussolini to the steps of the main entrance – something he had never done before – and shook his hand with great warmth.

As Mussolini attempted to get into his car, Captain Paolo Vigneri of the Carabinieri blocked his path and guided him by the elbow to a waiting ambulance parked in the drive. When the rear door opened, a startled Mussolini saw three more Carabinieri sitting on the side banks. A further fifty Carabinieri were hiding in the bushes on standby under the command of Lieutenant Colonel Giovanni Frignani, but they were not needed. Boratto, Mussolini's driver, had been called to the porter's lodge on the pretext that he was wanted on the telephone and was locked inside. He was not let out until midnight.[8]

Vigneri forced Mussolini into the ambulance, which then raced secretly through the streets of Rome until it reached the Podgora army barracks in Trastevere. From there, Il Duce was placed under house arrest on the island of Ponza, but a week later he was transferred to the more secure isle of La Maddalena, off the north tip of Sardinia. With no fight left in him, this island exile appealed to his Napoleonic ego,[9] and he passed the time reading the twenty-four-volume complete works of Nietzsche – a birthday present from Hitler. Predictably, he was impressed by Nietzsche's ideas about the superman, the whipping of women and the will to power.[10]

For years, Mussolini had continuously broadcast a formal proclamation from the King and Badoglio. It was a hot summer's night, and in the streets of Rome the people burst into song, laughed, and many wept with joy. They believed the fascist nightmare was over and that Mussolini's fall meant the end of the war. Far from putting up a fight, the 4 million Fascist Party members meekly accepted the change of regime. Even the leader's newspaper, the *Popolo d'Italia*, replaced the usual photograph of Mussolini that always appeared on the front page with Badoglio's image. Throughout

Italy, people released their built-up anger, smashing Mussolini's statues and ransacking fascist offices. Anti-Fascists murdered ten Fascists in the immediate aftermath; 1,200 more found themselves evicted from their homes and employers fired 4,765 from their jobs.[11]

Discredited by his earlier support for Mussolini, King Victor Emmanuel clung on to his throne after the dictator's fall. The King feared a German invasion as much as an Allied victory. After years of condoning the pro-German policy of the Fascists, his position with the Allies was probably untenable. However, his dismissal of Mussolini gave him an opportunity for redemption, and it was within the King's authority to appoint a moderate government to win the confidence of both the Italian people and the Allies. Being old, suspicious and out of touch, the King decided instead to impose stricter censorship and martial law in an attempt to appease the Nazis and stay in power. Over the following week, the army shot 81 people and wounded 320. Most were anti-fascist strikers and communists.[12]

The King's daughter-in-law, Crown Princess Marie-José of Italy, secretly reached out to the Allies to arrive at a separate peace. The saturnine Princess, whose oval face had sharp cheekbones and defiant eyes, was trapped in an unhappy marriage to Crown Prince Umberto, and she had enjoyed a brief fling with Mussolini. Mussolini's son Romano discovered a letter in 2018, which quotes his mother, Rachele, stating that there was a romantic interlude between her husband and Princess Marie-José.[13] According to gossip, the Princess swam naked in a swimming pool to seduce Mussolini. However, outside the bedroom, Marie-José had little time for Fascism.

Attracted to secrecy and political manoeuvring, the Princess attempted to meet American agents by using Monsignor Giovanni Battista Montini, a senior Vatican diplomat, as the intermediary. Monsignor Montini – who was elected Pope Paul VI in 1963 – was distrusted by Mussolini for meddling in government. Neither the King nor her husband Prince Umberto supported the Princess's schemes, and after her conspiracy failed, they sent her to Sarre on the Swiss border; there she was kept isolated from any further intrigues.

Hitler's reaction was one of visceral anger when he heard about the King's coup d'état against Mussolini, and he demanded the immediate occupation of Rome. For Hitler, Mussolini's arrest was his worst nightmare, as it threatened his belief in the concept of 'an intangible and sacred leader'.[14] Behind Hitler's emotion was the knowledge that his destiny was now inextricably linked to Mussolini's. 'He [Hitler] said he was oppressed day and night with anguish,' wrote Albert Speer, the Nazi architect who had become one of the Führer's closest freinds.[15] In private, Hitler told Goebbels that Mussolini had been a weak dictator who had not followed his advice to eliminate the monarchy, complaining that he had fallen victim to an international conspiracy of aristocrats and Jews.[16]

Mussolini's fall from power created a profound legitimacy crisis for the Nazi regime, and every effort was made in Germany to locate Il Duce's precise whereabouts, as Hitler became determined to reinstate the Italian dictator. The Nazis liberally distributed bribes using forged banknotes and they even consulted clairvoyants. To foil Hitler's search, Badoglio had him moved again, by plane and an ambulance disguised with Red Cross markings. His new prison was a luxurious suite at the Camp Imperatore Hotel, high up in the mountains of Gran Sasso, which was accessible only by cable car. Here 200 soldiers guarded him and had orders to kill him if he attempted to escape. He was often seen at the window of his suite, studying the landscape with binoculars. He seemed relieved to be a prisoner without further responsibility.[17] One of his favourite subjects was disloyalty, and he found solace in a biography of Jesus which he read with great attention and found 'astonishing analogues'[18] between his betrayal and that of Christ.[19]

During captivity, he made a half-hearted attempt at suicide and failed.[20] He then self-pityingly wrote that it was a law of life that the populace would tear down yesterday's idol, only to regret it later.[21] While Mussolini was ruminating his fall from power, the King was determined to keep the former dictator away from the Allies, who wanted to put him on trial, and the Germans, who intended to restore him. Churchill gave a realistic assessment of the tragic dilemma faced by the Italian leadership:

> So, the Italian position has to be that although an internal revolution had taken place in Italy, they were still the allies of Germany and were carrying on a common cause with them. This was a very difficult position to maintain day after day with the pistol of the Gestapo pointing at the nape of so many necks.[22]

The new Prime Minister Badoglio moved quickly to reassure Hitler in a telegram, promising that Italy would remain Germany's ally. Still, Hitler viewed the regime change with contempt, and he was not keen to deal with the politician who had betrayed Mussolini. Badoglio was determined to undermine the popular cult of Mussolini and ordered the press to print lurid details about Mussolini's relationship with Clara Petacci, which dented Il Duce's magnetic image. The Prime Minister was a double-dealer, and he began secret peace talks with the Allies, who also distrusted him. He dared not surrender unconditionally as Churchill and Roosevelt demanded, nor did the Italians particularly want to continue fighting on the side of the Germans. Badoglio was terrified of the Nazi reprisals. With little room to manoeuvre, he swayed as much as the King, and even inspired a new word in an English dictionary of neologisms: the verb to 'Badogliate'.[23]

Finally, on 8 September 1943, Victor Emmanuel publicly announced an armistice with the Allies. The following day, fearing a German advance on Rome, the King and Prime Minister abandoned the city and boarded a boat near Pescara which took them south to Brindisi, still held by the Italian army. The King gave the crown jewels to a trusted aide and sent forty freight cars of royal possessions to Switzerland for safekeeping. However, he left the Italian forces without orders and confusion reigned. The press made unfavourable comparisons with King George VI and Queen Elizabeth, who refused to leave London during the Blitz, and *Time Magazine* dubbed him 'The Little King'.[24]

The war continued, and eight new German divisions arrived in Italy to support the three already stationed there. Hitler's priority was to defend Germany at the new front which had opened up in Southern Italy. If the King and Badoglio possessed any strategic insight, they might have worked with the Allies to prevent the German invasion. Instead, Italy was turned into a battlefield as Hitler's troops marched into Rome and took over. A nine-month occupation followed: an ordeal of deprivation, hunger and oppression for many, of collaboration for some, of resistance, torture, imprisonment and death for others. German officials and soldiers unleashed the anti-Italian sentiment which they had subdued while Italy remained an ally. For Goebbels, the racially inferior Italians were just 'a people of gypsies'.[25] On average 160 Italian civilians died every day as a direct result of the occupation.[26] Altogether between 7,000 and 12,000 Italian soldiers were killed by the Germans in the aftermath of the armistice, and the Nazis took a further 600,000 to work camps in Germany.[27] There, denied the status of POWs, they became 'military internees' and were subjected to appalling treatment and starvation – worse even than the Russian prisoners – to reflect the belief that Italy had betrayed the Third Reich.

As the tide of war turned against Germany, Hitler became more malignant towards any dissenters. The Führer was suspicious that Prince Philipp of Hesse had co-operated with the Italian Royal Family's overthrow of Mussolini. The German press attacked the Italian King: 'Thus the Liar King Betrays the Duce' ran the headline in *Der Völkische Beobachter*, the Nazi Party newspaper.[28] Posters appeared glued to the walls of Philipp's home, the Bellevue Palace in Kassel, insulting the Italian Royal Family and his wife, Princess Mafalda.

By early 1942, the cracks had started to appear in the once-solid relationship between the Nazi elite and the German nobility. On one side, the social-climbing Hermann Göring and Heinrich Himmler employed aristocratic officers to inflate their narcissism, but Joseph Goebbels and Robert Ley despised them. Ley's speech published in Goebbel's *Der Angriff* was a visceral attack:

> Degenerate to their very bones, blue-blooded to the point of idiocy, nauseatingly corrupt, and cowardly like all nasty creatures – such is the aristocratic clique which the Jew has sicced on National Socialism … We must exterminate this filth, extirpate it root and branch.[29]

After Germany lost most of its territorial gains in Eastern Europe during 1943, the nobility had outlived their usefulness to the Nazi regime, except perhaps to serve as scapegoats. Himmler had ranted in an unguarded moment to his doctor:

> Hitler gave me the order to finish off all the German princes and to do so immediately. He suggested that the most important of them should be charged with espionage and high treason, others with committing sexual perversions. The People's Court will thereby sentence them to death. Goebbels wants the hangings to take place in Berlin before the Imperial Palace. The princes should be herded on foot down the Unter den Linden. The German Work Front will provide the necessary personnel, who will spit on them and in this way give expression to the anger of the nation … We will blame the defeat in the East on them. The property of the princes will be divided between party members and Old Fighters.[30]

With their recent military reverses looming disastrously, Nazi paranoia amplified, and on 19 May 1943, Hitler issued the 'Decree Concerning

Internationally Connected Men'. The Nazis never published or circulated the document widely, but it specified that princes and others with international ties could not hold positions in the party, state or armed forces. In practice, many aristocrats remained for the time being unimpeded in their jobs, but the Nazi bureaucracy started to monitor their overseas family and business connections. Hitler then personally decided whether that person should 'retire'.

On the night of 7 September 1943, Prince Philipp of Hesse dined with Hitler at Wolf's Lair, the Führer's East Prussian headquarters, and stayed there until the early hours of the morning. Duplicitously, Hitler had continued to treat Philipp with outward friendliness, but spies were watching the Prince continuously. Speer observed: 'Prince Philipp was sending information to the Italian royal house. He [Hitler] had himself kept an eye on him ... and ordered his telephone tapped.'[31]

When Italy surrendered to the Allies, Hitler ordered Philipp's arrest and he was escorted to the 'guest bunker' where the SS guards kept him in the dark, 'both literally and figuratively'.[32] Within twenty-four hours the Prince was dispatched to Gestapo headquarters in Berlin. Not since the murder of Ernst Röhm had Hitler turned on so close a friend. Goebbels wrote in his diary:

> The Führer is fully convinced that Prince Philipp of Hesse was fully informed of the measures planned by the King [Victor Emmanuel III of Italy]. He is an unfaithful traitor. Once upon a time, he couldn't praise Il Duce enough to high heaven, now he can't do enough to damn him to hell. He would do the same to us, given the opportunity.[33]

Gestapo Headquarters, Berlin. 9 September 1943.

Reich Main Security Headquarters is a building depicted in many Hollywood films. In *Valkyrie*, it is a concrete plaza draped with swastika flags, with a sweeping staircase that climbs upwards to the offices of the Nazi elite. It becomes a grand hotel of the art deco style in *Hitler's SS: Portrait in Evil*. However, such depictions are false. In truth, the architecture of the evil was far more mundane – five storeys of red brick – it looked like any ordinary Berlin mansion block occupying a moderately attractive tree-lined street. However, perception is everything, and the building had the power to intimidate.

Here, the Gestapo promoted the message that if you crossed the state, they would get you. Informers and spies were everywhere. It could be anyone: your postman, the old lady in the corner shop, or a jealous co-worker. Wise men kept their mouths shut and their unseeing eyes looking straight ahead in trepidation. Self-censorship became a necessity for survival. The Nazis' greatest weapon was the fear they created. They deliberately spread the word of their calculating brutality towards anyone in 'protective custody'. Downstairs, in the cellars of Gestapo headquarters, inventive torture reached new heights: interrogation encompassed water-boarding, electric shocks and hanging a prisoner up by the arms with their wrists tied behind their backs to dislocate their shoulders.

In the cells of the Reich Security, Prince Philipp met Heinrich Müller, Head of the Gestapo. 'Gestapo Müller' was a striving workaholic police-man who never took a holiday,[34] a killer bureaucrat who found solace in transforming reports of denouncements, torture and secret executions into red tape and statistics.[35] Mixing competence with violence, he hunted down anyone suspected of treason towards the Führer.[36] A smallish man with dark hair and thin lips, his grey-blue eyes would fix on intended victims with unwavering scrutiny. Very ordinary looking, he tended to leave no impression on the memory.[37] Back in 1931, as a member of the Munich police, Müller had successfully hushed up the scandal surrounding the suspicious suicide of Hitler's niece Geli Raubal and proved himself dependable.[38] Another game-changing moment came with the arrest of over 20,000 Jews during the *Kristallnacht* ('Night of the Broken Glass') in 1938, which he organised. Promotion followed such inverted successes as morality capsized in Germany.

Heinrich Müller observed Prince Philipp with cold curiosity.[39] Müller instructed Philipp that the Prince of Hesse no longer existed. That man was dead, along with all memory of him. In his place, he would now be mere 'Herr Wienberg'. They removed the labels in his clothes which revealed his real name and sealed his papers. The Prince was forbidden to speak about his family or background. Political discussion was completely censored, and any breaches of these rules would have serious penalties; he became a living ghost.[40]

Philipp convinced Müller to allow him the name of 'Wildhof', rather than the Jewish-sounding Weinberg. Wildhof derived from a favourite family hunting ground on their estate in Hessen, and it was the name used by family members when they travelled incognito. The Prince knew that if something happened to him, his family would discover his fate.[41] Philipp was immediately dispatched to the Flossenbürg concentration camp in a truck, deliberately arriving at night, and for the next two years, the guards held him in conditions which he later described as 'hermetic concealment from the outside world'.[42]

Villa Wolkonsky, Rome. 23 September 1943.

On 23 September, Philipp's wife Princess Mafalda received a phone call from the German High Command saying they had an important message for her from her husband. They asked her to please come to the German military headquarters at the Villa Wolkonsky on the Esquiline Hill to receive it. The villa's gardens were an oasis of flowers and chirping crickets,[43] and as her car drew up to the door, an SS officer stepped out to greet her. Elegantly dressed in a silk suit, the good-natured Princess had walked into a trap.

Mafalda had recently visited Bulgaria in early September to console her sister Queen Giovanna over the death of her husband, Tsar Boris III of Bulgaria. When she heard about the peace deal, she panicked and flew immediately back to Rome, to find that the rest of her family had escaped to Brindisi for safety. Mafalda left her children in the care of Monsignor Montini inside the Vatican.

Princess Mafalda never entered the villa. The SS officer explained to her: 'Your husband called and said that he will soon arrive at the airfield here in Rome and that he wanted to speak to you there.'[44] Immediately, the Princess was escorted by two guards to the airport just outside Rome. At the terminal, the guards left her in a waiting room with two women. When she tried to exit the room, the women stopped her. Mafalda now realised she was a prisoner.

Later, the guards escorted her to a plane and told her that she was going to Munich to meet Philipp.[45] Instead, the aircraft landed at the iconic Tempelhof airfield in Berlin. Built to overawe and intimidate, it emerged out of the landscape with its colossal limestone facades, its vast, menacing halls filled with soldiers. The airport had become a symbol of Hitler's 'world capital' of Germania – part of Speer's reconstruction of Berlin during the 1930s. Gestapo agents escorted the terrorised Princess through this Nazi megastructure straight to their detention centre near Lake Wannsee, situated to the west of the capital and reached via the new Fritz Lang-style highways.

Baptised the *Schlimmste Hündin* ('worst bitch') by Joseph Goebbels, Mafalda found herself the Gestapo's captive. They charged her with not informing the German government of Italy's separate peace as soon as she knew about it, which was her duty since she was a German citizen through her marriage. For fourteen days, she slept on the floor, while being repeatedly interrogated. On 20 October, crying incessantly out of sheer terror, she was taken to the concentration camp at Buchenwald and incarcerated under the pseudonym 'Frau von Weber'.[46]

Buchenwald Concentration Camp, Germany.
20 October 1943.

Sited on the northern slope of the Ettersberg mountain, Buchenwald was built 5 miles outside of Weimar. Encircled by electrified barbed-wire fences, ominous watchtowers and a chain of sentries equipped with machine guns, it was one of the largest concentration camps. The SS often shot prisoners randomly and hanged inmates in the crematorium area. Worked to death in the infamous Buchenwald quarry, Jewish prisoners received the cruellest treatment. They became emaciated shaven wretches shuffling around in wooden clogs. The eyes of these listless prisoners grew mean with terror.[47]

Housed in a special compound, Princess Mafalda was incarcerated with other prominent prisoners, including former Austrian Chancellor Kurt von Schuschnigg and industrialist Fritz Thyssen. The inmates together pledged that if any one of them made it out, the others would tell their respective families what happened to them.[48] Confused and informed that her husband was dead, Princess Mafalda found herself addressed by the guards as a widow. Worried incessantly about her children – Moritz, Heinrich, Otto-Adolf and Elizabeth – she was permitted to pen letters which the guards then intercepted. She spent all her time writing to family members and to senior Nazis, including Hitler and Himmler, with whom she had once been on friendly terms. No one Mafalda wrote to ever read the letters. Officials only allowed the Princess to write in the hope that she would incriminate herself.[49] However, the only evidence of Philipp and Mafalda's betrayal is a secret note that was discovered hidden in an address book. A cryptogram consisting of sets of numbers and short phrases:

1: The king will soon be there.
2: I am afraid.
169: We're off.
221: Forward.
222: But nothing.
224: It is peace![50]

The codes might have been entirely innocent; just because they were exchanging information doesn't mean they were guilty of treason. Indeed, the evidence of Philipp and Mafalda's role in a conspiracy against either Hitler or Mussolini was fragile. In truth, Hitler kept them as hostages to use them as pawns in a game he was playing with the Italian King. He was determined to intimidate Philipp and ordered Himmler to launch an investigation. Himmler, in turn, ordered police chief Prince Josias of Waldeck-Pyrmont to carry out a search of the Hesse residences.[51]

Waldeck and a dozen Gestapo men arrived at the Bellevue Palace in Kassel at 6.30 a.m. They forced the Prince's secretary, Adelheid Friege, out of her bed in terror, and searched every corner of the Palace, confiscating letters and papers. Waldeck declared, 'search until you find something, and if you don't find something, then make it up.'[52] Fourteen cases of valuables including jewellery, priceless furniture and furs were packed up and removed. It was not without irony that Prince Philipp, who had been such a vital 'cog in the Nazis' art plundering bureaucracy',[53] should now find himself robbed.

The Gestapo ordered a distraught Adelheid to appear at their headquarters and instructed her to help translate the Prince's Italian correspondence. Later, the guards questioned her about Philipp's homosexual activities. Waldeck was determined to make his sexuality an additional pretext for his arrest and tried to intimidate another servant, Herr Hollenberg, into testifying that Philipp was a homosexual. Hollenberg loyally protested and spent two months confined in one of the basement cells at Gestapo HQ, before being sent to a concentration camp for eleven months.[54]

Waldeck's malevolent jurisdiction also included a supervisory role over Buchenwald, and he made regular inspections of the concentration camp. Another prisoner at the camp was Johannes Hayes, a former aide to Waldeck, who witnessed him meeting Princess Mafalda inside the barracks:

As he [Waldeck] left the room, the princess [Mafalda] was standing before him. She was dressed very badly … He looked her up and down and then went out. The princess did not speak to him. But he must have recognised her … he was often a guest of Prince Philipp of Hesse.[55]

Another observer added that Waldeck 'Had no sympathy for the incredibly distressed woman'.[56]

Prince Philipp and Princess Mafalda's three youngest children – Heinrich, Otto-Adolf and Elizabeth – left the Vatican and were escorted from Rome to Germany under the care of SS Lieutenant Colonel Herbert Kappler, the head of Gestapo operations in the Holy City. Kappler was a menacing creature who supervised the persecution of Rome's Jews, extracting a ransom of 50kg in gold from them. He was also complicit in the murder of 335 Italian men and boys in the Argentine Caves: a reprisal for resistance activity in the area.[57] Fortunately, the children made it to the home of their paternal grandmother, Princess Margaret of Hesse, at Friedrichshof Castle, and Prince Philipp's sister-in-law, Princess Sophie of Hesse, took care of them.

Flossenbürg Concentration Camp, Germany. 1943.

Outside Waldeck's malicious dominion, life for Philipp was more comfortable. Inside a forbidden zone and surrounded by dense forests, the Nazis called the camp at Flossenbürg 'Bavarian Siberia'. Hitler picked the location for its remoteness. Local Franconia peasants were careful not to talk or enquire about it. Like Buchenwald, the camp housed politically prominent prisoners, including thirteen British secret agents.[58]

Segregated from the other prisoners, Philipp retained elevated privileges. He still wore his civilian clothes, and the guards who arrested him carried his luggage – which consisted of three suitcases and a toilet kit – into the camp. Housed in a double cell that included a washbasin, a table and a window, he ate the same food as the SS guards, and his captors even built him a wooden-fenced enclosure outside his cell where he could sit in the sun. Here, he peered through a crack and watched the rest of the camp unseen.[59]

This outside world had an 'atmosphere of death'.[60] The smell of rotten food sometimes filled the air, potent enough to make some prisoners gag and vomit.[61] Regular prisoners dressed in the zebra uniform of blue and grey, their names forgotten as the guards addressed them by the numbers sewn onto their jackets.

Every day, the inmates woke up fearful of the daily grind. Their routine was split into segments marked by the blast of sirens.[62] In the surrounding quarries, prisoners worked to death[63] extracting the white-flecked granite that the Nazis were using to rebuild Berlin.[64] Indiscriminately, guards tormented or shot them. Seven hundred died every week.[65] Hangings occurred only a few feet away from Philipp's window, and the guards led the condemned out to be strangled naked.

These killings frequently occurred six at a time, and the guards rarely waited for the death of one prisoner before stringing up another. Daily he 'could hear off and on, a soft cracking, something like a shot being fired'.[66] It turned out to be executions in the distance. He mostly sat in his cell all day looking out his window at the *Leichenstransporte* ('transport of the corpses'). Fortunately, he was protected because Hitler still thought he might be useful again.[67]

14

DOWNFALL

Stockholm, Sweden. February 1942.
As the Duke of Coburg's daughter, Princess Sibylla, had married into the Swedish Royal Family – she was in direct succession to become Queen of Sweden one day – Charles Edward continued to provide the Nazi regime with the soft power of royal connections. The relationship between 'neutral' Sweden and Hitler's regime was effective. Sweden was a major supplier of iron to Nazi Germany, it helped launder stolen Jewish gold to pay for war supplies, and some Swedes even volunteered for the German army. Churchill complained that King Gustaf V of Sweden was 'absolutely in the German grip', and he charged Sweden with playing both sides for profit.[1] As Hitler was about to initiate Operation Barbarossa, the German codename for the invasion of Soviet Russia, he needed to keep Sweden as an ally.

The Duke of Coburg and the German ambassador to Sweden, Prince Victor zu Wied, were close friends and worked as a double act. As a consequence of their intervention, King Gustaf applied pressure on the Swedish Parliament to aid Hitler's Russian invasion. Wied sent a 'Most Urgent – Top Secret' message to Berlin that the King had informed him personally that the transit of German troops through Sweden would be allowed: 'The King's words conveyed the joyful emotion he felt. He had lived through anxious days and had gone far in giving his support to the matter. King Gustaf had even threatened abdication.'[2] When Hitler attacked the Soviet Union on 23 August 1942, the King of Sweden, whose hatred of communism was paramount, sent the Führer a congratulatory letter as the German Blitzkrieg started to devastate Soviet Russia.

Although both Gustaf V and the Crown Prince Gustaf Adolf were pro-German, Sweden's Crown Princess, the former Lady Louise Mountbatten (the sister of Lord Mountbatten and Princess Andrew (Alice) of Greece), loathed the Nazis. The Swedish Royal Family's tennis coach was in the pay of Walter Schellenberg, the Nazi spymaster. This undercover agent passed on to Schellenberg and Hitler private family conversations – how Princess Louise had condemned Nazi Party 'barbarism' while the Crown Prince hoped the British would 'come to their senses' and make peace with Hitler, otherwise 'the red flag would soon be flying from Swedish castles'.[3]

For Hitler, the attack on the Soviet Union proved disastrous; the Battle of Stalingrad raged throughout the winter of 1942 to 1943 and became one of the most brutal conflicts of the Second World War. The Third Reich was bled dry and forced into retreat after the Red Army killed, wounded or captured 400,000 German soldiers.

Meanwhile, Princess Louise's neutral status in Sweden provided a boon for all the family scattered across Germany, Britain and Greece who could not write to each other directly. Louise acted as a conduit and helped clear their letters to each other. This postal service was not a simple matter of forwarding the messages, as Louise had to copy out every note and re-address it from herself. As a mark of their gratitude, her family gave Louise (by then Queen of Sweden) a gold envelope-shaped case on which they engraved all the names of the relatives she had quietly helped.[4]

Friedrichshof Castle, Germany. October 1943.

In October 1943, Princess Sophie of Hesse received bad news – her husband Christoph was dead. With the Allied invasion of Italy, Prince Christoph had been serving with the *Jagdgeschwader 53* (fighter squadron) of the Luftwaffe in Castelgandolfo outside Rome. On 7 October 1943, the Prince was flying to Berlin when his aircraft, a Siebel 104, collided with a hill near Forli. Rescuers took two days to find Christoph's body, which they buried on the hillside where the plane crashed. After Hitler had passed the May 1943 Decree Against Internationally Connected Men, it was remarkable that Christoph was still a serving officer. Despite the arrest of his brother and sister-in-law, Prince Philipp and Princess Mafalda, and the dismissal of his two brothers, Prince Wolfgang and Prince Richard, from their army units, Christoph remained a highly committed Nazi.[5]

Heinrich Himmler sent the menacing General Siegfried Taubert to offer his condolences to Princess Sophie and her mother-in-law, Princess Margaret of Hesse, at Friedrichshof Castle. Sophie had withdrawn to the castle with her four children at the start of the war. After the arrest of Philipp and Mafalda by the Gestapo, she had also taken over their day-to-day care.

General Taubert ran Wewelsburg Castle, a type of ideological–political training camp and school for the SS leadership. Its work focused on sinister pseudoscientific research into Germanic early history and genealogy – all intended to underpin the racial teachings of the Nazi movement. Taubert sent a report to Himmler, dated 30 November 1943, stating he was shocked at Sophie's 'terrible appearance; she has become thin and looks to be suffering a great deal, probably because she is expecting her fifth child'. It was a nervous and strained meeting, with Sophie and Margaret feeling extremely vulnerable. Taubert observed that 'both ladies are wracking their brains' with concern for Philipp and Mafalda.[6]

On hearing the news, Princess Alice arrived as quickly as she could from Greece to comfort her daughter.[7] Alice wrote to her son Philip in the British navy about Sophie, using her sister Crown Princess Louise of Sweden as a go-between:

> As you know, I went to Tiny [Princess Sophie's nickname], who is so brave when she is with her children and us, being her usual self and making jokes but her hours in her room alone are hardly to be endured, and made of all who love her suffer so much for her that I realise how much easier it is to bear one's own suffering than to share another's. I never suffered after 'the accident' [the 1937 Hesse plane crash] as I did those three weeks with Tiny and I certainly shall not forget them as long as I live. Her children are perfectly adorable, you would love them, and the new baby is too sweet for words.[8]

The entire family, even back in Britain, was concerned about Sophie. Her grandmother Victoria, Lady Milford Haven (née Princess Victoria of Hesse), wrote from Kensington Palace:

> Poor dear Tiny … She loved her husband & had been anxious about him ever since he was in Sicily … I am sorry for Mossie (Princess Margaret of Hesse) too, this is the 3rd son she has lost in the war, the two eldest in the last one & now her favourite in this one. This is now the 7th relative of mine who has lost his life flying.[9]

Victoria was pleased that her daughter Princess Alice had travelled to Germany: 'Luckily they both have good nerves as they are so near

Frankfurt, which has lately not been a pleasant neighbourhood.'[10] However, once Alice returned to Athens, she was completely cut off from the rest of her family. Threatened by the collapse of Italy, German control over Greece intensified, and thousands died of famine as the Germans looted and burned Athens.

Days later, a US army bomb dropped on the chapel near Friedrichshof Castle. When it exploded it killed Princess Marie Alexandra, the wife of Prince Wolfgang of Hesse. The ceiling had collapsed under the weight of the building, leaving her body almost unrecognisable. Despite his wife's death, Wolfgang travelled to Berlin in an attempt to save Philipp and Mafalda. Reichsmarschall Göring refused to see him, but he did meet Paul Körner, Göring's former chauffeur. Körner, who had now risen to become a state secretary in the Prussian Justice Department, stated that Göring was 'not reachable' and 'everything is chaotic here. It is best to do nothing, otherwise you will only endanger your family.' Sophie also contacted her old friend Emmy Göring, but she just told her that her husband knew where they were, but he 'was not permitted to speak about it'.[11] Emmy tried to be reassuring and claimed that the authorities were looking for a villa for Mafalda, and when they found one, she would contact Sophie to bring the children to their mother.

HMS Wallace, Mediterranean Sea. June 1943.

In June 1943, Prince Philip was serving on HMS *Wallace* as it prepared to assist in the invasion of Sicily, covering the landings of the Eighth Army while American and British airborne forces attacked from the skies. At one point, he might have been involved in shelling his brother-in-law Christoph just before his plane crash. Sophie later told a newspaper reporter, 'We have reason to believe that at one time during the Allied invasion of Sicily my brother and my uncle [Prince Philip and Lord Mountbatten] were fighting on the same sector of the island as my husband [Prince Christoph] was serving.'[12]

HMS *Wallace* was subjected to a prolonged and severe dive-bombing by Luftwaffe planes that summer and was almost continuously at action stations. Philip, now promoted to first lieutenant, was in the thick of the action. Harry Hargreaves, one of the yeomen on board, witnessed his bravery and quick thinking: 'On one occasion we were under attack from enemy aircraft for over-two-and-a-half hours without any help being given or expected, and Prince Philip coolly directed most of the operations from the bridge.'[13]

On 8 July, the night sky was particularly bright, and HMS *Wallace* became a sitting target for German bombers. Philip, always resourceful, started to build a wooden raft on the ship's deck with the crew. It was a decoy which they attached smoke floats to and launched over the side, making it look like the flaming debris of HMS *Wallace* drifting in the water. Their ship steamed away, cut its engines and lights, and waited until it heard the approaching enemy aircraft. Hargreaves described what happened next:

> The sound of the aircraft grew louder until I thought it was directly overhead and I screwed up my shoulders in anticipation of the bombs. The next thing was the scream of the bombs, but at some distance. The ruse had worked, and the aircraft was bombing the raft. I suppose he was under the impression that he had hit us in his last attack and was now finishing the job. Prince Philip saved our lives that night.[14]

When HMS *Wallace* was ordered home for a refit in Malta, Philip remained on standby, waiting for a new ship to come into service, and returned to London.

Windsor Castle. 25 December 1943.

Having 'nowhere particular to go' that Christmas, Prince Philip accompanied his young cousin, David, the new Marquess of Milford Haven, to Windsor Castle to watch the Royal Family's Christmas pantomime, *Aladdin*. Princess Elizabeth was in the starring role as the principal boy, and Princess Margaret played Roxana. The 17-year-old Elizabeth made her first stage entrance by bursting unexpectedly out of a laundry basket dressed in a Chinese kimono and white silk pantaloons. Everyone laughed when the cast sang in a slapstick Chinese laundry scene, particularly the 22-year-old Prince Philip, who sat in the front row with his cousin, the Duchess of Kent.[15]

Princess Elizabeth was a well-balanced young woman, an all-rounder. Not brilliant but sensible and composed. Not intellectual, but intelligent and grave. Since meeting Philip at Dartmouth on 22 July 1939, she had thought a lot about him. 'Guess who is coming to see us?' said the Princess to Marion Crawford, her nanny turned governess.[16] When he arrived, to Crawford's eyes he had 'greatly changed' since Dartmouth. 'It was a grave and charming man who sat there, with nothing of the rather bumptious boy … He looked more than ever, I thought like a Viking, weather-beaten and strained, and his manners left nothing to be desired.'[17] However, Crawford noticed that Elizabeth had a 'sparkle about her none of us had ever seen before'. After the pantomime, Elizabeth, Margaret, David and Philip turned on the gramophone and rolled back the carpet in the crimson drawing room. They all 'frisked and capered away till near 1.00 a.m.,' wrote Sir Alan Lascelles.[18] That Christmas weekend was a defining moment. In Elizabeth's bedroom, a photograph of Philip materialised, and a reciprocal one of her appeared in his bag.[19]

At first, the King and Queen were aghast at any potential match between Philip and Elizabeth. They considered him 'rough, ill-mannered, uneducated and would probably be unfaithful'.[20] However, the exiled King George II of Greece started to press hard for his cousin Philip's position as a suitor to the future Queen and urged George VI to take the matter seriously. The King resisted the pressure: 'We're going to tell George that P. had better not think any more about it for the present.'[21]

When Philip was in London, he either stayed with his grandmother, Lady Milford Haven, at Kensington Palace, or at the Mountbattens' home in Chester Square. Weekends were spent at his cousin Marina's country house, Coppins. Both the Duchess of Kent and Lord Mountbatten considered Philip their protégé and started to do everything possible to encourage the burgeoning romance. When he was at Coppins, Elizabeth was seldom far away, and she was about to turn 18 on 21 April.

Meanwhile, Philip reactivated his request for British citizenship, and was posted to Newcastle to help oversee the finishing touches to HMS *Whelp*, a new W-Class destroyer, which was commissioned for service on 17 April 1944. The presence of a Greek prince in the Newcastle docks attracted the attention of an ambitious young local reporter called Olga Franklin; she tracked Philip down to the small bed and breakfast where he was staying:

Few workers in a North-East shipyard are aware the tall, ash-blond first lieutenant, RN, who travels by bus to work among them each day is a royal prince. Citizens have been equally unaware that this 23-year-old naval officer, Prince Philip of Greece, has been living quietly in a hotel while standing by on a British destroyer. Prince Philip, who has the looks of a typical Prince of Hans Andersen fairy tale, will certainly have been noticed by many a girl worker at the shipyard ... This is the first time the Prince has been interviewed in this country ... and I thanked him for the good-humoured and kindly way he accepted 'exposure'.[22]

If Olga had known the real importance of the 'Greek prince', she would have secured a bigger scoop.

The mood during the summer of 1944 started to become optimistic; the war had turned in the Allies' favour. The Red Army was surging towards Germany from the east, the Italians had switched sides, and the presence of America provided both muscle and money. That August, Philip found himself partaking in the Allied landings in the South of France.

There was a sense of exhilaration, although the general public did not know about the secret D-Day preparations that were set for 6 June. Twenty-four thousand British, American and Canadian troops under the command of General Dwight Eisenhower would kick-start the liberation of Europe by landing on the Normandy beaches. Churchill, plagued by memories of the Gallipoli campaign – a catastrophic 29-year-old logistical mistake which led to 45,000 deaths in the First World War – wished his wife Clementine goodnight with the words: 'Do you realise that by the time you wake up in the morning 20,000 men may have been killed?' However, when Churchill addressed the House of Commons at 6 p.m., it was to announce an astounding success as the Allied forces marched towards Germany.

Buchenwald Concentration Camp, Germany. 24 August 1945.

On 24 August 1944, as the Allied powers advanced into Germany, they bombed the ammunition factory inside the camp at Buchenwald killing over 400 prisoners. The blast seriously wounded Princess Mafalda, whom the camp guards had imprisoned in a building adjacent to the factory. She was left buried up to her neck in debris with severe burns to her arm. In the chaotic aftermath, two fellow Italian prisoners pulled her from the rubble and recognised who she was. The Princess said, 'I'm dying. Remember me not as a princess but as your Italian sister.'

The guards brought her to the on-site brothel, which doubled as an infirmary. The camp doctor, Dr Gerhard Schiedlausky, was a sadist who had conducted experiments with 'serums' on living prisoners. Ninety per cent of the time, these try-outs proved fatal. He now sutured her arm but made no further effort to help her. After two days of agony, her wounds turned gangrenous, and he performed an amputation on her injured arm. Princess Mafalda lost too much blood and never regained consciousness.

Princess Mafalda's body was sent, naked, to the crematorium, where Father Joseph Thyl placed it in a wooden coffin: Number 262. He cut a lock of her hair, which he sent to her family, and her fellow prisoners buried her, with no name and no ceremony. Confirmation of her death did not come until after the Axis powers surrendered to the Allies in April 1945. Six years later, Italian prisoners held at Buchenwald identified Mafalda's burial site, and her family reburied her in the chapel near Friedrichshof Castle.[23]

Dachau Concentration Camp, Germany. April 1945.

In April 1945, after a year and a half of solitary confinement in Flossenbürg concentration camp, Prince Philipp of Hesse was transferred to Dachau in a green police transport wagon together with Fabian von Schlabrendorff, a lawyer and member of the German resistance to Hitler. At Dachau, Philipp joined an elite group of 120 VIP prisoners – the *Prominenten* (Celebrities) – who were secreted, out of view, in an isolated building that was formerly a schoolhouse. This elite group lived in relative comfort, although they slept together in dormitories of fifteen people. Beyond their wall was a city of barracks, filled with miserably thin and exhausted inmates – many too weak to stand. There was also a constant risk from American bombs. Almost every night, like clockwork, the sirens would screech, and bombs rained down on the camp.

Among this group of captives were former Austrian chancellor Kurt von Schushnigg, ex-French premier Léon Blum and industrialist Fritz Thyssen. There were also several captured British soldiers, including British intelligence officer Captain Sigismund Payne-Best, Lieutenant Colonel Jack Churchill and SOE officer Peter Churchill. Imprisoned aristocrats included Countess Nina von Stauffenberg, whose husband Klaus had plotted to assassinate Hitler, and Prince Xavier de Bourbon-Parma, the pretender to the Spanish throne, who had worked with the French Resistance. They even detained the Kaiser's nephew, Prince Frederick Leopold of Prussia, for listening to enemy radio stations, after being betrayed by servants in his castle for being gay. On arrival at the camp, he was assigned the job of cleaning the camp latrines and nearly died from diphtheria. After he recovered, he worked as a batman and errand boy for the camp brothel.[24]

The stress of incarceration forged strong bonds between the prisoners. For ten days the *Prominenten* stayed at Dachau. Then the group secretly moved around central Europe in a convoy of four buses, trucks and cattle-cars at night, their windows sinisterly blacked out and with nothing to eat. The experience was harrowing, as *Obersturmführer* (First Lieutenant) Ernst

Bader and the twenty SS men who were responsible for camp executions guarded them. Bader was a tall, thin man with sharp cheekbones; he dressed in the grey uniform of the SS fighting corps. A cold-eyed monster, Bader frequently screamed at the prisoners to stop complaining and to move faster. He was under orders to liquidate the *Prominenten* if necessary, and a portable gas chamber travelled with the party.[25]

The Allies were liberating many parts of Europe. Refugees were on the road and there was constant bombing. Nazi command still sent soldiers to the front, but it was evident that the German war machine was breaking down. For the cramped passengers in the trucks, it seemed the roads got narrower and steeper, and the vehicles regularly stopped. At one point, they all had to get out and push one of the trucks up a sharp hill.[26] Rumours were rife that a fanatical Nazi group would establish an Alpine zone to fight to the end using guerrilla tactics, and they would become their hostages.

Philipp was known to be a committed Nazi, a close friend to both Hitler and Göring. Therefore, the rest of the group viewed him with suspicion. Fey von Hassell, a young German aristocrat, incarcerated because of her father's role in the Stauffenburg plot to kill Hitler, wrote, 'I was surprised to encounter Prince Philipp of Hesse in that particular crowd.' There was an element of pity because of Mafalda's tragic death. Several other prisoners had learned of her death before Philipp did, and Fey recalled, 'I did not have the heart to tell him of her sad end. I just shook my head, leaving the unpleasant task to someone else.'[27]

Karinhall, Schorfhiede Forest outside Berlin. 28 April 1945.

Göring woke on the morning of 28 April at his country estate at Karinhall, north of Berlin. A convoy of Luftwaffe trucks, although desperately needed for more urgent wartime duties, were loaded with his looted treasures and Göring patiently watched them leave. An army engineer then wired the house with explosives, and left Göring to detonate the house himself. This vast shrine to the Reichsmarschall's vanity exploded into flames as Göring stepped into his black Mercedes limousine and drove towards Berlin. He never looked back. He left to join Hitler at the Reich Chancellery.[28]

By now, it was clear that Germany had lost the war. In Berlin, Hitler had not left his eighteen-room bunker, 55 feet under the Reichstag, for three months. The Soviet army's 2.5 million troops and 6,150 tanks approached the city from the east, while to the west, German city after city had started to fall to the British and the American armies. The Allies were racing to see who would be the first to capture the Nazi capital.

Hitler's Bunker, Berlin. 28 April 1945.

The Führer put incredible pressure on people in the bunker to commit suicide. As he handed out cyanide capsules, he demanded oaths from his colleagues to take their lives after he was dead. These fatal instructions were part of Hitler's so-called 'Nero decree' policy. He also ordered the destruction of the German infrastructure to prevent its use by the Allies – a commanded deliberately ignored by Albert Speer.

Hitler wanted his secrets to disappear, whether written down in files or hidden 'inside' people. One of his last acts was to issue a command to assassinate the Duke of Coburg. In his roles as President of the German Red Cross and Secretary of the Kaiser Wilhelm Society, Charles Edward knew a great deal: the horrors of the Nazi euthanasia programme, the experiments taking place inside the concentration camps and German nuclear research secrets. Charles Edward never knew that Hitler wanted him killed; therefore, he never disowned or criticised Hitler later.

On the night of 28 April, Hitler married Eva Braun, his mistress for sixteen years, and on the following day the couple poisoned themselves and their dogs by swallowing cyanide capsules, and Hitler also shot himself in the head. Hitler and Braun's bodies were hastily cremated in the chancellery garden to prevent the advancing Soviet forces from publicly stringing up their bodies, like Mussolini and his mistress, Clara Petacci. Only Goebbels, his wife and their children famously joined Hitler in the suicide pact.[29]

Villabassa, Austria. 28 April 1945.

Meanwhile, the *Prominenten* convoy complete with its SS guard arrived at Villabassa, a village in the South Tyrol on the Italian–Austrian border. Here, it was confronted by the regular German troops under the command of General Heinrich von Vietinghoff. He had just received the news that Germany had negotiated a delicate ceasefire with the Allies and on no account was he going to allow the slaughter of prisoners to take place under his jurisdiction. When news of Hitler's suicide broke, the SS unit under Bader yielded to the German army, which in turn handed the prisoners over to the Americans on 4 May 1945. Four days later, Germany surrendered unconditionally to the Allied forces.[30]

The Americans had no idea who this strange ensemble cast were. Aristocratic and prominent names like Hesse, Stauffenberg, Schushnigg and Thyssen went unrecognised. The group was transferred to the comfortable Hotel Braies just across the border in Italy, with its kitchens stocked with American canned food and chocolate, as well as cigarettes. Soon, an intrigued flock of journalists and war correspondents descended on the hotel, realising there was the potential for a story.[31]

Prince Philipp of Hesse's troubles continued after the ceasefire. On 10 May, Prince Philipp and the German members of the group were taken to Verona airport in eight comfortable military buses for a two-hour flight to Naples, where they boarded a ferry and were taken across the bay to the Hotel Paradise Eden on the island of Capri. Against the stunning backdrop of the Mediterranean, the Americans now started to question and identify the group.

The Allies formally arrested Philipp in the spring of 1945. As the former Governor of Hesse, he had ranked number fifty-three on America's list of most-wanted Nazis. Philipp was moved to another interrogation centre at the Château de Châtenay near Paris and then moved again to camp Ashcan (Allied Supreme Headquarters for Axis Nationals) on 6 July at the Palace Hotel in Mondorf-les-Bains, Luxembourg. The hotel held fifty-two high-ranking Nazis including Göring, Speer and Ribbentrop. Here, their shoelaces, ties and belts were removed in order to prevent any suicide attempts and the regime was strict despite the luxurious surroundings.[32]

THE RECKONING

Coburg Castle. April 1945.

The Second World War was almost over, and the Allies – Britain, France, America and Russia – started to divide Germany into four occupation zones. Most of George VI's German relatives lived in the American Occupied Zone, and the town of Coburg fell under the jurisdiction of General George Patton. Charles Edward, Duke of Coburg, was placed under house arrest at Coburg Castle and Stefan Heym, from the army's psychological warfare unit, was quickly sent to interview him:

> The Duke believed until recently that Germany would win the war. He thinks Hitler did a wonderful job in Germany. Only trouble is that he 'overshot the mark.' Hitler should have managed his *Drang nach Osten* (Drive to the East), by measures short of war. The method used in eliminating the Jews was harsh, but he thinks it was necessary to remove the Jewish influence from the German theatre, art, newspapers etc.

When Heym asked Charles Edward what he thought the percentage of Jews in Germany had been, he replied: 'about ten per cent' and presented a list of outrageous 'demands':

> The United Nations should furnish Germany with raw materials so that I can rebuild its industries, become a great nation and thus be in a position to pay war damages. No one in Germany should be punished for war crimes because no German is guilty of any war crimes, says the Duke.[1]

Heym felt that Charles Edward had lost all touch with reality, 'yet he [Charles Edward] had simply stayed loyal to the ideas he had acquired twenty years earlier'.[2]

Five categories of war criminal existed: Major Offender, Offender, Lesser Offender, Follower and Exonerated Person. In November, the American military prosecutors charged Charles Edward as a Major Offender with 'crimes against humanity' for his complicity in Hitler's Final Solution. As President of the German Red Cross, he had collaborated in the Nazi programme of forced euthanasia. The Americans understood that the capture of Charles Edward would have considerable political implications. The Duke of Coburg was cousin to the British King, and the grandfather to the future King of Sweden. His arrest quickly became public knowledge and an article appeared in the *New York Times*:

> Charles Edward, Duke of Saxe-Coburg and Gotha, and a grandson of Queen Victoria, is under house arrest and the Allies confiscated his estates, American military government officials announced today. The duke was President of the German Red Cross and a General in the Storm Troopers. His high rank in the German hierarchy places him in the categorical arrest class.[3]

Charles Edward was taken to Bamburg POW camp and imprisoned with other Nazi officials under extremely harsh conditions. A doctor's medical report detailed that the 62-year-old Duke had chronic spinal arthritis and a basal cell carcinoma on his left eye.[4]

In London, the indomitable Princess Alice was determined to rescue her Nazi brother.

Marlborough House, London. April 1946.

Princess Alice and her husband, Lord Athlone, had returned from Canada in April 1946 to a very different London. The exciting wealthy London of the 1930s was gone, and the war had bankrupted the city, bombed-out buildings and houses pitted thick with shrapnel scars. It was drab, gloomy and down-at-heel. A town of survivors forced to queue for buses, cinemas and food. The Athlones' Kensington Palace apartment was uninhabitable, and they had sold Brantridge Park with its pre-war ghosts. Alice and Lord Athlone stayed with Queen Mary at Marlborough House, which as winter approached became a refrigerator. They lived in 'overcoats and snowboots'.[5]

The Princess immediately began to work on her Nazi brother's behalf. Alice was 'nothing if not resilient'[6] and the Princess mobilised royal courtiers, who used Balmoral and Buckingham Palace writing paper to pressurise the Foreign Office to rescue Charles Edward. Still, her attempts to whitewash his far-right politics with royal letterheads did not fool officials:[7]

> Princess Alice spoke to me about her the Duke [Charles Edward] the other day, she said that the latter – by his own estimation at any events – had done quite a lot to try to improve Anglo-German relations during the inter-war period in his capacity as President of the Anglo-German society, the German Red Cross and various ex-servicemen's associations. I gather that the Duke rather hoped that the Foreign Office had apparently [said] about [Herbert von] Dirksen that the latter had, in his capacity as Ambassador, done his best to improve Anglo-German relations, so would we say something to that effect.[8]

She also lobbied British officials in the British Occupied Zone. In a letter to Sir Brian Robertson, the Deputy Military Governor of the British Zone, Alice expressed her fears about her brother:

> Fate has been cruel to him, but I am fully aware of his great folly in getting himself so deeply involved in the Nazi Party as President of the German Red Cross … This has, of course, landed him in his present predicament. But it is absurd to consider him a Nazi insider.[9]

In a second letter, Alice suggests that Robertson should 'bring pressure to bear on the right quarters'.[10]

Alice then started to lobby American officials in Germany and sent out a stream of correspondence to General Lucius D. Clay, Eisenhower's deputy, expressing her concern for her brother's welfare and health. She even hired a German lawyer and argued that the Allies should release Charles Edward on humanitarian grounds, because he had severe arthritis and cancer of the eye. Ideally, Alice wanted her brother released into the care of his daughter Princess Sibylla in Sweden, or his wife in Coburg: 'All of us are anxious to remove him from camp life to a place where he can receive more individual attention.'[11]

In September 1946, Alice travelled to Sweden to stay with her niece Sibylla. She also met with the head of the Swedish Red Cross, Count

Folke Bernadotte, who had just returned from Germany and heard reports that Charles Edward's health was 'satisfactory'. Alice mused in a letter to Robertson if her brother's recent health scare was a 'purposeful exaggeration',[12] but concluded that 'Nothing matters if we can only get him home'.[13] She was realistic about his situation: 'I am afraid that a string of Nazi titles will undo every effort on our part.'[14]

Charles Edward's trial started in 1946. Still, it would not conclude for three more years. During that timeframe, the denazification courts reviewed 2.5 million Nazi officials. Thirty-five thousand cases were for individuals classified as dangerous perpetrators, such as the Duke. The British Foreign Office could not lie for the Princess and provided the denazification tribunal with a damning report about his Nazi activities, going right back to his role in the murderous Freikorps militias.[15]

Alice was also refused permission from the King to travel to Coburg. George VI considered his German cousin a delicate problem. Nonetheless, Alice was determined to whitewash her brother's Nazi past, so she ensured that the Duke's friends and aides attested to his 'peace work'.

Friedrichshof Castle and Wolfsgarten Castle, Germany. 29 March 1945.

General Patton's Third Army had reached Friedrichshof Castle on 29 March, and on 12 April, Prince Wolfgang of Hesse was arrested and sent to Darmstadt POW camp. Meanwhile, the billeted American troops helped themselves to the castle's wine cellars. They ignited fires in the courtyard to cook the family's pet peacocks on a rotisserie and the castle became a GI rest camp.[16] Almost immediately, the soldiers began looting and taking 'souvenirs' from the castle as American soldiers walked off with bits of family silver, and a convoy of trucks removed the best furniture for Allied headquarters.[17] Even a priceless Rubens painting went missing, but the 100-room castle was so vast and crammed with treasures that the Americans thought it would take thirty men six months to inventory – so they didn't bother and preferred to help themselves.[18]

By 19 April, the Americans ordered the remaining members of Hesse's family to leave the castle. Princess Margaret, Princess Sophie and the nine children had just four hours to pack, and they could only take food and clothing. Princess Margaret of Hesse was 73 years old, ill with pneumonia, and refused to leave her home. An American soldier overseeing the requisition barked, 'If that old girl does not come down at once, I'll go up and shoot her.'[19] She moved into her land agent's twelve-bedroomed 'cottage' just outside the gates of Friedrichshof.

Princess Sophie and all nine children took refuge with Prince Ludwig and Princess Peg of Hesse and by Rhine at Wolfsgarten Castle, north of Darmstadt. They travelled in a cart with the nine children hidden under straw.[20] Allied bombs had almost destroyed Darmstadt and damaged much of the property belonging to the family. Wolfsgarten became an oasis of calm in the turmoil of the Allied occupation.[21]

Princess 'Peg' was an Englishwoman, born the Hon. Margaret Geddes, and was a friend of the British royals. She had married Prince Louis after meeting him on a skiing holiday in Bavaria, and she had stayed in Germany, despite the risks, throughout the war. Afterwards, Peg and Louis took in numerous aristocratic and royal refugees. Tatiana Metternich abandoned her house in Bohemia to the Red Army and fled to the safety of Wolfsgarten. The Kaiser's granddaughter, Princess Cecilie of Prussia, also took refuge there and even met her future husband, an American monuments, fine arts and archives officer called Clyde Harris from Texas. On the day of the wedding, the Hohenzollern Black Eagle flag flew over the castle in the bride's honour.

Princess Sophie also found love amongst the castle refugees. Three years after her husband's plane crash, she met Prince George William of Hanover, largely thanks to Princess Peg's matchmaking skills.[22] George was finishing his doctoral studies at Göttingen University before becoming the headmaster of the Salem School when it reopened later that year. He was the brother of the exiled Queen Frederica of Greece, and part of that multinational Anglo-German royal clique where everyone seemed related to each other. In Britain, Queen Mary expressed her pleasure that the 'pretty little widow Tiny' had found a new husband, and thought with five children already, they would need a large house.[23]

Darmstadt POW Camp, Germany. 1945.

After leaving the temporary prison camp on Capri, the Allies moved Philipp around a series of twenty-two different POW internment camps. His treatment varied: sometimes it was harsh, at other times he became a privileged prisoner. However, the Counter-Intelligence Corps and the International Military Tribunal lawyer Robert Kempner regularly cross-examined Philipp as they built their case against him. Philipp eventually ended up interned in the same Darmstadt POW camp as his brother Wolfgang, which was also closer to the rest of his family.

The camp was a vast complex with 20,000 prisoners. Former SS officers formed a self-appointed police force that imposed order amongst
the chaos. Prisoners lived in tents, and the conditions were as brutal as
Bamberg when the temperature dropped.[24] However, Philipp cultivated
friendships with the artists and sculptors; and he claimed later that he
wanted to devote himself to the arts and avoid politics. To pass the time,
prisoners were given musical instruments and allowed to stage plays and
operettas. For one surreal evening, former SS officers dressed up in drag
and took on the female roles to perform *The Merry Wives of Windsor* for the
other inmates. Prince Louis and Princess Peg regularly visited Philipp, and
over Christmas, in 1946, he enjoyed a week-long holiday to Wolfsgarten.[25]

Peg noted that Philipp 'outwardly looks well and seems unchanged …
but the death of his wife under such gruesome circumstances have greatly
shaken him inwardly, if not fully ground him down. A freedom-loving
artistic nature, of course, suffers from years-long imprisonment more than
the average person.'[26]

Despite the presence of Prince Wolfgang, Philipp became weakened,
demoralised and subject to swift mood changes. At one moment, he
imaged himself being fully exonerated; at darker moments, he knew the
Allies planned to put senior Nazis on trial at Nuremberg.[27] At an earlier
hearing of prisoner guards complicit in the Hadamar sanitorium killings,
the judges sentenced three of the seven defendants 'to be hanged by the
neck until dead'.[28]

London. July 1945.

In London, the people finally recognised the war was over. Four million service personnel had been demobbed and returned to civilian life.
Mistaken political consensus predicted Churchill would be swept back
to power on a tide of emotion after the war, a grateful nation thanking
him for his wartime contribution. Labour's landslide election victory on
5 July 1945 came as a shock, even to the Labour Party. Churchill had
misread the post-war public appetite for social reform and fallaciously
claimed that it would require 'some form of Gestapo' to impose socialism
on Britain.[29]

The press proved themselves rotten tipsters, by prophesying a massive
Conservative majority of 100. Lord Beaverbrook heard the surprise news
while dining at Claridge's just as he was expecting to toast Churchill's
return with champagne. Labour won an extra 239 seats in Parliament and
the Conservatives lost 190 seats.[30] Symbolically, as Clement Attlee drove

cautiously into Buckingham Palace's forecourt to take up his premiership in his modest Standard saloon, a chauffeur-driven Rolls-Royce swooped past in the opposite direction. Puffing on his Havana cigar, Churchill sat in the back seat, rejected by the nation for his politics, although his popularity remained high. Attlee's total lack of charisma, in comparison to the power of his new political position, remained a puzzle to Churchill, who never appreciated his quiet competence.[31] Droll insults were heaped upon the new Prime Minister as Churchill's crushing wit described him privately: 'Mr Attlee is a very modest man. But then he has much to be modest about',[32] 'A sheep, in sheep's clothing,' and 'an empty taxi arrived at 10 Downing Street, and when the door opened, Attlee got out'.[33]

On the day of Churchill's departure, the King wrote in his diary, 'A very sad meeting.'[34] George VI told Churchill that the British people were very ungrateful 'after the way they had been led in the War'.[35] George VI's mood was glum as he privately struggled over the future of the monarchy.[36] He must have mused over the security of his Crown and the steadfastness of Attlee's untested socialist government. The Second World War had thrown people together as never before, and the mood was for change as social transformation swept through Britain. People even dared to question the point of having a Royal Family. Class dominated society in 1945: it subjugated and divided the country. The left-wing *Daily Mirror* accused the aristocracy of being 'treacherous upper crust riff-raff'[37] who championed Hitler.

Since Victory in Europe (VE) Day on 8 May 1945, when the Allies celebrated Germany's unconditional surrender of all its armed forces, irrefutable evidence of Nazi brutality appeared in the news footage from Auschwitz, Dachau and other concentration camps, which horrified the world. George VI and Churchill established a steadfast public relations campaign to prevent pre-war contacts between the House of Windsor and the Third Reich ever becoming known.

Marburg Castle, Germany. July 1945.

Under what was known as the Goldcup Plan, the Allies had been plotting the capture of secret German documents for several years. British Lieutenant Robert Currie, who worked at the Foreign Office, had devised a joint policy with the Americans for dealing with any vital archives. He drafted a blacklist of high-value targets focusing on the records of Hitler and Ribbentrop, and by January 1945 the mission employed 287 officers and 900 soldiers.[38]

In July 1945, a group of international historians led by Colonel 'Tommy' Thomson of the British Foreign Office and Dr W.R. Perkins of the US State Department started to sift through the official German archives at Marburg Castle in Hesse: 485 tonnes of documents and 60 tonnes of books.[39] Soon, documents relating to Anglo-German family relations started to make unsolicited appearances. First, an unwelcomed account of the Hesse family's visit to Britain in 1936 emerged; next, the historians discovered letters exposing Hitler's attempt to use the Kaiser as an intermediary between Germany and his British royal cousins. Several damning telegrams then appeared that recorded that the Duke of Windsor had met Nazi officials in Lisbon in 1940.[40]

While in Germany, Thomson was approached by a mysterious German called Carl von Loesch, who had worked as the understudy to Hitler's personal interpreter Dr Paul Otto Schmidt. When the State Secretary at the German Foreign Office, Ernst von Weizsäcker, evacuated his office, Loesch removed microfilm of the most secret German archives from 1933 onwards, packed them in a metal container and buried them in the grounds of a country estate in Mühlhausen, Thuringia. In return for revealing this secret treasure, Loesch wanted to elude any trial and be flown to Britain to start a new life. His mother had been English, and he had been born in London.[41]

For Currie, finding Loesch was a miracle. As early as 30 April 1945, a top-secret CIOS (Combined Intelligence Objective Subcommittee) memorandum described how Loesch had hidden thirty cases of German Foreign Office documents and recommended that it was a priority to find him 'if possible'. On 14 May, just five days after Germany's unconditional surrender, Loesch, Thomson, Dr Ralph Collins of the US State Department and a bodyguard called Captain Albert Folkard drove towards a forest near Mühlhausen to retrieve the buried documents. Thomson wrote:

> We had to descend, rather uncomfortably, a steep ravine banked with pine trees. Our guide halted at a certain spot, and he and Captain Folkard with iron bars soon scraped the soil from a waterproof cape covering a large battered metal can. This Captain Folkard brought to the top of the declivity and place under guard at the mansion.[42]

An armoured car took the canister containing thirty rolls of microfilm back to Marburg Castle. The documents detailing the Duke and Duchess of Windsor's wartime activities were marked B15, from B002527 to

B003018. The Duke was portrayed as a man who was dissatisfied with his position, disloyal to the Royal Family and unpatriotic. Most of the material came from their stopovers in Madrid and Lisbon, where their loose tongues and snide remarks were recorded by German diplomats. Not only was the Duke highly critical of Churchill, but he believed that if he had remained King, he would have stopped the war. He even hoped that the severe bombing of British cities would force Churchill to negotiate with Nazi Germany.[43]

Edward immediately resigned from his governorship of the Bahamas after the war ended. He and Wallis checked into their favourite suite at Waldorf Towers in New York, unaware of the incriminating discoveries at Marburg. For the next twelve years, the British government, Churchill and George VI fought a battle both diplomatically and politically with the Americans to prevent the Duke's actions ever becoming public. Churchill wrote first to President Eisenhower requesting a full embargo on sensitive information for at least ten or twenty years.[44] Then to Attlee, 'I earnestly trust it may be possible to destroy all traces of these German intrigues.' The new Labour Prime Minister was equally willing to aid the cover-up, considering the documents had 'little or no credence' and 'might do the greatest possible harm'.[45] The unanimous decision within the Cabinet was to destroy them.

That summer, Attlee was a guest of the King and Queen at Balmoral, for the traditional Prime Minister's weekend. George VI was delighted by Attlee's attitude towards the Duke of Windsor when they discussed the irksome ex-king during their walks across the Scottish moors. He told Queen Mary that Attlee 'agrees with me that he [the Duke of Windsor] cannot live here permanently owing to his wife and he is not prepared to offer D a job here or anywhere'.[46]

Certain critical documents still remained undiscovered, including details of the Duke of Windsor's private conversation over tea at Berchtesgaden on 22 October 1937. Before the war, the Duke had spent time with his German cousins Charles Edward, Duke of Coburg, and Prince Philipp of Hesse. Both were now on trial for war crimes thanks to their intimacy with Hitler and the Nazi Party. Rumours circulated that the Duke of Windsor and Prince Philipp met in secret to discuss a negotiated peace settlement.[47] George VI himself was also compromised. He was party to the diplomatic activities of his younger brother, the Duke of Kent, who also met Prince Philipp of Hesse in Florence in 1939, and possibly Lisbon in 1940.[48]

George VI now fought to save the tainted reputation of the House of Windsor, and Anglo-German family ties quickly became a sensitive subject. The King instigated a clean-up operation designed to save the family from 'archival embarrassment'.[49] Two royal agents – Major Anthony Blunt and Sir Owen Morshead – were dispatched to Germany by George VI as early as August 1945 to gather up incriminating evidence and transfer any documents to the safety of Windsor Castle.

Sir Owen Morshead was a highly decorated army officer and had the urbane charm of a palace courtier, moderately good looks, and a predisposed deference, which the Windsors appreciated.[50] Anthony Blunt was the newly appointed Surveyor of the King's Pictures. He was a former member of British Intelligence – the counterintelligence branch, MI5. He also spoke German and was a third cousin to Queen Elizabeth, the Queen Mother. Blunt and the Queen often shared gossipy evenings in the royal box at Covent Garden opera.[51] The Queen, like many at the Palace, observed Blunt's champagne socialism with wry scepticism, not knowing the depth of his commitment. However, while at Cambridge University, the Russians secretly recruited Blunt into a Soviet spy ring along with Guy Burgess, Kim Philby and Donald Maclean.

Friedrichshof Castle. August 1945.

Morshead and Blunt made an unlikely but flamboyant duo as they landed at Frankfurt airport on 3 August 1945. Officially, they were to retrieve from Friedrichshof Castle the so-called 'Vicky letters'. These were the letters between Queen Victoria and her eldest daughter Vicky, who married the German Emperor Frederick and was the mother of Kaiser Wilhelm II.[52] However, many historians argue that Blunt was searching for the Duke of Windsor's correspondence to his cousin Prince Philipp of Hesse. Such letters might reveal the Duke's Nazi sympathies, including the fact that he passed secrets to Hitler. A witness statement supports this theory of a cover-up. Historian Douglas Price was stationed at Friedrichshof in the summer of 1945 when serving as an aide to General Dwight D. Eisenhower. He often visited the library, and in one corner Price found an ornate cabinet which contained letters between the Hesse family and the Duke of Windsor, dating back to when he had been Prince of Wales. Rumours have persisted that these were the real documents that Blunt was looking to retrieve.[53]

Blunt and Morshead landed in Germany and headed first to Wolfsgarten for three days. They showered the Hesse family, whom Morshead knew, with gifts including 'vitamin preparations, toilet paper, soap, tea, coffee, matches ... and chocolate'[54] – all luxuries that in Germany were now sorely missed. Then Morshead visited the elderly Princess Margaret, who regardless of her English origins now loathed the British after her three sons had died in both world wars. Morshead had to convince the Princess that the documents he was looking for would be safer at Windsor Castle. Accompanying him was Princess Sophie, and the pair had clambered into a borrowed Rolls-Royce with a cluster of children, their pet dog and a tame wild boar called Bambi. Morshead's considerable charm, gifts of chocolate and Princess Sophie's presence did the trick. Princess Margaret signed a document allowing for the papers stored at Friedrichshof to be released.[55]

Occupied by the Americans, Friedrichshof Castle was now under the management of Captain Kathleen Nash. She was short, plump, unassuming and dishonest. On her enlistment papers, Nash stated her age as 30; in fact, Nash was nine years older. She had also neglected to mention that she had two grown-up children from a marriage that had ended in divorce.[56] She had further encouraged the looting at the castle, and at the 4 July celebrations 'dolls, harmonicas, stockings and dresses [were] taken from the castle' and given away to US military units as 'prizes at parties, bingo games, and so forth'.[57]

Captain Nash had probably never met anyone quite like Blunt or Morshead before. In one version of the story, Blunt insisted that Churchill supported their mission. When Nash left the room to phone headquarters to check these facts, Morshead and two British privates loaded two trunks containing the documents from the library onto an army truck and drove off into the night. In another version, promoted by journalist and espionage expert Chapman Pincher, Nash refused Blunt and Morshead entry to the castle, so Princess Margaret directed the pair to a backdoor entrance where the two men broke in and retrieved the letters at night. Whatever the truth is to the story, crates of documents were removed and sent back to the Royal Archives at Windsor.[58]

Kathleen Nash had a good reason for prohibiting any access to Friedrichshof. Together with her lover, Colonel Jack Durant, a handsome 38-year-old hard-drinking staff officer, she had discovered the Hessian crown jewels which had been secretly buried in the castle cellar for safety. While Blunt and Morshead were attempting to search for embarrassing royal letters, Nash was secretly shipping this valuable plunder worth millions back to the United States.

Nash discovered the jewels when a member of her staff, Roy Carlton, found two electrical wires running directly into what appeared to be a solid foundation wall in the cellar. As the brickwork looked very recent, Nash ordered Carlton to take a sledgehammer and smash through the wall. Together, they found a secret room containing 1,238 bottles of vintage wine dating back to 1834. When they removed the bottles, they noticed a second potential hiding place on the floor. Digging down into the concrete, Carlton unearthed a casket the size of a wine box. Using a crowbar to open it, he then punched through a zinc lining to reveal dozens of small brown paper packages inside.[59] Nash and Carlton just stood stunned – then burst out laughing. Inside were priceless royal heirlooms. Nine studded diamond tiaras, a wristwatch that glittered with so many gems it was hard to tell the time, a bracelet with 365 large diamonds, two Fabergé eggs, a 12-carat diamond ring, various necklaces and hundreds of other gold and platinum pieces. Someone had individually wrapped the jewels and placed them in a zinc-lined casket for protection.[60]

After paying Roy Carlton off with a few items to keep him quiet, Nash and Durant hatched a plan to break down all the pieces and sell whatever they could to dealers in London and Switzerland, and then mail the rest back to the United States. A total of thirty packages were sent to family members in the United States.[61] It was arguably the heist of the century: valued in 1945 at £2 million, the jewels would in today's terms be worth £30 million. Looting German treasures was legally ambiguous: 'The American soldiers took "souvenirs", and those in the Red Army took "loot".'[62] The Western Allies prohibited the seizing of art and cultural property, and compared to the Soviet trophy brigades they behaved marginally better. When the Hesse family discovered their jewels were missing, the American military police were informed and immediately started their investigations. By then Kathleen Nash had left Germany and was back home in the United States, where she and Durant were living it up at La Salle Hotel in Chicago.[63]

Questioned by both military and FBI investigators, and given a lie detector test, Kathleen broke down and revealed the locations of the missing jewels: a house in Wisconsin and lockers at the Chicago railway terminal.[64] The police sent what remained of the stolen jewels to the Pentagon, where officials made an inventory. Secretaries who worked there took delight in modelling the jewels for court photographers. Military chiefs who viewed the haul were dazzled, but one piece was damaging evidence to the Hesse family's reputation – a large Nazi emblem in solid gold.[65]

The case against Nash and Durant came before the military court in October 1946. Nash received a five-year sentence, and Durant, as the most senior ranking officer, got fifteen years.[66] Strangely, despite being probably the most significant jewel theft of the century, the publicity was minimal. The *New York Times* gave a detailed report, but the robbery made American troops stationed in Germany look like dishonest looters, and the story quickly died. Journalists made no connections between Prince Philipp of Hesse, Princess Sophie or Prince Philip, despite the fact Philip had started to feature regularly in London's society columns.

Buckingham Palace. January 1946.

Prince Philip of Greece's involvement with the war ended when his ship HMS *Whelp* sailed back to Britain in January 1946, and he quickly reunited with his sweetheart. The first night he obtained leave, he headed to Buckingham Palace, where Princess Elizabeth entertained him at dinner and her giggling sister Margaret acted as a chaperone. He could not believe his good fortune and wrote to the Queen:

> I am sure I do not deserve all the good things that have happened to me ... To have been spared the war and seen victory, to have been given the chance to rest and re-adjust myself, to have fallen in love completely and undeservedly ... The generous hospitality and the warm friendliness did much to restore my faith in permanent values and brighten up a rather warped view of life.[67]

The Queen was not entirely impressed with the letter; she found Philip's family connections to Germany extremely unwelcome. She loathed Germans: to her, they were vermin, solely responsible for starting the war. Of all the nations in the world from which her daughter could have chosen a husband, she must have hoped Elizabeth would have cold-shouldered the Germans.

Two months later, Philip packed a bag and travelled across Europe to slip into Germany and attend his sister Sophie's wedding to Prince George William of Hanover on 23 April 1946. He came loaded with essential provisions from Britain as well as the traditional wedding gifts. Sophie had not seen Philip for nine years, and when they had last met in 1937, he had been just 16 years old. The Princess was shocked to see how closely he resembled their late father Prince Andrew of Greece, who had died in 1944, with 'the same mannerisms, movements, ways of standing, walking laughing ... The

colossal sense of humour, really seeing the funny side of things always ...'[68]
He told his sister that he was thinking about getting engaged.

The following month, Philip was back in England. On 29 May, the
press photographed him standing beside Princess Elizabeth at the wedding
of her lady-in-waiting Jean Gibbs to Andrew Elphinstone (Elizabeth's
cousin on her mother's side). Their courtship was entering a more serious
mode, so the Queen invited Philip to Balmoral for three weeks – which
amounted to putting the young suitor through his paces under the various guises of deerstalking, sporting events, royal formalities, horse riding
and games of charades. Antlers, stags' heads, hides hung as tapestries, brass
bedsteads and paintings of Landseer dogs filled the castle. There was no
running water or private bathrooms in any of the bedrooms, and staff
brought guests hot water – brownish peat water – in cans. The enormous Victorian loos had mahogany armrests and basketwork lids, and
when you pulled the handle, it set off volcanic gurgles.[69] However, a long
romantic walk ended with a proposal, as Philip and Elizabeth sat on the
heather beside a loch. Philip dared to bypass the King's traditional permission to ask his bride directly. He oozed an appealing quality of rudeness
in a world of deference, unbound by the conventions Princess Elizabeth
slavishly observed.[70]

Guests at Balmoral, however, found Philip somewhat 'unpolished'[71] as
he possessed no plus fours and went shooting in flannel trousers, and even
had to borrow a gun, while the gamekeepers muttered about his 'rather
erratic' shooting style.[72] However, the King agreed in principle to let them
marry. Still, he insisted on no formal announcement until the following
year, when the family had completed an overseas royal tour together to
South Africa, by which time Elizabeth would be 21. It was a carefully
planned delaying tactic. The King felt his daughter was too young, while
in the Queen's mind Philip was still a 'Charlie Kraut'[73] whose sisters were
all married to former Nazi officers. When speaking to her disciples in the
royal household, she secretly called him 'The Hun'. It was a severely with-
ering term to use after the bloody war that had just ended.

The Queen's brother, the Honourable David Bowes-Lyon, led a group
of peers, including Lords Salisbury, Stanley and Eldon, who opposed
the match. 'Who is this exiled and penniless Prince of Greece?' they
demanded. They declared him a nobody, 'a prince of nowhere'.[74] In their
view, Philip was spiky, arrogant and Teutonic; a rootless and penniless son
of a disreputable minor Danish-German-Greek dynasty. The Princess's
cousin, Margaret Rhodes, regarded him as a 'foreign interloper out for the

goodies'[75] as Philip's total income from the navy was just £11 a week.[76] A pauper prince, his grandmother, Lady Milford Haven, paid for his tailor's bills at Gieves & Hawkes in Savile Row, and during a Christmas visit to Sandringham before the wedding, he wore his late father's repaired hand-me-down clothes and borrowed a bow tie.[77]

The Queen's superficial sweetness hid an imperial iron will, and she devised a so-called 'cricket list' or 'First XI' of suitable young gentlemen and paraded them before her daughter at weekends, hoping this might spark some romantic interest. 'There was a whole battalion of lively young men,' stated Lady Anne Glenconner.[78] They included Sonny Blandford, the Duke of Marlborough, Johnny Dalkeith, heir to the Duke of Buccleuch, and 'Porchy' Porchester, heir to the Earl of Carnarvon, but the Queen's marital mission failed.[79] Princess Elizabeth's most prominent and only act of rebellion was her choice of husband. Faced with her daughter's unexpected strength of will, Queen Elizabeth was forced, for once, to give in. She complained to her dear friend, Lady Hardinge: 'The trouble is that Philip is so impossibly attractive, and Lilibet [Princess Elizabeth] just cannot see beyond that.'[80]

Soon, there was a standoff between the British Establishment's old guard and this young naval officer. Although the aristocracy surrounding the Royal Family did what they often did concerning an outsider and closed ranks, Philip refused to let them intimidate him.

A PRECARIOUS DYNASTY

Westminster Abbey, London. 20 November 1947.
Winston Churchill timed his unpunctual entrance to perfection. The former Prime Minister and his wife, Clementine, appeared just moments before the royal wedding party were due to arrive.[1] An ear-splitting roar grew from the crowded streets surrounding Westminster Abbey, growing increasingly loud and thunderous, cheering not the Royal Family, but Churchill. The noise filled the nave and transepts. As the Churchills walked up the scarlet carpet, all 2,500 guests inside the abbey – including four foreign kings, five queens and the Shah of Iran – rose to their feet. Just two years after the Second World War, everyone stood for Churchill. His political rival, Prime Minister Attlee, could only look on in grim frustration.[2] Churchill felt himself the greater man, trouncing Attlee's diligence with the iambic pentameter of his oratory and his insatiable hunger for glory. With the entire world watching, the incumbent Prime Minister found himself eclipsed by his predecessor. Although there had been much public grumbling about the cost of this wedding, Churchill had pronounced, quoting Ulysses in *Troilus and Cressida*, 'Millions will welcome this joyous event as a flash of colour on the hard road we have to travel.'[3] Attlee agreed with him, believing that a ceremonial monarchy was an excellent democratic alternative to either fascism or communism.[4]

Princess Elizabeth was about to marry Prince Philip of Greece, who had anglicised his name to Lieutenant Philip Mountbatten RN. Philip wasn't ethnically Greek, but had a mix of German and Danish blood, and his actual surname was Schleswig-Holstein-Sonderburg-Glücksburg. The couple were third cousins as great-great-grandchildren of Queen Victoria, and both were part of that enmeshed Anglo-German family network which the war had stretched to breaking point. Any British blood that the bride had came from Queen Elizabeth, her mother. If on the day of the royal wedding, anyone was unwise enough to mention the 'German' side of the family, they did so discreetly.

Inside Westminster Abbey, the old privileged elite looked unrivalled and seemed untouchable. Captured on film in full technicolour, the mother of the bride gave Winston Churchill a regal smile reserved for her closest allies.[5] Neither Queen Elizabeth nor Churchill had wanted this wedding. Beaming for the cameras under a concoction of apricot ostrich feathers and with her ample bosom wrapped in a matching silk dress with gold brocade, she, like Churchill, had graciously accepted her defeat over the issue of Philip.

The congregation sat expectantly, and the thin November sunshine patterned the walls with bright colours through the stained-glass window. The court ladies wore stunning long dresses, elbow-length white gloves and tiaras, while the men wore morning dress. There were visiting maharajahs in silk turbans; Arab sheikhs arrived dressed in their white robes; officers showed off bright red-and-blue uniforms, their rows of medals glinting under the ceiling lights. Dowagers looked like Christmas trees decked out in the family diamonds that had been removed from storage and dusted down. Queen Juliana of the Netherlands caused a stir, making scathing comments disparaging the jewellery. The pieces were 'so dirty',[6] she kept saying, noticing that many diamonds weren't sufficiently polished. The style was down-at-heel glamour, and anyone fortunate enough to have a new dress drew envious eyes. The eccentric Lady Munnings sat through the whole service with her Pekinese dog, Black Knight, concealed in her muff.[7]

Outside, the people in the streets were waiting. The public had initially been hostile to Prince Philip, and a poll in the *Sunday Pictorial* taken in January 1947 found that 40 per cent of the people surveyed were against Princess Elizabeth's wedding to Philip because of his Greek nationality and family background with ties to fascism. However, gradually the mood changed, and dissenting voices died out because Elizabeth was in love. Many people just wanted to get out the bunting and have a knees-up. The night before the wedding, some Londoners had laid out their old Blitz mattresses and blankets, so they could sit through the darkness and reserve good vantage points to watch the pageant pass. In the morning, women washed in hot water from vacuum flasks before putting on their make-up.[8] There were picnic breakfasts, families cooking bacon over little stoves and the smell of coffee filled the air.[9] A myriad of homemade periscopes, simple mirrors attached to sticks, danced like 'crystallised sunshine'[10] above the dense crowds when the light finally broke through the clouds. The people had waited for hours, singing 'All the Nice Girls Love a Sailor', and it seemed the war was finally over.[11]

The King had been concerned about how to propagandise this royal wedding, as the Establishment in post-war Britain was not entirely sure about the monarchy's popularity. Under a Labour government and without Churchill to protect them, George VI felt their embarrassing German relatives – on both sides of the aisle – might threaten the family's stability. To believe in the royal fairy tale, an excellent reputation was essential, and in 1947, King George became preoccupied with the consequences of his family's German connections. Four areas could still prove uncomfortable and potentially scandalous. Firstly, the fact that the King had suggested back-door peace talks with Hitler, via two royal intermediaries – the Duke of Kent and Prince Philipp of Hesse. Secondly, the Duke of Windsor's impulsive visit to Hitler in 1937 and the damaging evidence found in the Marburg File. Thirdly, the unwavering support the Duke of Coburg gave Hitler. And finally, the wartime activities of Prince Philip's Nazi brothers-in-law.

As a consequence of these wartime misdemeanours, Philip's side of the aisle looked empty as the Queen had banned Philip's three sisters – Sophie, Margarita and Theodora – from the guest list, considering them a public relations catastrophe. They remained out of sight in their various Bavarian castles, writing letters of protest at not being invited.[12] Philip had only four close family members in attendance: his mother, Princess Alice of Greece, and his maternal grandmother, Lady Milford Haven, who sat alongside his uncle and aunt, Lord and Lady Mountbatten.

Philip stood waiting at the altar, fortified by a morning gin and tonic. He had quietly entered the abbey through the Poet's Corner door and wore his British naval uniform, which was slightly shabby. This usual 'after-the-war look' was the correct form in post-war austerity Britain,[13] but it glinted with a new Garter badge pinned to his jacket.[14] The groom's uncle, Lord Mountbatten, had skilfully played up Philip's 'Britishness' to the British press barons. Jock Colville, Churchill's Private Secretary, wrote in his diary, 'An effort has been made to build him up as the nephew of Lord Louis Mountbatten, rather than a Greek prince.'[15] George VI had completed Philip's 'transmogrification'[16] from a foreign prince into an Englishman by creating him the Duke of Edinburgh, Earl of Merioneth and Baron Greenwich the day before the wedding. It was a useful camouflage.

Princess Elizabeth had got what she wanted. She was clearly in love, and Philip was tall, with piercing blue eyes and blond hair, exuding confidence, in control and rebellious. When the Princess arrived at the abbey, the crowds reacted with a second wave of approval. It took the bride's ethereal beauty to upstage Churchill. When the Irish State Coach drew up outside, Princess Elizabeth stepped out, looking 'shy and attractive'.[17] The wedding gown was a triumph for the designer, Norman Hartnell, who roamed the London art galleries for inspiration and found a Botticelli figure in clinging ivory silk.[18] The result cost £1,200 (£40,000 in today's money), and 300 clothing coupons.[19] The fashion maestro announced to a xenophobic nation that the ivory silk dress was made from patriotic Nationalist Chinese silkworms and not those of evil Japan after press speculation had erupted.[20] It was the worst possible time, even for silkworms, to be allied to an enemy country.

On the bride's side of the aisle, there were two conspicuous absentees. The first was her great-uncle, Charles Edward, Duke of Coburg, although his sister Princess Alice, Countess of Athlone, was a prominent guest sitting next to Queen Mary. Furthermore, amongst the white orchids in the bride's bouquet was a sprig of myrtle grown at Queen Victoria's seaside home, Osbourne House. It was a family tradition, as Prince Albert had imported the myrtle bush from Coburg.[21]

The second family member missing was the bride's uncle, the Duke of Windsor. George VI was insistent on his brother's continued banishment to France. Unknown to the British public at the time was the extent of the Duke's interest with the Nazi Party during the 1930s. To protect the monarchy, George VI and Queen Elizabeth conducted an almost religious censorship of public records to ensure his treachery remained a secret. However, the Queen flatly declared that she would not attend her daughter's wedding if the loathsome Duke were present.[22]

Coburg. December 1947.

After the wedding, George VI finally permitted Princess Alice, Countess of Athlone, to visit her brother in Germany. That December, Alice and her husband made the journey across war-shattered Europe to Coburg. Charles Edward had been released from prison and was living with his wife Princess Victoria Adelaide, Duchess of Coburg, in a tiny cottage near

Callenburg Castle, one of their homes which had been requisition by the Americans for refugees. 'It was sad and sordid,' concluded Alice.[23]

Alice found her brother a broken man and crippled with arthritis. His son Prince Hubertus, a courier pilot in the Luftwaffe, had been fatally shot down by Russians on the Eastern Front and the Soviets had seized the family estates in Gotha, which was now part of East Germany. Princess Alice and Lord Athlone stayed at a local hotel and they did everything in their power to help Charles Edward. They hassled the local American officials – who were 'all odious' – to provide the Duke and Duchess with better accommodation, which worked. After many rebuffs, Charles Edward and Victoria Adelaide moved into a more comfortable house in Coburg.

Despite the horrors of the concentration camps, Alice's anti-Semitism and racism remained unfaltering, and in her memoirs she wrote:

> In our efforts to do something for Uncle Charlie, Grandpa [Lord Athlone] and I humiliated ourselves by dining with the US Governor of Coburg, a Syrian by birth. We also called on and lunched with his successor, a Jewish-French American whom we did not think a suitable representative of his great country nor the sort of person one would select to instruct the Germans in democracy![24]

Charles Edward still had to face a denazification trial. After the publicity surrounding the Nuremberg Trials – where an international panel of judges had sentenced twenty-four leading Nazis such as Ribbentrop and Göring to death for participating in the Holocaust and other international war crimes – he was fearful about the verdict. However, the Allied Control Council Law No. 10 of December 1945 authorised the German courts to pass sentence on atrocities committed during the war years by German citizens against other German nationals. The Duke of Coburg fell into this category, and the prosecution team charged Charles Edward with 'crimes against humanity' as a Category 1 'Major Offender', which carried the death sentence.

As Charles Edward was in the hospital having the malignant tumour near his left eye treated, he was tried in absentia.[25] His wife Victoria Adelaide testified on his behalf. She stated that Charles Edward agreed with Hitler's efforts to lead the German people out of their misery after the First World War. However, he had only stayed loyal to the Nazi Party because he thought the party would eventually negotiate peace terms. Although he considered resigning from his presidency of the German

Red Cross, he never did so because it was dangerous to resign from posts in Hitler's Germany.[26]

In August 1949, the courts exonerated Charles Edward of complicity in actual war crimes. They declared him 'an important Nazi' and only his failing health saved him from another lengthy prison sentence.[27] He was eventually sentenced to the lesser crime of being a Category 4 'Fellow Traveller' and fined. Another factor for leniency towards him was the fact that, in April 1946, his daughter Sibylla had a baby boy, the future King Carl XVI Gustaf of Sweden. It would have been embarrassing for the Swedish Royal Family to have a war criminal for their King's grandfather.

After the war, the Duke and Duchess spent most of their time at the picturesque Greinburg Castle on the Danube River in Austria, where they tried to rewrite history.[28] Victoria Adelaide claimed in an interview that the Duke never entertained leading Nazis because he was a 'very modest and shy man'.[29] While Charles Edward boldly stated that 'on my foreign trips I never made any propaganda' for the Nazis.[30]

To the end, Princess Alice fervently believed 'her brother had been a victim of history', otherwise 'how could she logically explain his actions'.[31] She wrote: 'Fate plays a part in our lives and sometimes forces us into situations to which we must adapt ourselves – often against our inclinations. Several members of my family, including my own brother, found themselves encompassed by the fatal hands of fortune.'[32]

To avoid fines and ruinous taxes, Charles Edward decided to resign as the primary beneficiary of the Coburg Foundation which he had established in 1920. Control of the duchy and the family's two remaining castles of Greinburg and Callenberg, together with their farming estates and substantial real estate, passed to his son Prince Friedrich Josias of Saxe-Coburg and grandson Prince Andreas. As well as great inherited wealth, his heirs received a bitter legacy. Andreas wrote about his grandfather: 'Yet, victim or not, he willingly associated with the regime and supported Hitler's rise to power. There is nothing that can absolve him ...'[33]

Darmstadt POW Camp. 15–17 December 1947.

Between 15 and 17 December 1947, Prince Philipp of Hesse was cross-examined by the Denazification Tribunal inside the Darmstadt POW camp. Although the Americans monitored the trials, Dr Hans Quambusch chaired the five-member German tribunal[34] and prosecutors charged Philipp with three significant offences: 'helping bring Hitler to power, convincing Mussolini to accept the *Anschluss*, and facilitating the murders at Hadamar.'[35]

The tribunal classified him as a 'Major Offender' Category 1. Meanwhile, the criminal court in Frankfurt started to collect evidence to support a murder charge. The prosecutors pointed to his various posts and honours: *Oberpräsident* (Governor), *SA-Obergruppenführer* (Senior Group Leader), recipient of the Nazi Golden Party Badge, as well as his activities as a go-between with international leaders including Mussolini and Prince Paul of Yugoslavia.[36]

Although the tribunal was not a show trial like Nuremberg, it attracted press attention. However, there were very few incriminating documents for the prosecutors to find as the Allies had bombed the Governor's office in Kassel, and the Nazis had confiscated many records in 1943 when the Gestapo had arrested Philipp and Mafalda.[37] Philipp's defence lawyer, Fabian von Schlabrendorff – who Philipp had met in Flossenbürg concentration camp in April 1945 – paraded seventeen sympathetic witnesses before the judges in the gloomy makeshift courtroom. They were mostly old and influential friends who pointed out the terrible hardships Philipp had suffered since Mafalda's death and the popularity of the Hesse family locally.[38]

Schlabrendorff was a brilliant choice politically. He had been a member of the German resistance, and like so many Germans, Philipp attempted to present himself as a fellow member using his Gestapo arrest as proof of his defiance towards Hitler's regime.[39] Questions nevertheless became intense when prosecutors questioned Philipp about his involvement in the T-4 euthanasia programme and the persecution of Jews.[40]

The Darmstadt tribunal found Philipp guilty of being a Category 2 'Offender'. This ruling classed him as a Nazi militant activist and profiteer, with a prison sentence of up to ten years performing reparation or reconstruction work as well as other restrictions including loss of voting rights, a ban on holding public office, a ban on owning a car and a forfeiture of 30 per cent of his property. In the end, Dr Quambusch sentenced him to a mere two years, counting his 'political incarceration after 8 May 1945' as time served.[41] Philipp walked free that day. In summing up, the judges stated:

> With his compete repudiation and total obliviousness of the mentality of other people, he was in all earnestness filled with madness. With regards to foreign governments, he thought he could push through the same clumsy ruses and use the brutally violent methods with which he

successfully deceived honest people. With all his evil instincts that gave rise to inexpressible suffering, he proved at the end how deep people can sink if they have been robbed of their freedom.[42]

Philipp was unhappy with this verdict, and he hired a new lawyer, Ferdinand de la Fontaine, who argued that the Prince should be classified as a Category 5 'Person Exonerated', claiming he had worked with Crown Prince Umberto of Italy 'in toppling the Fascist regime' of Mussolini,[43] although there was no evidence to support his 'active resistance'.[44] The tribunal acknowledged that the Nazi regime had victimised him and his family. Finally, he was declared a Category 3 'Lesser Offender' with a reduced fine of 20,000 deutschmarks.[45]

As Philipp's financial affairs were muddled, proving the extent of his wealth was almost impossible. Ultimately, he delayed, obscured and confounded the authorities for five years and eventually paid 36,568 reichsmarks. This amount was a modest sum considering his estimated net worth at the time was at least 686,000 reichsmarks, which was a 'suspiciously low'[46] figure considering his assets. In 1950, his lawyers petitioned for a reduction in his sentence, and they were successful. He was placed in Category 4 as a 'Fellow Traveller', although he still considered himself victimised and remained bitter.[47]

Philipp's two brothers, Prince Wolfgang and Prince Richard, were also subjected to the denazification trials and received lenient sentences. Richard was initially placed in Category 3 'Lesser Offender' in April 1948, but had his sentence reduced the following year to Category 4 'Fellow Traveller'. Wolfgang had been released early in November 1946, and the tribunal completely exonerated him at his hearing in June 1948.

After the war, the Allies charged 3.5 million Germans they deemed part of the Nazi war machine, but they released 2.5 million without trial. Most of the million people left faced no harsher punishment than a fine, confiscation of property they had looted, or a temporary employment restriction. Of the twenty-four most senior Nazis prosecuted at Nuremberg, the court sentenced twelve to death by hanging on 16 October 1945, including Ribbentrop, while Göring escaped execution by swallowing a potassium cyanide capsule the night before.

The Allies were more fearful of the Soviet Union and the new Cold War than any latent Nazism inside Germany. It became vital to bolster West Germany against the Eastern Bloc beyond the Iron Curtain. Accordingly, the German courts downgraded many charges and allowed war criminals back into German society. By the end of 1946 alone, tribunals dismissed 70 per cent of all the tribunals' pending cases. By 1948, they had acquitted the vast majority of all Category 1–3 offenders. The summary proceedings of most trials left insufficient time to thoroughly investigate the accused, so that many of the judgements of this period have questionable value. As a result, the court system facilitated Germany's desire to forget their history. By 1949, only 300 Nazis remained in prison.

EPILOGUE

During the 1950s, the Hesse brothers, like many Germans, struggled in the post-war environment. Philipp and Wolfgang formed a partnership to oversee the family's considerable assets. The Hesse family was still incredibly wealthy, owning hotels, property, vineyards, and what is considered the most exquisite private art collection in Germany. Wolfgang as an ex-banker focused on the business side of the family estates, and it was his idea to turn Friedrichshof Castle into a luxury hotel in 1954. Philipp used his artistic talents to reconstruct their damaged property and catalogue the family's vast art collection. He turned Adolphseck Castle, an enormous baroque palace outside Fulda, into a museum and renamed it Fasanerie Castle. Today it contains much of the Hesse family's collection of porcelain, art and furniture.[1]

Prince Philipp completely retreated from public life and divided his time between his former villa in Rome and a restored medieval tower that stood amongst the ruins of the old castle next to Friedrichshof. He visited old friends such as the Duke and Duchess of Windsor in Paris and tended to associate with members of the old aristocracy, like the Bismarck family, who had tarnished reputations after the war. Philipp continued to elicit sympathy from extreme right-wingers until his death, aged 84, in Rome.

Princess Sophie of Hesse (now Princess George of Hanover) struggled in post-war Germany. Although excluded from her brother's wedding, she finally visited him at Windlesham House in Surrey in 1948, the private country home of Prince Philip and Princess Elizabeth until she became Queen. Princess Elizabeth and Princess Sophie became friends after a shopping trip in Knightsbridge with Sophie's two teenage daughters –

Christina and Dorothea of Hesse – and 'normal family relations were now resumed'.[2] Philip's remaining two sisters, Margarita and Theodora, visited later that year.

The Nazi connections of the Duke of Edinburgh remain a highly sensitive subject. Still, when the Coronation occurred on 2 June 1953, Sophie, Margarita and Theodora were permitted to attend the ceremony in Westminster Abbey with their mother Princess Andrew (Alice) of Greece. They sat in the royal box behind the Queen Mother and the British royal princesses – including Princess Alice, Countess of Athlone.

After walking free from the denazification courts, Charles Edward, Duke of Coburg, found himself permanently excluded by his British relatives. He watched the Coronation at a local cinema in Coburg. He died the following year on 6 March 1954 from cancer in his apartment on Elsässer Straße in central Coburg. His sister Princess Alice occasionally visited, but lived out the rest of her life at Kensington Palace and died in her sleep aged 97 years old. At the time of her death, she was the longest-living British princess of royal blood and the last surviving grandchild of Queen Victoria.

Queen Elizabeth II and Prince Philip, Duke of Edinburgh, did not make an official royal tour of West Germany until May 1965. They waited until twenty years after the end of the Second World War. Although they toured all the major cities, including Bonn, Cologne, Munich and Stuttgart, they studiously avoided the town of Coburg. A file in The National Archives at Kew reads: 'Saxe-Coburg-Gotha: denazification Duke and guardianship grandson'. Inspecting such documents is impossible, as the Foreign Office bars the general public. Other files relating to the interests of the Royal Family in the Saxe-Coburg properties in Austria and Germany also remain sealed. Both files are dated 1947, the year of the royal wedding.[3] Today, these files are exempt from the Freedom of Information Act and protected by Royal Privilege.

After the war, the King met the Duke of Windsor twice in October 1945 and made it clear that his residence in Britain would be unwelcome, and that there would be no special diplomatic appointment either in France or America, which his brother wanted.[4] When George VI died, the Duke returned to London to attend his brother's public funeral and to check that the family was going to maintain his allowance. During this visit, he described his mother, Queen Mary, as 'Mama as hard as nails but failing', and his brother's widow as 'Mrs Shirley Temple Senior'.[5] Queen Elizabeth, now the Queen Mother, took the view that if Edward had not abdicated, her husband would still be alive.

The Duke and Duchess of Windsor had no choice but to remain in France. Their home was a stately villa on the Bois de Boulogne in Paris, a picturesque farmhouse for weekends just outside Versailles called Le Moulin des Tuileries, and an apartment at the Waldorf Towers in New York. For the rest of their lives, they ate at the best restaurants, shopped at the best stores and never ran out of caviar. They rarely paid for anything, including tax, and perfected the art of sybaritic living. They were often bored, and their social circle often scratched over petty spites and who collaborated during the war.[6] One day at lunch, a head waiter offered to show the Duke a souvenir pencil from 1936 that the restaurant had made to celebrate Edward's coronation which had never happened. By all means, the Duke said, with what passed for a royal smile. The waiter produced a pencil, but it was now only 2 inches long. On top was Edward's crowned head and the Duke stared at it and whined: 'Oh look, Wallis. I'm all whittled away!'

The relationship between the Palace and the Duke of Windsor remained frosty until he died on 23 May 1972. The Duke acknowledged in his memoirs that he admired the Germans, but denied being pro-Nazi. He wrote the 'Führer struck me as a somewhat ridiculous figure with his theatrical posturing and bombastic pretensions',[7] but in private he told a friend, Lord Kinross, that 'I never thought Hitler was such a bad chap'.[8]

ACKNOWLEDGEMENTS

I would like to thank the following people who helped with the research and preparation of this book: Piers Blofeld at Sneil Land; Mark Beynon, Jess Gofton and Alex Waite at The History Press; and Dr Julie Wheelwright, Sarah Wise, Lesley Downer and Agnieska Wsol at City, University of London. I should also mention friends and family who have been supportive throughout this process: John Baldry, Sandy Culkoff, Mary-Jane Evans, Robert Hall, Caroline Haworth, Rachel Himbury, Angela Holden, Cecily Liu, Kathleen Palmer, Kim Palmer, Debyon Pinnock, Paula Read, Alan Reynolds, Patricia Turnbull, Deborah Wearn-Hall, Jacqueline Wearn and Caroline Winter-Jones.

The following archives and libraries also proved invaluable: The Bodleian Library at Oxford University (Queen Victoria's Journals); The Cadbury Research Library at Birmingham University (Neville Chamberlain's Papers); Cambridge University Library (Sassoon Papers); Chartwell House; Chichester Library; Churchill Archives at Churchill College, University of Cambridge; City, University of London Library; Chichester Library in West Sussex; FBI Archives; The Getty Archive; Hessian State Archive (Marburg and Wiesbaden in Germany); Macarthur Memorial Library; Institute for Contemporary History (Munich); National Archives and Records Administration (Maryland, USA); The National Archives at Kew (formerly the Public Records Office); The London Library; The Quaker Society of Friends Library; Royal Historical Society; Secret State Prussian Archives (Berlin); Sheffield University Library (Oswald Mosley Papers in the British Union Collection); The

United States Holocaust Memorial Museum; and the Wiener Library for the Study of the Holocaust at the University of London.

Most factual writers pluck fragments, large and small, from their predecessors' work. In writing this book I also found the works of the following historians and journalists extremely useful: Theo Aronson, Michael Bloch, Tim Bouverie, Sarah Bradford, Deborah Cadbury, Miranda Carter, Philip Eade, Greg King, Andrew Morton, John Parker, Jonathan Petropoulos, Andrew Roberts, Harald Sandner, Karina Urbach, John Van Der Kiste, Hugo Vickers, Sophie Watson, Sir John Wheeler-Bennett and Philip Ziegler.

The diaries and memoirs of Princess Alice, Countess of Athlone, Emmy Göring, Sir Henry Channon, Sir Robert Bruce Lockheart, Harold Nicholson, Princess Daisy of Pless, Lt Col Stewart Roddie, Rothay Reynolds, the Duke of Windsor and the Duchess of Windsor all provided invaluable insights into this period of history.

CHARACTER NOTES

To help the reader, I have included notes on the various Anglo-German royal cousins and their interweaving relationships. Several characters mentioned in this book also have the same first name.

Most confusing are the two princesses called Alice. The first is Princess Alice of Albany, who became Princess Alice, Countess of Athlone; and the second is Princess Alice of Battenberg, who became Princess Andrew of Greece and Denmark. She was the mother of Prince Philip, Duke of Edinburgh.

There are also a large number of royal Georges. First is King George V. Then his second eldest son was Prince Albert, Duke of York (nicknamed 'Bertie'), who assumed the name King George VI on becoming sovereign. Finally, there was George VI's youngest brother, Prince George, Duke of Kent.

There are also two Philips: Prince Philipp of Hesse and Prince Philip of Greece, who later became the Duke of Edinburgh.

House of Saxe-Coburg and Gotha

QUEEN VICTORIA
   Queen of the United Kingdom.
PRINCE ALBERT OF SAXE-COBURG-GOTHA
   Queen Victoria's husband.
PRINCE ERNST, DUKE OF SAXE-COBURG-GOTHA
   Prince Albert's elder brother.

PRINCESS VICTORIA (THE EMPRESS FREDERICK)

Eldest daughter of Queen Victoria and Prince Albert. She married the German Emperor Frederick and was the mother of Kaiser Wilhelm II.

EDWARD VII

Queen Victoria's eldest son.

PRINCE ALFRED, DUKE OF EDINBURGH AND SAXE-COBURG-GOTHA

The second-eldest son of Queen Victoria. He became the sovereign Duke of Saxe-Coburg-Gotha when his uncle Prince Ernst died.

GRAND DUCHESS MARIA OF RUSSIA

The eldest daughter of the Russian Tsar who married Prince Alfred, Duke of Edinburgh. She later became the Duchess of Saxe-Coburg-Gotha.

PRINCE ALFRED OF EDINBURGH AND HEREDITARY PRINCE OF SAXE-COBURG-GOTHA

Alfred was the only son of Duke Alfred and Grand Duchess Maria. He was known in the family as 'Affie' and died following a suicide attempt.

PRINCE LEOPOLD, DUKE OF ALBANY

Queen Victoria and Prince Albert's youngest son who died from haemophilia.

PRINCESS HELEN, DUCHESS OF ALBANY

Helen was the wife of Prince Leopold. Born Princess Helen of Waldeck and Pyrmont (in Germany).

DUKE CHARLES EDWARD OF SAXE-COBURG-GOTHA

Born Prince Charles Edward, Duke of Albany, he inherited the duchy of Saxe-Coburg and Gotha and became a German national. During the First World War, Parliament declared him a traitor, and he lost his British titles. He joined the Nazi Party in 1933.

PRINCESS ALICE, COUNTESS OF ATHLONE

Alice was the sister of Charles Edward. She married her cousin Prince Alexander of Teck and lived in England. The couple became the Earl and Countess of Athlone in 1917.

House of Windsor

In 1917, the British branch of the House of Saxe-Coburg-Gotha changed its surname to Windsor as the First World War caused a wave of anti-German feelings.

GEORGE V
  Edward VII's eldest son.
QUEEN MARY
  Born Princess Mary of Teck. Although she had a German title before she married, her parents always lived in England.
EDWARD VIII (DUKE OF WINDSOR)
  George V's eldest son. He was formerly known as Edward, Prince of Wales, before he became King Edward VIII. After he abdicated he assumed the title Duke of Windsor. Within the family he was called 'David'.
WALLIS, DUCHESS OF WINDSOR
  The Duchess was born Bessie Wallis Warfield. She divorced Ernest Simpson to marry the Duke of Windsor. The Royal Family denied her the title of Her Royal Highness.
GEORGE VI
  George V's second-eldest son. He was born Prince Albert and became the Duke of York. He was crowned King in 1936 and assumed the name George VI.
QUEEN ELIZABETH (DUCHESS OF YORK AND LATER
QUEEN MOTHER)
  Born Lady Elizabeth Bowes-Lyon, she married Prince Albert, Duke of York. Following Edward's abdication, Elizabeth was crowned Queen Consort in 1937. When her husband died, she assumed the title Queen Elizabeth, the Queen Mother.
PRINCESS ELIZABETH (LATER QUEEN ELIZABETH II)
  The eldest daughter of George V and Queen Elizabeth. Elizabeth married Philip Mountbatten (formerly a Prince of Greece and Denmark) and was crowned Queen Regnant in 1953.
PRINCE GEORGE, DUKE OF KENT
  George V's fourth son.

PRINCESS MARINA, DUCHESS OF KENT

Born Princess Marina of Greece and Denmark, she married Prince George, Duke of Kent. She was also the first cousin of Prince Philip, Duke of Edinburgh.

The House of Glücksberg

The Glücksbergs (or to give them their full name: Schleswig-Holstein-Sonderburg-Glücksberg) were the royal house of Greece, although they were of Danish and German descent.

PRINCE ANDREW OF GREECE AND DENMARK

The fourth son of King George I of the Hellenes (Greece) and forced into exile in Paris with his wife Princess Alice of Battenberg in 1922. They had four daughters: Margarita, Theodora, Cecilie and Sophie, and one son, Philip.

PRINCESS MARGARITA OF GREECE AND DENMARK

The eldest daughter of Prince Andrew and married to Prince Gottfried of Hohenlohe-Langenburg. Prince Gottfried served in the German army and was a Nazi Party member.

PRINCESS THEODORA OF GREECE AND DENMARK

The second daughter of Prince Andrew and married to Prince Berthold, Margrave of Baden.

PRINCESS CECILIE OF GREECE AND DENMARK

The third daughter of Prince Andrew and married to the pro-Nazi hereditary Grand Duke Georg Donatus of Hesse and by Rhine.

PRINCESS SOPHIE OF GREECE AND DENMARK

The fourth daughter of Prince Andrew and married to Prince Christoph of Hesse, a committed Nazi Party member. The couple named their first son Karl Adolf in honour of the Führer. After the death of her first husband, she remarried Prince George of Hanover.

PRINCE PHILIP OF GREECE AND DENMARK (PHILIP, DUKE OF EDINBURGH)

In 1947, Philip assumed British citizenship and adopted the surname of his uncle, Lord Louis Mountbatten, in preparation for his wedding to Princess Elizabeth. George VI also created him Duke of Edinburgh.

The Houses of Hesse and Mountbatten (formerly Battenberg)

There were three branches of the House of Hesse in Germany and Britain:

The Hesse-Darmstadt Branch

GRAND DUKE GEORG DONATUS OF HESSE AND BY RHINE
 A member of the Nazi Party. Georg, his wife (the former Princess
 Cecilie of Greece) and three children all died in a plane crash in 1937.
PRINCE LOUIS OF HESSE AND BY RHINE (GRAND DUKE
OF HESSE)
 Georg Donatus's brother who married a British woman, the Hon. Margaret
 Geddes (nicknamed 'Princess Peg'). She lived in Germany throughout the
 Second World War. Louis succeeded his brother as Grand Duke in 1937.

The Hesse-Kassel Branch

PRINCESS MARGARET 'MOSSIE' OF PRUSSIA (THE
LANDGRAVINE OF HESSE)
 The granddaughter of Queen Victoria and youngest daughter of the
 Empress Frederick of Germany. She married Prince Frederick Charles
 of Hesse. The couple had six sons: Frederick Wilhelm, Maximilian,
 Christoph, Philipp, Wolfgang and Richard.
PRINCE CHRISTOPH OF HESSE
 He married Princess Sophie of Greece and Denmark. In 1930, he
 joined the Nazi Party.
PRINCE PHILIPP OF HESSE
 He married Princess Mafalda of Savoy, the daughter of the Italian King,
 in 1925. He then joined the Nazi Party in 1930.

The Mountbatten (Battenberg) Branch

The Battenberg family was the morganatic branch of the Hesse-Darmstadt
dynasty created when Prince Alexander of Hesse married a commoner,

Julia Hauke. Julia and her descendants received the lesser title of Princess (or Prince) of Battenberg. In 1917, the Battenbergs changed their surname to Mountbatten.

PRINCE LOUIS OF BATTENBERG (1ST MARQUESS OF MILFORD HAVEN)

Married his cousin Princess Victoria of Hesse and by Rhine. The couple lived in Britain and became the Marquess and Marchioness of Milford Haven in 1917.

PRINCESS VICTORIA OF HESSE (MARCHIONESS OF MILFORD HAVEN)

Victoria was the granddaughter of Queen Victoria and born in Germany. When she married her cousin Prince Louis of Battenberg, she moved permanently to England. Her sister, Princess Alix of Hesse, became the Empress Alexandra of Russia and was executed by the communists at Ekaterinburg with her family in 1918. She was the grandmother of Prince Philip, Duke of Edinburgh.

PRINCESS ALICE OF BATTENBERG (PRINCESS ANDREW OF GREECE AND DENMARK)

Prince Louis's eldest daughter who married Prince Andrew of Greece and Denmark.

GEORGE MOUNTBATTEN, 2ND MARQUESS OF MILFORD HAVEN

The eldest son of Prince Louis. He married Countess Nadejad de Torby.

LOUISE, QUEEN OF SWEDEN

Born Princess Louise of Battenberg, she became Lady Louise Mountbatten in 1917 when her family relinquished their German titles. She married the Crown Prince Gustaf Adolf of Sweden and became Queen of Sweden in 1950.

LORD LOUIS MOUNTBATTEN (EARL MOUNTBATTEN OF BURMA)

Younger son of Prince Louis and born a Prince of Battenberg until his family relinquished their German titles. He became plain Lord Louis Mountbatten in 1917. Still, he made up for this demotion by marrying the wealthy heiress Edwina Ashley and becoming Viceroy of India and Earl Mountbatten of Burma in 1947.

An abridged family tree of the houses of Windsor, Hesse and Saxe-Coburg-Gotha.

Queen Victoria had eight children and forty-two grandchildren, which makes this a very simplified family tree. Its purpose is to show the close relationships between the book's central characters.

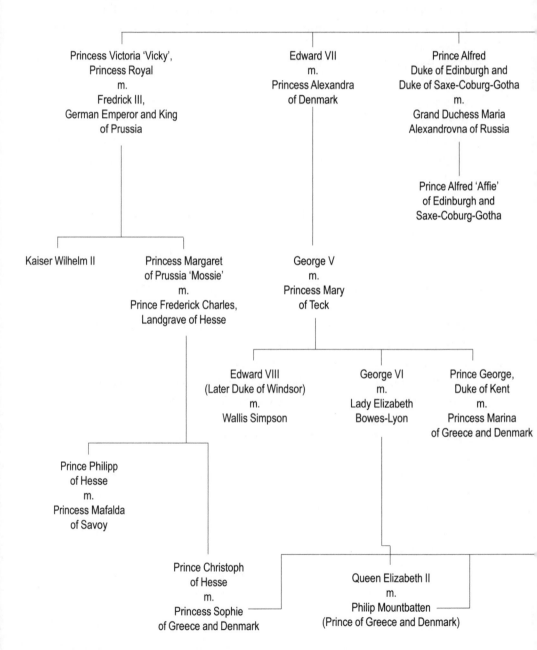

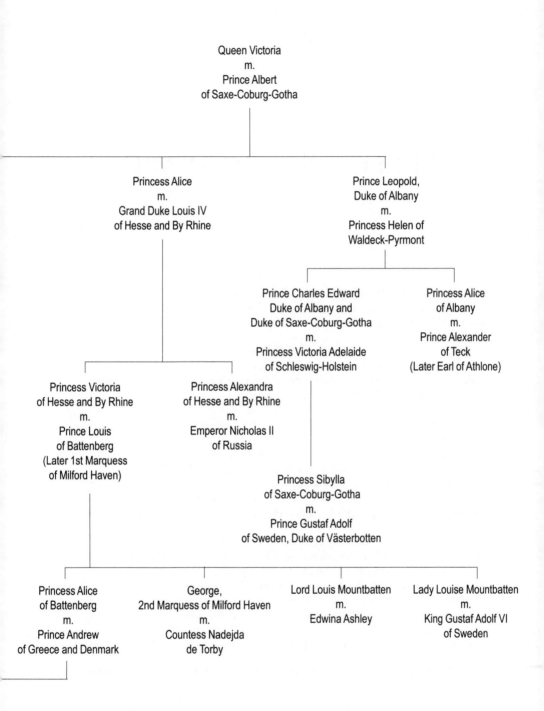

SELECT BIBLIOGRAPHY

Albright, M. (2018). *Fascism: A Warning.* William Collins.

Queen Alexandra of Yugoslavia. (1956). *For a King's Love.* Doubleday.

Queen Alexandra of Yugoslavia. (1960). *Prince Philip: A Family Portrait.* Hodder and Stoughton.

Alford, K. (1994). *The Spoils of World War II: The American Military's Role in the Stealing of European Treasures.* Birch Lane Press.

Princess Alice, Countess of Athlone. (1966). *For My Grandchildren.* Evans Brothers.

Allen, M. (2000). *Hidden Agenda.* M. Evans and Co.

Allen, P. (1983). *The Crown and the Swastika.* Hale.

Prince Andreas of Saxe-Coburg and Gotha. (2015). *Memoirs: I Did It My Way...* Europhistory.com.

Aronson, T. (1994). *Royal Family at War.* John Murray.

Aronson, T. (2014). *Princess Alice, Countess of Athlone.* Thistle Publishing.

Bailey, C. (2019). *The Lost Boys.* Viking.

Balfour, M. (1972). *The Kaiser and His Times.* Norton Library.

Balfour, N. and Mackay, S. (1980). *Paul of Yugoslavia: Britain's Maligned Friend.* Hamish Hamilton.

Bartlett, V. (1933). *Nazi Germany Explained.* Victor Gollancz.

Lord Beaverbrook. (1966). *The Abdication of Edward VIII.* Hamish Hamilton.

Beevor, A. (2007). *Berlin: The Downfall 1945.* Penguin.

Bentinck, N. (1922). *The Ex-Kaiser in Exile.* Hodder.

Bielenberg, C. (1998). *When I Was a German, 1934–1945.* University of Nebraska Press.

Lord Birkenhead. (1969). *Walter Monckton: The Life of Viscount Monckton of Brenchley.* Weidenfeld and Nicolson.

Bischoff, G. and Ambrose, S. (1992). *Eisenhower and the German POWs: Facts Against Falsehood.* Louisiana State University Press.

Bloch, M. (1984). *Operation Willi: The Plot to Kidnap the Duke of Windsor. July 1940.* Weidenfeld and Nicholson.

Bloch, M. (Ed.) (1986). *Wallis and Edward: Letters 1931–1937: The Intimate Correspondence of the Duke and Duchess of Windsor.* Weidenfeld and Nicolson.

Bloch, M. (1988). *The Secret File on the Duke of Windsor.* Brown Book Group.

Bloch, M. (1994). *Ribbentrop.* Bantam Press.

Bloch, M. (2012 Reissue). *The Duchess of Windsor.* Hachette Digital.

Bocca, G. (1954). *The Woman Who Would Be Queen.* Rinehart.

Bolitho, H. (1938). *Further Letters of Queen Victoria, From the Archives of House of Brandenburg-Prussia.* Thornton Butterworth.

Boothroyd, B. (1971). *Philip: An Informal Biography.* Longman.

Botting, D. (1985). *In the Ruins of the Reich.* George Allen & Unwin.

Bouverie, T. (2019). *Appeasing Hitler: Chamberlain, Churchill and the Road to War.* The Bodley Head.

Boyd, J. (2017). *Travellers in the Third Reich.* Elliott & Thompson.

Bradford, S. (2011). *George VI.* Penguin.

Brendon, P. (2016). *Edward VIII: The Uncrowned King.* Penguin.

Brendon, P. and Whitehead, P. (2000). *The Windsors: A Dynasty Revealed 1917–2000.* Pimlico.

Brereton, H. (1950). *Gordonstoun.* The University Press Aberdeen.

Brooke-Shepherd, G. (1987). *Royal Sunset: The Dynasties of Europe and the Great War.* Weidenfeld and Nicolson.

Bryan, J. and Murphy, C. (1979). *The Windsor Story.* Granada.

Bryant, C. (2017). *Entitled: A Critical History of the British Aristocracy.* Transworld.

Bullitt, O. (1973). *For the President – Personal and Secret: Correspondence between Franklin D. Roosevelt and William C. Bullitt. With an introduction by George F. Kennan.* Andre Deutsch.

Burn, M. (2003). *Turned Towards the Sun: An Autobiography.* Michael Russell.

Cadbury, D. (2015). *Princes at War: The British Royal Family's Private Battle in the Second World War.* Bloomsbury.

Cadbury, D. (2017). *Queen Victoria's Match Making.* Bloomsbury.

Carter, M. (2001). *Anthony Blunt: His Lives.* Macmillan.

Carter, M. (2009). *The Three Emperors.* Penguin.

Cecil, L. (1996). *Wilhelm II, Emperor and Exile 1900–1941.* Vol. 2. University of North Carolina Press.

Churchill, W. (1948). *The Gathering Storm.* Houghton Mifflin.

Churchill, W. (1959). *Great Contemporaries.* Fontana Paperback Edition.

Prince Christopher of Greece. (1938). *Memoirs of Prince Christopher of Greece.* Hurst & Blackett.

Connell, B. (1935). *Manifest Destiny: A Study in Five Profiles of the Rise and Influence of the Mountbatten Family.* Cassell & Co.

Cookridge, E. (1968). *From Battenberg to Mountbatten.* John Day.

Corbitt, F. (1956). *Fit for A King.* Odhams.

Corti, E. (1954). *Alexander von Battenberg.* Cassell & Co.

Corti, E. (1957). *The English Empress: A Study in Relations between Queen Victoria and her Eldest Daughter, Empress Frederick of Germany.* Cassell & Co.

Costello, J. (1988). *Mask of Treachery.* William Morrow.

Costello, J. (1991). *Ten Days to Destiny.* William Morrow.

Courcy, A. de (2004). *Diana Mosley.* Vintage.

Craig, G. and Gilbert, F. (1953). *The German Foreign Office from Neurath to Ribbentrop: The Diplomats 1919–39.* Princeton University Press.

Crankshaw, E. (2002). *Gestapo: Instrument of Tyranny.* Greenhill Books.

Crawford, M. (1952). *Little Princesses.* Cassells.

Crowson, N. (1998). *Fleet Street, Press Barons & Politics: The Journals of Colin Brooks 1932–1940.* Camden Fifth Series. Vol. 11. Royal Historical Society.

Cust, L. (1930). *King Edward VII and His Court*. E.P. Dutton.

Princess Daisy of Pless. (1931). *From My Private Diary*. J. Murray

Princess Daisy of Pless. (1936). *What I Left Unsaid*. Cassell & Co.

Deacon, R. (1979). *The British Connection*. Hamish Hamilton.

Defries, H. (2001). *Conservative Party Attitudes to Jews 1900–1950*. Routledge.

De Pough, L. (1979). *My Blue Notebooks*. Andre Deutsche.

De Waal, E. (2011). *The Hare with Amber Eyes*. Vintage.

Dietrich, O. (2010). *The Hitler I Knew*. Pen and Sword.

Dodd, M. (1940). *My Years in Germany*. Victor Gollancz.

Dodd, M. (1939). *Through Embassy Eyes*. Harcourt, Brace and Company.

Döhring, H., Wilhelm, K. and Plain, A. (2018). *Living with Hitler*. Greenhill Books.

Donaldson, F. (1986). *Edward VIII*. Weidenfeld and Nicolson.

Dormus, M. and Romane, P. (Ed.) (2007). *The Essential Hitler*. Bolchazy-Carducci.

Dorrell, S. (2006). *Blackshirt: Sir Oswald Mosley and British Fascism*. Viking.

Duff, D. (1985). *Queen Mary*. Collins.

Eade, P. (2012). *Young Prince Philip: His Turbulent Early Life*. Harper Press.

Egremont, M. (2013). *Siegfried Sassoon: A Biography*. Picador.

Eilers, M. (1987). *Queen Victoria's Descendants*. Clearfield.

Ellis, W. (1997). *Robert Worth Bingham and the Southern Mystique: From Old South to the New South and Beyond*. Kent State University Papers.

Evans, R. (2005). *The Third Reich in Power*. Allen Lane.

Evans, R. (2008). *The Third Reich at War*. Penguin.

Evans, S. (2016). *Queen Bees: Six Brilliant and Extraordinary Society Hostesses Between the Wars*. Two Roads Books.

Faber, D. (2008). *Munich: The 1938 Appeasement Crisis*. Simon and Schuster.

Farago, L. (1971). *The Game of the Foxes*. David Mckay Company.

Farrell, N. (2003). *Mussolini: A New Life*. Weidenfeld and Nicolson.

Fielding, D. (1968). *Emerald and Nancy: Lady Cunard and her Daughter*. Eyre & Spottiswoode.

Fisher, C. (1995). *Cyril Connolly*. St Martin's Press.

Fjellman, M. (1968). *Louise Mountbatten, Queen of Sweden*. George Allen and Unwin.

Flavin, M. (1996). *Kurt Hahn's Schools & Legacy*. The Middle Atlantic Press.

Ford, H. (1920). *The International Jew: The World's Foremost Problem*. Dearborn.

Freeman, G. (2008). *The Forgotten 500: The Untold Story of the Men Who Risked All for the Greatest Rescue Mission of World War II*. Penguin Books.

Freitag, C. (2015). *Ritter, Reichsmarschall & Revoluzzer. Aus der Geschichte eines Berliner Landhauses* (From the History of a Berlin Country House). Friedenauer Brücke.

Friedrich, O. (1995). *Before the Deluge: A Portrait of Berlin in the 1920s*. Harper Perennial.

Fritzsche, P. (1992). *A Nation of Fliers: German Aviation and Popular Imagination*. Harvard University Press.

Fromme, B. (1990). *Blood & Banquets: A Berlin Social Diary*. Carol Publishing Group.

Fulford, R. (1981). *Beloved Mama: Private Correspondence of Queen Victoria and the German Crown Princess 1878–1885*. Evans Brothers.

Fussell, P. (2002). *Uniforms: Why We Are What We Wear*. Houghton Mifflin.

Gay, P. (2001). *Weimar Culture: The Outside as Insider*. W.W. Norton & Company.

Gelardi, J. (2011). *From Splendor to Revolution: The Romanov Women 1847–1928*. St Martin's Press.

Getty, J.P. (1976). *As I See It: The Autobiography of J. Paul Getty*. Prentice-Hall.

Gilbert, M. (1976). *Companion to Winston S. Churchill*. Vol. 5. 1922–39. Heinemann.

Gilbert, M. (1979). *Exile and Return*. Weidenfeld and Nicolson.

Giudice, G. (1971). *Benito Mussolini*. Turin.

Goeschel, C. (2018). *Mussolini and Hitler: Forging of the Fascist Alliance*. Yale University Press.

Goldsmith, B. (1980). *Little Gloria … Happy at Last*. Macmillan.

Göring, E. (1967). *An der Seite meines Mannes (*At the Side of my Husband). Schültz.

Göring, E. (1972). *My Life with Göring*. David Bruce and Watson.

Griffiths, R. (1983). *Fellow Travellers of the Right: British Enthusiasts for Nazi Germany 1933–1939*. Oxford University Press.

Gun, N. (1969). *Eva Braun: Hitler's Mistress*. Leslie Frewin.

Gustche, W. (1991). *Kaiser im Exil: Der Letzte Deutsche Kaiser Wilhelm II. In Holland. Eine Kritische Biographie* (Emperor in Exile: The Last German Kaiser Wilhelm II. In Holland. A Critical Biography). Hitzeroth.

Hamilton, F. (1950). *The Vanished Pomps of Yesterday*. Hodder & Stoughton.

Hanson, N. (2009). *First Blitz: The Secret German Plan to Raze London to the Ground in 1918*. Corgi.

Harding, H. (1967). *Loyal to Three Kings*. William Kimber.

Harding, T. (2015). *The House by the Lake*. Penguin Random House.

Hart-Davis, D. (2007). *The King's Counsellor: Abdication and War: The Diaries of Sir Alan Lascelles*. Entry: 26 December 1943. Phoenix.

Hart-Davis, R. (1981). *Sassoon Diaries 1920–1922*. Faber and Faber.

Hartnell, N. (1955). *Silver and Gold*. Evans Brothers.

Heck, A. (2001). *A Child of Hitler: Germany in the Days When God Wore a Swastika*. Renaissance House.

Henderson, N. (1940). *Failure of a Mission: Berlin 1937 to 1939*. Hodder and Stoughton.

Herf, J. (2008). *The Jewish Enemy: Nazi Propaganda During World War II and the Holocaust*. Harvard University Press.

Hesse, F. (1954). *Hitler and the English*. Allen Wingate.

Hesse, F. (1979). *Das Vorspiel zum Kriege*. (The Prelude to War). Stranberg.

Hessen, H. (1994). *Der Kristallene Lüster*. (The Crystal Chandelier). Piper.

Hessen, W. (Ed.) and Hessen, R. (1986) *Aufzeichnungen* (Records). Privatedruck.

Hichens, M. (2016). *Abdication: The Rise and Fall of Edward VIII*. Book Guild Publishing.

Hicks, P. (2012). *Daughter of Empire: Life as a Mountbatten*. Phoenix.

Higham, C. (2005). *Mrs Simpson: Secret Lives of the Duchess of Windsor*. Sidgwick and Jackson.

Higham, C. and Mosely, R. (1991). *Elizabeth and Philip: The Untold Story of the Queen of England and Her Prince*. Doubleday.

Hitler, A. (1926). *Mein Kampf* (My Struggle). Eher Verlag.

Hoey, B. (2012). *Her Majesty: 60 Regal Years*. Diamond Jubilee Edition.

Hoey, B. (2008). *Mountbatten: The Private Story*. The History Press.

Hohne, H. (1979). *Canaris: Hitler's Master Spy*. Doubleday.

Holstein, F. (1955). *The Holstein Papers*. Vol. 1. Cambridge University Press.

Hough, R. (Ed.) (1975). *Advice to a Granddaughter: Letters from Queen Victoria to Princess Victoria of Hesse*. William Heinemann.

Hough, R. (1983). *Edwina, Countess Mountbatten of Burma*. Weidenfeld and Nicolson.

Hough, R. (1984). *Louis and Victoria: The Family History of the Mountbattens*. Weidenfeld and Nicolson.

Howard, A. (1987). *RAB: The Life of R. A. Butler*. Jonathan Cape.

Hull, I. (2008). *The Entourage of Kaiser Wilhelm II, 1888–1918*. Cambridge University Press.

Hutchinson, G. (1939). *Challenge*. Hutchinson & Co.

Hutton, M. (2013). *Life in the 1940s.* Amberley Publishing.

James, R. (Ed.) (1993). *Chips: The Diaries of Sir Henry Channon.* Phoenix.

Jenkins, R. (2001). *Churchill.* Macmillan.

Jennings, C. (2007). *Them and Us: The American Invasion of British High Society.* Sutton Publishing.

Jonas, K. (1961). *The Life of Crown Prince William.* Routledge.

Judd, D. (2012). *George VI.* I.B. Tauris & Co.

Kahn, A. (1950). *Betrayal: Our Occupation of Germany.* Ksiazkai Wiedza.

Kahn, D. (1978). *Hitler's Spies.* Hodder and Stoughton.

Katz, O. (1933). *Brown Book of the Reichstag Fire and Hitler Terror.* Alfred A. Knopf.

Katz, R. (2003). *Battle for Rome: The Germans, the Allies, the Partisans, and the Pope.* Simon and Schuster.

Keegan, J. (1989). *The Second World War.* Viking.

Keenan, G. (1967). *Memoirs 1925–50.* Little, Brown and Co.

Kennedy, A. (1956). *My Dear Duchess: Social and Political Letters to the Duchess of Manchester 1958–1869.* John Murray.

Kerr, M. (1934). *Prince Louis of Battenberg: Admiral of the Fleet.* Longmans, Green and Company.

Kershaw, I. (1999). *Hitler 1889–1936. Hubris:* W.W. Norton & Company.

Kershaw, I. (2000). *Hitler 1936–1945: Nemesis.* Allen Lane.

Kershaw, I. (2004). *Making Friends with Hitler: Lord Londonderry and Britain's Road to War.* Penguin.

Kershaw, I. (2008). *Hitler: A Biography.* W.W. Norton & Company.

Kessler, H. (2011). *Journey to the Abyss: The Diaries of Count Harry Kessler, 1880–1918.* Vintage Books.

Kessler, H. (2013). *Walter Rathenau: His Life and Work.* Beston Press.

Keynes, J. (1919). *The Economic Consequence of Peace.* Macmillan.

King, D. (2017). *The Trial of Adolf Hitler: The Beer Hall Putsch and the Rise of Nazi Germany.* Macmillan.

King, G. (1996). *The Man Who Killed Rasputin: Prince Youssoupov and the Murder that Helped Bring Down the Russian Empire.* Birch Lane Press.

King, G. (1999). *The Duchess of Windsor: The Uncommon Life of Wallis Simpson.* Citadel Press.

King, G. (2003). *Wallis: The Uncommon Life of the Duchess of Windsor.* Aurum Press.

King, G. (2007). *Twilight of Splendour: The Court of Queen Victoria During Her Diamond Jubilee Year.* John Wiley & Sons.

King, G. and Woolmans, S. (2013). *The Assassination of the Archduke.* St Martin's Press.

Kirkpatrick, Sir Ivone. (1959). *The Inner Circle: Memoirs.* Macmillan.

Klein, M. (1994). *Ernst von Salomon. Eine Politisch Biographie.* (A Political Biography). Limberg.

Kohut, T. (1982). *Kaiser Wilhelm II and his Parents.* [Quoted in *Kaiser Wilhelm II: The Corfu Papers.* Ed. Röhl, J. and Sombart, N. Cambridge University Press.]

Kohut, T. (1991). *Wilhelm II and the Germans.* Oxford University Press.

Kollander, P. (2005). *I Must Be a Part of this War: A German American's Fight Against Hitler and Nazism.* Fordham University Press.

Kynaston, D. (2007). *Austerity Britain 1945–51.* Bloomsbury.

Lamar, C. (1996). *Wilhelm II: Emperor and Exile, 1900–1941.* Vol. 2. UNC Press Books.

Lambton, A. (1989). *The Mountbattens: The Battenbergs and Young Mountbatten.* Constable.

Lane, P. (1980). *Prince Philip.* Robert Hales.

Larson, E. (2012). *In the Garden of Beasts: Love and Terror in Hitler's Berlin*. Black Swann.

Lee, S. (1923). *King Edward VII*. Vol. 1. Macmillan.

Lee, S. (1925). *King Edward VII*. Vol 2. Macmillan.

Lees-Milne, J. (1988). *The Enigmatic Edwardian: The Life of Reginald, 2nd Viscount Esher*. Sidgwick and Jackson.

Leibovitz, C. and Finkel, A. (1997). *The Chamberlain–Hitler Collusion*. Merlin Press.

Litchfield, D. (2015). *Hitler's Valkyrie: The Uncensored Biography of Unity Mitford*. The History Press.

Lockhart, R. Young, K. (Ed.) (1973). *The Diaries of Sir Robert Bruce Lockhart 1915–1938*. Vol. 1. Macmillan.

Longford, E. (1964). *Queen Victoria*. Harper and Row.

Lough, D. (2015). *No More Champagne: Churchill and His Money*. Head of Zeus.

Lovell, M. (2002). *The Mitford Girls: The Biography of an Extraordinary Family*. Abacus.

Lowndes, S. (Ed.) (1971). *Maria Belloc Lowndes Diaries, Diaries and Letters of Maria Belloc Lowndes*. Chatto and Windus.

Lyon, A. (2016). *Constitutional History of the UK*. Routledge.

Mabell, Countess of Airlie. (1962). *Thatched with Gold*. (Ed. Ellis, J.). Hutchinson.

MacDonogh, G. (2000). *The Last Kaiser: William the Impetuous*. Weidenfeld and Nicolson.

McDonough, F. (1998). *Neville Chamberlain, Appeasement, and the British Road to War*. Manchester University Press.

Mack Smith, D. (1995). *Mussolini*. Phoenix.

Macmillan, H. (1984). *War Diaries*. Macmillan.

Macmillan, H. (1966). *Winds of Change 1914–1939*. Macmillan.

Macmillan, M. (2014). *The War that Ended Peace*. Profile Books.

Maxwell, E. (1954). *R.S.V.P.: Elsa Maxwell's Own Story*. Little Brown.

Mallwitz, P. (Ed.) (1986). *Stefan Heym: Reden an den feind* (Talking to the Enemy). Fischer.

Malony, A. (2005). *The Forties: Good Times Just Around the Corner*. Michael O'Mara.

Manvell, R. Fraenkel, H. (2011). *Goering: The Rise and Fall of the Notorious Nazi Leader*. Skyhorse.

Queen Marie of Romania. (1935). *The Story of My Life*. Vol. 1. Cassell.

Magnus, P. (1964). *King Edward the Seventh*. John Murray.

Martin, R. (1973). *The Woman He Loved*. Simon and Schuster.

Marr, A. (2011). *The Diamond Queen*. Macmillan.

Maser, W. (2000). *Hermann Göring*. Uitgeverij Aspekt.

Massie, R. (1991). *Dreadnought*. Random House.

Medd, J. (2002). *The Cult of the Clitoris: Anatomy of a National Scandal*. Vol 9. John Hopkins University Press.

Middlemas, K. and Barnes, J. (1969). *Baldwin: A Biography*. Weidenfeld and Nicolson.

Milton, R. (2007). *Best of Enemies*. Icon Books.

Mitchell, O. (2008). *Hitler's Stormtroopers and the Attack on the German Republic, 1919–1933*. McFarland & Company.

Modin, Y. (1994). *My Five Cambridge Friends*. Headline.

Monger, D. (2012). *Patriotism and Propaganda in First World War Britain*. Liverpool University Press.

Montgomery Hyde, H. (1991). *Walter Monckton*. Sinclair-Stevenson.

Moorcroft-Wilson, J. (2013) *Siegfried Sassoon: Soldier, Poet, Lover, Friend. A Life in One Volume*. Duckworth Overlook.

Lord Moran. (1966). *Winston Churchill: The Struggle for Survival 1940–1965.* Houghton Mifflin.

Morgan, J. (1991). *Edwina Mountbatten: A Life of Her Own.* Harper Collins.

Morrow, A. (1983). *The Queen.* William Morrow.

Morton, A. (2015). *17 Carnations: The Windsors, the Nazis and the Cover-up.* Michael O'Mara.

Mosley, O. (1968). *My Life.* Thomas Nelson and Sons.

Muggeridge, M. (Ed.), Count Ciano (1939). *Ciano's Diary.* Heinemann.

Mussolini, B. (2000). *Memoirs 1942–1943.* Orion Publishing Group.

Nicolson, H. (1952). *George V, His Life and Reign.* Constable.

Nicolson, H. (1984). *King George V.* Constable.

Nicolson, N. (Ed.) (1967). *Harold Nicolson: Diaries and Letters 1930–1939.* Collins.

Nicolson, N. (Ed.) (1967). *Sir Harold Nicolson: Diaries and Letters.* Vol. 2.

Nicolson, N. (Ed.) (2004). *The Harold Nicolson Diaries.* Weidenfeld and Nicolson.

Norwich, J. (Ed.) (2005). *The Duff Cooper Diaries 1915–1951.* Weidenfeld and Nicolson.

Packard, J. (1998). *Victoria's Daughters.* St. Martin's Griffin.

Padfield, P. (2014). *Hess, Hitler and Churchill: The Real Turning Point of the Second World War – A Secret History.* Icon.

Padfield, P. (1990). *Himmler: Reichsführer-SS.* Henry Holt and Company.

Pakula, H. (1984). *The Last Romantic: A Biography of Queen Marie of Romania.* Simon and Schuster.

Pakula, H. (1999). *An Uncommon Woman.* Phoenix Press.

Parker, J. (1988). *King of Fools.* A Futura Book.

Parker, J. (1990). *Prince Philip: Critical Biography.* Sidgwick & Jackson.

Patch, H. and Van Emden, R. (2009). *The Last Fighting Tommy.* Centenary Anniversary Edition. Bloomsbury.

Petropoulos, J. (2006). *Royals and the Reich.* Oxford University.

Pimlott, B. (2002). *The Queen: Golden Jubilee Edition.* HarperCollins.

Ponsonby, A. (1943). *Henry Ponsonby, Queen Victoria's Private Secretary: His Life from His Letters.* Macmillan.

Ponsonby, F. (1935). *My Recollections of Three Reigns.* Oldham Press.

Pope-Hennessy, J. (1959). *Queen Mary.* George Allen and Unwin.

Porter, D. (2005). *Howard Hughes: Hell's Angel.* Blood Moon.

Pugh, M. (2005). *Hurrah for the Blackshirts! Fascist and Fascism in Britain Between the Wars.* Jonathan Cape.

Rauchensteiner, M. and Litscher, M. (Ed.) (2000). *The Das Heeresgeschichtliche Museum in Wien* (The Museum of Military History in Vienna). Styria.

Reynolds, Q. (1963). *By Quentin Reynolds.* McGraw Hill.

Reynolds, R. (1939). *When Freedom Shrieked.* Victor Gollancz.

Rhodes, J. (Ed.) (1967). *Chips: The Diaries of Sir Henry Channon.* Weidenfeld and Nicolson.

Ridley, J. (2013). *Bertie: A Life of Edward VII.* Vintage.

Roberts, A. (1997). *The Holy Fox: The Life of Lord Halifax.* Phoenix.

Roberts, A. (1994). *Eminent Churchillians.* Phoenix.

Roberts, A. (2011). *Salisbury: Victorian Titan.* Faber and Faber.

Roberts, A. (2018). *Churchill: Walking with Destiny.* Allen Lane.

Roberts, J. (2007). *Five Gold Rings: A Royal Wedding Souvenir Album from Queen Victoria to Queen Elizabeth II.* Royal Collection Enterprises Ltd.

Roddie, S. (1932). *Peace Patrol.* Christophers.

Röhl, J. (2014). *Kaiser Wilhelm II.* Cambridge University Press.

Rose, K. (1975). *The Later Cecils.* Weidenfeld and Nicolson.

Rose, K. (1983). *King George V.* Weidenfeld and Nicolson.

Rose, N. (2001). *The Cliveden Set: Portrait of an Exclusive Fraternity.* Pimlico.

Rose, N. (1986). *Chaim Weizmann: A Biography by Norman Rose.* Viking.

Rushton, A. (2018). *Charles Edward of Saxe-Coburg: The German Red Cross and the Plan to Kill 'Unfit' Citizens.* Cambridge Scholars Publishing.

St Aubyn, G. (1979). *Edward VII, Prince and King.* Collins.

Sandner, H. (2010). *Hitler's Herzog: Carl Eduard von Sachsen-Coburg-Gotha.* (Hitler's Duke: Charles Edward of Saxe-Coburg-Gotha). Shaker Media.

Sassoon, S. (1930). *Memoirs of an Infantry Officer.* Faber and Faber.

Schmidt, P. (2016). *Hitler's Interpreter: The Memoirs of Paul Schmidt.* New Translated Edition. The History Press.

Sebba, A. (2011). *That Woman: The Life of Wallis Simpson Duchess of Windsor.* Phoenix.

Seymour, M. (2014). *Noble Endeavours.* Simon and Schuster.

Shard, M. (2004). *Hitler's Spy Princess.* The History Press.

Shaw, K. (1999). *Royal Babylon: The Alarming History of European Royalty.* Broadway.

Shawcross, W. (2009). *Queen Elizabeth, The Queen Mother: Official Biography.* Macmillan.

Shawcross, W. (2012). *Counting One's Blessings: The Selected Letters of Queen Elizabeth, The Queen Mother.* Macmillan.

Shirer, W. (1962). *The Rise and Fall of the Third Reich: A History of Nazi Germany.* Simon and Schuster.

Shirer, W. (2004). *Berlin Diary: Journal of a Foreign Correspondent.* Black Dog & Leventhal Publishers.

Sinclair-Loutit, K. (2009). *Very Little Luggage* [unpublished memoir].

Skyes, C. (1972). *Nancy: The Life of Lady Astor.* Harper & Row.

Snyder, L. (1976). *Encyclopaedia of the Third Reich.* McGraw-Hill.

Speer, A. (1970). *Inside the Third Reich.* Macmillan.

Speer, A. (2009). *Inside the Reich.* Weidenfeld and Nicolson.

Spencer Shew, B. (1955). *Queen Elizabeth, The Queen Mother.* Hodder and Stoughton.

Stephen, J. (1978). *The Russian Fascists: Tragedy and Farce in Exile, 1925–1945.* Harper and Row.

Susmel, E. and Suseml, D. (Eds) (1951). *Opera Omnia by Benito Mussolini.* La Fenice.

Taylor, A. (1972). *Lord Beaverbrook.* Hamish Hamilton.

Lord Templewood. (1976). *Nine Troubled Years.* Greenwood Press.

Toland, J. (1976). *Adolf Hitler.* Vol. 1. Doubleday.

Topham, A. (1992). *Distant Thunder: Intimate Recollections of the Kaiser's Court.* A Clio History Book.

Trevelyan, G.M. (1947). *The Wedding of Her Royal Highness Princess Elizabeth and Lieutenant Philip Mountbatten RN.* Official Souvenir Programme.

Trevelyan, R. (1981). *Rome 1944.* Martin Secker and Warburg.

Tuchman, B. (1980). *Proud Tower: Portrait of the World Before the War, 1890–1914.* Macmillan.

Ullrich, V. (2013). *Hitler: A Biography.* Vol. 1: Ascent. The Bodley Head.

Urbach, K. (2015). *Go-Betweens for Hitler.* Oxford University Press.

Vanderbilt, G. and Furness, T. (1958). *Double Exposure: A Twin Autobiography.* David McKay.

Van der Kiste, J. (2013). *Alfred: Queen Victoria's Second Son.* Fonthill.

Van der Kiste, J. (2014). *Kaiser Wilhelm: Germany's Last Emperor.* Sutton Publishing.

Van der Kiste, J. (2015). *The Last German Empress: A Life of Empress Augusta Victoria, Consort of Emperor William II*. Createspace.

Van der Kiste, J. (1999). *The Romanovs 1818–1959*. Sutton Publishing.

Vansittart, R. (1958). *The Mist Procession*. Hutchinson.

Vickers, H. (2000). *Alice, Princess of Greece*. Viking.

Vickers, H. (1985). *Cecil Beaton: The Authorised Biography*. Weidenfeld and Nicolson.

Viktoria Luise, Duchess of Brunswick. (1965). *Ein Leben als Tochter de Kaiser* (A Life as the Daughter of the Emperor). Hannover.

Viktoria Luise, Duchess of Brunswick. (1967). *Im Glanz der Krone*. (In the Splendour of the Crown). Hannover.

Viktoria Luise, Princess of Prussia. (1977). *The Kaiser's Daughter*. Prentice Hall.

Von Ilsleman, S. (1967). *Der Kaiser in Holland* (The Kaiser in Holland). Vol. 1. Biederstein.

Wachsmann, N. (2015). *KL: The History of the Nazi Concentration Camps*. Abacus.

Wainwright, W. (2017). *Reporting on Hitler: Rothay Reynolds and the British Press in Nazi Germany*. Biteback.

Warwick, C. (2016). *George and Marina, Duke and Duchess of Kent*. Revised edition. Albert Bridge Books.

Watson, S. (1997). *Marina: The Story of a Princess*. Phoenix.

Weinberg, G. (2004). *A World at Arms: A Global History of World War II*. Cambridge University Press.

Weisbrode, K. (2013). *Churchill and the King*. Viking.

Wheeler-Bennett, J. (1936). *Hindenburg: The Wooden Titan*. Macmillan.

Wheeler-Bennett, J. (1959). *King George VI*. Reprint Society.

Wheeler-Bennett, J. (1974). *Knaves, Fools and Heroes: In Europe Between the Wars*. Macmillan.

Wiebe, M. (Ed.) (2004). *Benjamin Disraeli Letters*. Vol. 2. University of Toronto Press.

Crown Prince Wilhelm of Germany. (1922). *Erinnerungen* (Memories). Vol. 1. Thornton Butterworth.

Wilson, A. (2014). *Victoria: A Life*. Atlantic Books.

Wilson, A. (1939). *Walks and Talks Abroad: The Diary of a Member of Parliament in 1934–36*. Oxford University Press.

Wilson, E. (1983). *The Forties*. Farrar, Straus & Giroux.

Wilson, J. (2011). *Nazis Princess: Hitler, Lord Rothermere and Princess Stephanie von Hohenlohe*. The History Press.

Wilson, J. (2006). *Hitler's Alpine Retreat*. Pen & Sword.

The Duchess of Windsor. (1980). *The Heart Had Its Reasons*. Sphere Books.

The Duke of Windsor. (1947). *A King's Story: The Memoirs of the Duke of Windsor*. G.P. Putnam & Sons.

Lord Winterton. (1953). *Orders of the Day*. Cassell.

Wiskemann, E. (1966). *The Rome–Berlin Axis*. The Fontana Library.

Witte, S. (1921). *Memoirs of Count Witte*. Heinemann.

Wulff, L. (1947). *Queen of Tomorrow*. Samson Low.

Yarnall, J. (2011). *Barbed Wire Disease: British & German Prisoners of War, 1914–19*. Spellmount.

Young, K. (Ed.) (1973). *The Diaries of Sir Robert Bruce Lockhart*. Vol. 1. Macmillan.

Young, K. (Ed.) (1980). *The Diaries of Sir Robert Bruce Lockhart*. Vol. 2. Macmillan.

Ziegler, P. (1981). *Diana Cooper*. Hamish Hamilton.

Ziegler, P. (1990). *King Edward VIII: The Official Biography*. Collins.

Zinoveiff, S. (2014). *The Mad Boy, Lord Berners, My Grandmother and Me*. Vintage.

Archive References & Abbreviations

FO	British Government Foreign Office.
HHStaw	*Hessisches Hauptstaatsarchiv* (Hessian Main State Archives) in Wiesbaden, Germany.
HO	British Government Home Office.
HStAM	*Hessisches Staatsarchiv* (Hessian State Archives) in Marburg.
IfZG	*Institut für Zeitgeschichte* (Institute for Contemporary History) in Munich, Germany.
NARA	National Archives and Records Administration, College Park in Maryland, USA.

NOTES

Introduction

1. *Secret History: Hitler's Favourite Royal*. (2007). Television Documentary. Channel 4.
2. Bischoff, G. and Ambrose, S. (1992). p.9.
3. Ibid. p.78.
4. Botting, D. (1985). p.159.
5. Keenan, G. (1967).
6. Botting, D. (1985). p.161.
7. Kahn, A.D. (1950).
8. Emerich, J. (1998). p.59.
9. Rushton, A.R. (2018). p.4.
10. Urbach, K. (2015). p.309.
11. Callan, P. (2007). 'Hitler's Puppet Prince.' *Daily Express*. 24 November 2007.
12. Bridges, A. (2015). 'Queen's visit to Germany recalls Albert and Victoria in Coburg'. *The Daily Telegraph*. 22 June 2015.
13. Princess Alice, Countess of Athlone. (1966). p.280.
14. Solomon, Z. (1985). 'General Patton: Hero or Anti-Semite?' *Jewniverse*. 19 April 1985.
15. Ibid.
16. Bischoff, G. and Ambrose, S. (1992). p.33.
17. Urbach, K. (2015). p.2.
18. Rushton, A.R. (2018). p.9.
19. Princess Alice, Countess of Athlone. (1966). p.280.
20. Ibid. p.281.
21. Urbach, K. (2015). p.309.
22. Kollander, P. (2005). p.109.
23. Botting, D. (1985). p.157.
24. *Bunte Bühm für die Wehrmacht*. (17 April 1945) . Radio Programme. (Quoted in Mallwitz, P. (Ed.) (1986). *Stefan Heym: Reden an den feind* (Talking to the Enemy). Fischer. p.332).
25. Urbach, K. (2015). p.157.
26. Ibid. p.309.
27. Ibid.

28. Oltmann, J. (18 January 2001). *Seine Königliche Hoheit der Obergruppenführer* (His Royal Highness of the Upper Group Leaders).
29. Urbach, K. (2015). p.309.
30. Ibid. p.309.
31. Ibid. p.311.
32. Letter to General Sir Brian Robertson. Correspondence regarding the Duke of Saxe-Coburg-Gotha. 28 May 1946. FO 1030/302.
33. Letter from Princess Alice, Countess of Athlone to General Sir Brian Robertson. Correspondence regarding the Duke of Saxe-Coburg-Gotha. 20 September 1946. FO 1030/302.
34. Princess Alice, Countess of Athlone. (1966). pp.281–82.
35. Reifenrath, J.W. (1997).
36. Hackett, D.A. (1997). *The Buchenwald Report.* Westview Press.
37. Urbach, K. (2016). pp.183–85.

Chapter One

1. Zeepvat, C. (2013). p.238.
2. Urbach, K. (2015). pp.27–8.
3. Princess Alice, Countess of Athlone. (1966). p.14.
4. Ibid. p.62.
5. Aronson, T. (2014). p.31.
6. Ibid. p.71.
7. Princess Alice, Countess of Athlone. (1966). p.65.
8. Urbach, K. (2015). pp.27–8.
9. Princess Alice, Countess of Athlone. (1966). p.66.
10. Pakula, H. (1984). p.43.
11. Gelardi, J. (2011). p.138.
12. Aronson, T. (2014). p.106.
13. Ibid. p.113.
14. Urbach, K. (2016). pp.28–30.
15. *Leipziger Neueste Nachrichten* (Leipziger Latest News). 22 April 1899.
16. Urbach, K. (2015). p.28.
17. Aronson, T. (2014). p.108.
18. Hough, R. (Ed.) (1975). p.144.
19. Urbach, K. (2015). p.29.
20. Aronson, T. (2014). p.111
21. Princess Alice, Countess of Athlone. (1966). p.84.
22. Lee, S. (1925). p.741.
23. Princess Alice, Countess of Athlone. (1966). p.90.
24. Ibid. p.90.
25. Ibid. p.37.
26. Rushton, A.R. (2018). p.14.
27. Urbach, K. (2015). p.31.
28. Röhl, J. (2014). p.18.
29. Aronson, T. (2014). p.115.
30. Ibid. p.115.
31. Wiebe, M. (Ed.) (2004). p.77.
32. Topham, A. (1992). p.30.
33. Princess Alice, Countess of Athlone. (1966). p.97.

34. Aronson, T. (2014). pp.117–18.
35. Princess Daisy of Pless. (1931). p.285.
36. Princess Alice, Countess of Athlone. (1966). p.92.
37. Van der Kiste, J. (2015). p.34.
38. Kessler, H. (2011). p.199.
39. Princess Alice, Countess of Athlone. (1966). p.91.
40. Ibid. p.92.
41. Ibid. p.86.
42. Van der Kiste, J. (1999). p.165.
43. Röhl, J. (2014). p.10.
44. Ibid. pp.4–5.
45. Topham, A. (1992). p.26.
46. Ibid. pp.26–7.
47. *The Times.* 16 June 1888.
48. Corti, E. (1957). *The English Empress: A Study in Relations between Queen Victoria and Her Eldest Daughter, Empress Frederick of Germany.* Cassell & Co. p.302.
49. Seymour, M. (2014). p.106.
50. Ibid.
51. RA Z 45/36 V to QV 8/5/89. Quoted in Pakula, H. (1999). p.564.
52. Pakula, H. (1999). p.621.
53. Seymour, M. (2014). pp.126–27.
54. Pakula, H. (1999). pp.621–25.
55. Letter from Queen Victoria to Empress Vicky. 7 November 1879. Quoted in Fulford, R. (1981). p.57.
56. Van der Kiste, J. (2014). p.40.
57. Roberts, A. (2011). p.484.
58. Massie, R. (1991). p.268.
59. Wilson, A.N. (2014). p.469.
60. Aronson, T. (2014). p.126.
61. Wilson, A.N. (2014). p.571.
62. Princess Alice, Countess of Athlone. (1966). p.102.
63. Ibid. p.101.
64. Röhl, J. (2014). p.574.
65. Cust, L. (1930). p.28.
66. Ridley, J. (2013). pp.367–69.
67. Princess Alice, Countess of Athlone. (1966). p.115.
68. Letter from Charles Edward Duke of Saxe-Coburg-Gotha to Princess Alice. 1 August 1902. RA ACA/10. Quoted in Urbach, K. (2015). p.31.
69. *The Graphic.* 20 February 1904.
70. Urbach, K. (2015). p.32.
71. Ibid. p.32.
72. RA Prince of Wales's Diary. 27 March, 5, 6 April 1913. Quoted in Ziegler, P. (1990). p.42.
73. The Duke of Windsor (1947). p.100.
74. Bolitho, H. (1937). p.45.
75. Letter from Princess Alice of Teck to Queen Mary. 18 September 1913. RA GV CC 53/399. Quoted in Ziegler, P. (1990). p.44.
76. RA Prince of Wales's Diary. 7 June 1914. Quoted in Ziegler, P. (1990). p.44.
77. RA Prince of Wales's Diary. 2 July 1914. Quoted in Ziegler, P. (1990). p.44.
78. Ibid.

79. King, G. and Woolmans, S. (2013). p.177.
80. Rauchensteiner, M. and Litscher, M. (Eds) (2000). p.63.
81. Carter, M. (2003). p.419.
82. Seymour, M. (2014). p.189.
83. Rushton, A.R. (2018). p.20.
84. Petropoulos, J. (2006). p.39.
85. Seymour, M. (2014). p.189.
86. Letter from Friedrich von Hochberg to Princess Daisy of Pless. 29 May 1917. Quoted in Pless, D. (1936). pp.91–92.
87. Carter, M. (2003). p.427
88. RA GV/PRIV/ GVD. 29 July 1914. Quoted in Carter, M. (2003). p.439.
89. Nicolson, H. (1984). p.247.
90. Princess Alice, Countess of Athlone. (1966). p.157.
91. Urbach, K. (2015). p.65.
92. Püschel, A. *Carl Eduard von Coburg*: BA thesis in Staatsarchive Coburg. Quoted in Urbach, K. (2015). p.66.
93. *John Bull*. 6 October 1917.
94. *Evening News*. 2 February 1935.
95. Sassoon, S. (1930). p.273.
96. *Evening News*. 2 February 1935.
97. Hanson, N. (2009). p.137.
98. Ibid. p.147.
99. *The Daily Mail*. 15 June 1917.
100. *The Times*. 15 June 1917.
101. Hanson, N. (2009). p.159.
102. Bradford, S. (2011). p.84.
103. Rose, K. (1983). p.171.
104. Urbach, K. (2015). p.66.
105. *The Times*. 1 September 1922.
106. Aronson, T. (2014). p.216.
107. HC Deb (18 November 1914). Vol. 68 cc. 437–38. Hansard.
108. Monger, D. (2012). p.234.
109. Princess Alice, Countess of Athlone. (1966). p.165.
110. Rose, K. (1983). p.174.
111. Linning, S. (2017). 'How the House of Windsor Was Born'. *The Daily Mail*. 23 February 2017.
112. Ibid.
113. Eade, P. (2011). p.22.
114. Monger, D. (2012). p.234.
115. Kerr, M. (1934). p.289.

Chapter Two

1. Ziegler, P. (1990). p.48.
2. The Duke of Windsor. (1947). p.111.
3. Ziegler, P. (1990). p.51.
4. The Duke of Windsor. (1947). p.111.
5. Ibid. pp.111–12.
6. Ziegler, P. (1990). p.67.

7. King, G. (2003). p.88.
8. Ziegler, P. (1990). pp.48–9.
9. Letter from Edward to Lady Coke. Coke Papers. 23 June 1917. Quoted in Ziegler, P. (1990). p.76.
10. The Duke of Windsor. (1947). p.124.
11. *Passchendaele: Fighting for Belgium* (2017). Ministry for Culture and Heritage.
12. Patch, H. and Van Emden, R. (2009). p.98.
13. Blundell, N. (2007). 'The Last Survivor re-lives the horrors of Passchendaele'. *The Daily Mail*. 28 July 2007.
14. The Duke of Windsor. (1947). p.112.
15. Patch, H. Van Emden, R. (2009). p.74.
16. The Duke of Windsor. (1947). p.123.
17. Ziegler, P. (1990). p.78.
18. The Duke of Windsor. (1947). p.124.
19. Letter from Edward to his father King George V. 31 July 1917. Quoted in The Duke of Windsor (1947). p.125.
20. RA Prince of Wales's Diary. 21 February 1916. Quoted in Ziegler, P. (1990). p.89.
21. Lees-Milne, J. (1988). p.301.
22. Piers Leigh Papers (1 November 1918). Quoted in Ziegler, P. (1990). p.90.
23. Carter, M. (2003). p.445.
24. Airlie, M. (1962). p.138.
25. Princess Alice, Countess of Athlone. (1966). p.160.
26. Kerr, M. (1934). p.289.
27. Eade, P. (2011). p.22.
28. Friedrich, O. (1995). p.23.
29. MacDonogh, G. (2000). p.414.
30. Carter, M. (2009). p.484.
31. Bentinck, N. (1922). p.23.
32. Macarthur Memorial. (2016). *Kaiser Wilhelm II: Part I by World War. Season Three*. July 2016.
33. Lamar, C. (1996). p.299.
34. 'Kaiser's Youngest Son Shoots Himself.' *The New York Times*. 19 July 1920.
35. Carter, M. (2009). p.491.
36. Ibid.
37. Lamar, C. (1996). p.302.
38. Urbach, K. (2015). p.143.
39. Letter from Carl Eduard to his sister Princess Alice. 15 November 1928. RA ACA/10. Quoted in Urbach, K. (2015). p.148.
40. Roddie, S. (1932). pp.88–89.
41. Princess Alice, Countess of Athlone. (1966). p.165.
42. Urbach, K. (2015). p.137.
43. Petropoulos, J. (2006). p.41.
44. Hessen, W. (Ed.), Hessen, R. (1986). *Aufzeichnungen* (Records). Privatedruck. Quoted in Petropoulos, J. (2006). p.44.
45. Roddie, S. (1932). pp.50–54.
46. Letter by Dorothy Dexter. 3 September 1923. Society of Friends Library. FEWVRC 1914–24, 10/3/7.
47. Letter from Lieutenant Colonel Roddie wrote to Field Marshall Sir William Wilson. Quoted in Roddie, S. (1932). pp.54–55.
48. Roddie, S. (1932). p.57.

Chapter Three

1. Friedrich, O. (1995). p.39.
2. Mitchell, O. (2008). p.47.
3. Hessen, W. (Ed.) and Hessen, R. (1986) *Aufzeichnungen* (Records). Privatedruck. pp.129–31. Quoted in Petropoulos, J. (2006). pp.129–31.
4. Friedrich, O. (1995). pp.44–45.
5. Ibid. p.45.
6. Ibid. p.48.
7. Urbach, K. (2015). p.146.
8. Letter from Carl Eduard to his sister Princess Alice, Countess of Athlone. October 1919. RA ACA/10. Quoted Urbach, K. (2015). p.146.
9. Letter from Carl Eduard to his sister Princess Alice, Countess of Athlone. 15 November 1928. RA ACA/10. Quoted in Urbach, K. (2015). p.147.
10. Seymour, M. (2014). p.240.
11. Keynes, J. (1919). p.251.
12. Sandner, H. (2010). p.183.
13. Urbach, K. (2015). p.151.
14. Friedrich, O. (1995). p.112.
15. Kessler, H. (2013). p.5228.
16. Ibid. p.5024.
17. Ibid.
18. Ibid. p.5058.
19. Friedrich, O. (1995). p.113.
20. Ibid. p.113.
21. *Vossische Zietung.* 25 June 1922. Quoted in Kessler, H. (2013). p.5176.
22. Friedrich, O. (1995). pp.113–14.
23. Kessler, H. (2013).
24. Urbach, K. (2016). pp.152–53.
25. Ibid. p.152.
26. Friedrich, O. (1995). p.117.
27. Gay, P. (2001). p.20.
28. Urbach, K. (2016). p.153.
29. Kershaw, I. (2008). pp.125–26.
30. Hitler, A. (1926). p.615.
31. Urbach, K. (2016). p.156.
32. Letter from Carl Eduard to Princess Alice. 1 September 1923. RA ACA/10. Quoted in Urbach, K. (2016). p.155.
33. Friedrich, O. (1995). p.144.
34. Roddie, S. (1932). pp.233–34.
35. Ibid. p.234.
36. Urbach, K. (2016). p.154.
37. Ibid. p.149
38. Letter from Carl Eduard to Princess Alice. 27 November 1923. RA ACA/10. Quoted in Urbach, K. (2016). p.155.
39. Ullrich, V. (2013). p.73.

Chapter Four

1. Albright, M. (2018). p.63.
2. Katz, R. (2003). p.20.
3. British Government: Home Office (1927). *Churchill's speech in Rome.* 20 January 1927. HO 45/24893.
4. Fromme, B. (1990). p.138.
5. Fisher, C. (1995).
6. *The Spectator.* 18 October 2014.
7. Zinoveiff, S. (2014). p.87.
8. Seymour, M. (2014). p.245.
9. Petropoulos, J. (2006). p.68.
10. Clavichord Recital. (1922). *Nation.* 30 December 1922. pp.225 and 229.
11. Moorcroft-Wilson, J. (2013). p.417.
12. Letter from Prince Philip to Sassoon. (1921). University Library Cambridge. MS. Add. 390 9375/390. 17 October 1921.
13. Letter from Prince Philip to Sassoon. (1921). University Library Cambridge. MS. Add. 390 9375/391. 28 October 1921.
14. Letter from Prince Philip to Sassoon. (1923). University Library Cambridge, MS. Add. 390 9375/460. 2 August 1923.
15. Clavichord Recital. (1922). *Nation.* 30 December 1922.
16. Petropoulos, J. (2006). p.65.
17. Hart-Davis, R. (1981). pp.200–01.
18. Ibid. p.225.
19. Letter from Prince Philipp of Hess to Sassoon. (1921). University Library Cambridge. MS. Add. 9375/391. 28 October 1921.
20. Egremont, M. (2013). p.268.
21. Hart-Davis, R. (1981). p.216.
22. Ibid. p.227.
23. Petropoulos, J. (2006). p.71.
24. Wiskemann, E. (1966). pp.40–1.
25. Hart-Davis, R. (1981). p.227.
26. Von Ilsemann, S. (1968). p.51.
27. Warwick, C. (2016). p.64.
28. 'The Forgotten Prince'. *The Scotsman.* 25 August 2002.
29. Wilson, J. (2011). p.95.
30. Shaw, K. (1999). p.305.
31. Warwick, C. (2016). p.64.
32. Lee, A. 'Scandal of Forgotten Prince George, Duke of Kent and his Tormented Lovechild.' *Daily Express.* 15 July 2012.
33. Shaw, K. (1999). p.304.
34. Lockhart, R. (1973). p.215.
35. Warwick, C. (2016). pp.66–67.
36. Shaw, K. (1999). p.305.
37. Young, K. (Ed.) (1973). p.215.
38. Wilkes, R. (2002). 'A Dainty Dish to Set Before the Prince'. *The Telegraph.* 9 January 2002.
39. Higham, C. (2005). p.55.
40. King, G. (2003). p.92.
41. Fritzsche, P. (1992). p.125.

42. Petropoulos, J. (2006). p.92.
43. Eade, P. (2012). p.73.
44. Petropoulos, J. (2006). pp.88–91.
45. *File of Prince Christoph*. BAB (formerly BDC) SSF 94A. Lebenslauf. 21 February 1933. Quoted in Petropoulos, J. (2006). p.91.
46. *Victoria, Marchioness of Milford Haven Statement*, 8 May 1930. Bingswanger Papers, University of Tübingen. Quoted in Vickers, H. (2000). pp.181–84.
47. Vickers, H. (2000). pp.200–01
48. Hicks, P. (2012). p.19.
49. Vickers, H. (2000). pp.205–07.
50. Eade, P. (2012). p.203.
51. Vickers, H. (2000). p.242.
52. Eade, P. (2012). pp.77–78.
53. Ibid. p.203.
54. Rocco, F. 'A Strange Life: Profile of Prince Philip'. *The Independent*. 13 December 1992.
55. Goldsmith, B. (1980). pp.150–53.
56. Eade, P. (2012). p.63.
57. Ibid.
58. Goldsmith, B. (1980). p.151.
59. Higham, C. and Mosely R. (1991). p.81.
60. Ibid. pp.79–81.
61. Ullrich, V. (2013). p.316.
62. Jenkins, R. (2001). p.468.
63. Ibid. p.469.
64. Roberts, A. (2018). p.363.
65. Goldsmith, B. (1980). p.151.
66. Reynolds, R. (1939). p.9.
67. Wainwright, W. (2017). p.87.
68. Reynolds, R. (1939). p.33.
69. Ibid. p.11.
70. Larson, E. (2012). p.146.
71. Harding, T. (2015). p.76.
72. Letter from Paul von Hindenburg to Meissner. (13 August 1932). Quoted in Wheeler-Bennett, J. (1936).
73. Cecil, L. (1996). p.304.
74. Letter from Wilhelm to Houston Chamberlain. 3 June 1923. HS Chamberlain, *Briefe*, 2:274. Quoted in Cecil, L. (1996). p.318.
75. Wheeler-Bennett, J. (1974). pp.182–83.
76. Fromme, B. (1990). p.58.
77. Cecil, L. (1996). pp.335–36.
78. Ibid. p.336.
79. Sermon by Wilhelm at Doorn. 18 May 1930. Mackensen Paper's no. 263. Quoted in Cecil, L. (1996). p.334.
80. Gustche, W. (1991). p.131.
81. Petropoulos, J. (2006). p.116.
82. Maser, W. (2000). p.247.
83. Petropoulos, J. (2006). pp.124–25.
84. Göring, E. (1967). pp.32–33.
85. Parker, J. (1990). p.74.

86. Prince Heinrich of Hesse (1994). p.170. Quoted in Petropoulos, J. (2006). p.132.
87. Balfour, N. and Mackay, S. (1980). p.177.
88. Fussell, P. (2002). pp.24–25.
89. Brereton, H. (1950). pp.143–44.
90. Flavin, M. (1996). p.86.
91. Ibid. p.85.
92. Eade, P. (2012). p.86.
93. Flavin, M. (1996). p.110.
94. Eade, P. (2012). p.88.
95. Rocco, F. 'A Strange Life: Profile of Prince Philip'. *The Independent.* 13 December 1992.
96. Eade, P. (2012). pp.88–89.
97. Parker, J. (1990). p.56.
98. *Gordontoun Record* (Easter, 1947). p.4.

Chapter Five

1. Mosley, O. (1968). p.76.
2. Rose, N. (2001). p.115.
3. Jennings, C. (2007). p.232.
4. Ibid.
5. Parker, J. (1988). p.90.
6. Litchfield, D. (2015). p.96.
7. Rose, N. (2001). p.120.
8. Ibid. p.122.
9. Ibid. p.39.
10. Renehan, Jr. E. (2002). *Joseph Kennedy and the Jews.* The George Washington University. historynewsnetwork.org/article/697.
11. Nicholson, N. (Ed.) (1967). p.469.
12. Rose, N. (1986). p.149.
13. Boyd, J. (2017). p.197.
14. Rose, N. (2001). p.137.
15. *Princess Stephanie Hohenlohe Papers.* (Box 3). Quoted in Wilson, J. (2011). p.98.
16. Wilson, J. (2011). p.98.
17. Wachsmann, N. (2015). p.26.
18. Ibid. p.31.
19. Ibid. p.36.
20. Sinclair-Loutit, K. (2009). p.22.
21. Boyd, J. (2017). p.115.
22. Wilson, A. (1939). p.83.
23. Boyd, J. (2017). p.175.
24. Ibid. p.191.
25. Burn, M. (2003). pp.76–77.
26. Göring, E. (1972). p.70.
27. Spitzy, R. (1986). *So haben wir das Reich verspielt: Bekenntnisse eines Illegalen* (So We Have Gambled the Empire: Confessions of an Illegal). Munich and Vienna. p.408. Quoted in Urbach, K. (2015). p.180.
28. Urbach, K. (2015). p.175.
29. Ibid. p.178.

30. Letter from Otto II von Bismarck to Dr Dieckhoff. 22 August 1934. Otto II Bismarck papers. Friedrichsruh, AOBS. Quoted in Urbach, K. (2015). p.185.
31. Letter from the Duke of Coburg to Princess Alice. 15 April 1936. RA ACA/10. Quoted in Urbach, K. (2015). p.186.
32. Urbach, K. (2015). p.186.
33. Norwich, J. (Ed.). (2005). p.218.
34. Pugh, M. (2006). p.270.
35. Donaldson, F. (1986). p.195.
36. Pugh, M. (2006). p.270.
37. Knightly, P. (2003). 'The Truth About the Cambridge Spies'. *The Independent.* 11 May 2003.
38. Hutchinson, G. (1939). p.195.
39. *The Times.* 12 June 1935.
40. Martin, R. (1973). pp.171–72.
41. Parker, J. (1988). p.94.
42. Craig, G. and Gilbert, F. (1953). p.425.
43. Parker, J. (1988). p.93.
44. Hess, F. (1979). p.28. Quoted in Urbach, K. (2015). p.189.
45. Urbach, K. (2015). p.189.
46. Hess, F. (1979). p.43. Quoted in Urbach, K. (2015). p.189.
47. Bloch, M. (1994). pp.77–81.
48. Ibid. p.11.
49. Ibid pp.71–73.
50. DBFP 2/XIII. Nos. 289–90. (Documents on British Foreign Policy.) Quoted in Bloch, M. (1994). p.72.
51. Kershaw, I. (1999). p.558.
52. Bloch, M. (1994). p.48.
53. Higham, C. (2005). p.96.
54. Viktoria Luise, Duchess of Brunswick. (1967). p.162.

Chapter Six

1. Maxwell, E. (1954). p.295.
2. Bloch, M. (2012). p.461.
3. Higham, C. (2005). p.102.
4. Rhodes, J.R. (Ed.) (1967). p.41.
5. The Duchess of Windsor. (1980). p.8.
6. Keegan, J. (1989). p.151.
7. Balfour, N. and Mackay, S. (1980). p.93.
8. Higham, C. (2005). p.109.
9. Columbia Box 112. Letter from Prince Philipp of Hesse to Prince Paul. 1 January 1935. Quoted in Balfour, N. and Mackay, S. (1980). p.115.
10. Balfour, N. and Mackay, S. (1980). p.115.
11. Lowndes, S. (Ed.) (1971). pp.145–46.
12. Higham, C. (2005). pp.109–11.
13. Ibid. p.110.
14. Parker, J. (1988). pp.87–88.
15. Watson, S. (1997). pp.112–14.
16. Ibid. p.120.
17. Higham, C. (2005). p.111.

18. Sebba, A. (2004). p.104.
19. *Spying on the Royals.* (2007). Television Documentary. Channel 4.
20. Morton, A. (2015). p.48.
21. *Spying on the Royals.* (2007). Television Documentary. Channel 4.
22. Ibid. Interview with Professor Richard Aldrich.
23. Ibid.
24. Parker, J. (1988). p.67.
25. *Spying on the Royals.* (2007). Television Documentary. Channel 4.
26. Parker, J. (1988). p.97.
27. Morton, A. (2015). p.59.
28. Parker, J. (1988). pp.92–93.
29. Shard, M. (2004). pp.56–57.
30. Wilson, J. (2011). p.96.
31. Morton, A. (2015). p.55.
32. Ibid. p.56.
33. Harding, T. (2015). p.90.
34. Bartlett, V. (1933). p.12.
35. Griffiths, R. (1983). p.183.
36. Ibid.
37. Harding, H. (1967). p.61.
38. Parker, J. (1988). p.99.
39. German Documents: 5482/E3 82057-78.
40. Parker, J. (1988). p.101.
41. Donaldson, F. (1986). p.179.
42. Ibid. p.181.
43. Ibid. pp.179–80.
44. Higham, C. (2005). p.149.
45. Morrow, A. (1983). p.19.
46. Higham, C. (2005). p.150.
47. Morton, A. (2015). p.74.
48. Donaldson, F. (1986). p.183.
49. Vansittart, R. (1958). p.445.
50. King, G. (2003). p.149.
51. Sukhdev, S. (2015). 'Rendezvous at the Russian Tea Rooms'. *The Observer.*
     18 October 2015.
52. Admiral Wolkoff's file in The National Archives (KV 2/2258).
53. Deacon, R. (1979).
54. Ellis, W. (1997). p.183.

Chapter Seven

1. Hesse, F. (1954). pp.21–23.
2. Speer, A. (1970). p.72.
3. Allen, M. (2000). p.17.
4. Speer, A. (1970).
5. Allen, P. (1983). p.60.
6. Morton, A. (2015). p.79.
7. Ibid.
8. George S. Messersmith Papers. MSS 109 0809-00.

9. King, G. (2003). p.149.
10. Shawcross, W. (2009). p.366.
11. Morton, A. (2015). p.72.
12. 'Memorandum of the Foreign Secretary Anthony Eden'. 8 March 1936. Quoted in *Documents on British Foreign Policy 1919–1939, vol. XXI: The Rhineland Crisis and the Ending of Sanctions March–July 1936.* HMSO (1977). pp.60–66.
13. Lord Birkenhead. (1969). p.128.
14. King, G. (1999). p.153.
15. Lord Birkenhead. (1969). p.128.
16. King, G. (2003). pp.153–54.
17. Ibid. p.155.
18. Sotheby's Catalogue. Public collection. 36.
19. *Spying on the Royals.* (2007). Television Documentary. Channel 4.
20. Higham, C. (2005). p 161.
21. Donaldson, F. (1986). p.214.
22. Sebba, A. (2011). p.137.
23. Turkey Weller, G. (1936). *New York Times.* 20 September 1936.
24. Higham, C. (2005). p.161.
25. Ibid. p.169.
26. The Duke of Windsor. (1947). p.319.
27. Higham, C. (2005). p.170.
28. Ibid. pp.167–69.
29. Ibid. p.169.
30. Rev. Alan Don Diary. 4 November 1936.
31. Donaldson, F. (1986). p.235.
32. Middlemas, K. and Barnes, J. (1969). p.994.
33. Hansard's Parliamentary Debates. 10 December 1936.
34. The Duke of Windsor. (1947). p.333.
35. King, G. (2003). p.198.
36. Ibid. p.255.
37. Watson, S. (1997). p.142.
38. Higham, C. (2005). p.176.
39. Lord Birkenhead. (1969). p.141.
40. Roberts, A. (2018). p.409.
41. Ibid. p.408.
42. Ibid. pp.408–09.
43. Higham, C. (2005). p.181.
44. Dorrell, S. (2006). p.405.
45. Sebba, A. (2011). p.164.
46. Bloch, M. (Ed.) (1986). p.216.
47. Higham, C. (2005). p.183.
48. Ziegler, P. (1990). p.328.
49. Sebba, A. (2011). p.169.
50. *Spying on the Royals.* (2007). Television Documentary. Channel 4.
51. Ibid.
52. Dorrell, S. (2006). p.404.
53. Ibid. p.406.
54. Ibid. p.403.
55. The Duke of Windsor. (1947). p.384.

56. Bates, S. (2003). 'Monarch's Unheard Public Appeal to Hang onto the Throne'. *The Guardian*. 30 January 2003.
57. Dorrell, S. (2006). p.406.
58. James, R. (Ed.) (1993). p.95.
59. Lord Winterton. (1953). p.233.
60. Dorrell, S. (2006). p.404.
61. Donaldson, F. (1986). p.282.
62. Dorrell, S. (2006). p.406.
63. Higham, C. (2005). p.185.
64. Dorrell, S. (2006). p.406.
65. Roberts, A. (2018). p.411.
66. Ibid.
67. Ziegler, P. (1990). p.331.

Chapter Eight

1. Wilson, J. (2006).
2. Döhring, H., Wilhelm, K. and Plain, A. (2018). p.133.
3. Dorrell, S. (2006). p.406.
4. Parker, J. (1988). p.146.
5. Ibid. p.148.
6. King, G. (2003). p.258.
7. Higham, C. (2005). p 233.
8. Donaldson, F. (1986). p.323.
9. King, G. (1999). pp.265–66.
10. Parker, J. (1988). p.152.
11. Bocca, G. (1954). p.163.
12. King, G. (1999). p.271.
13. Ibid. p.274.
14. Cadbury, D. (2015). p.48.
15. Dodds, M. (1940). p.223.
16. Evans, R. (2005). pp.458–59.
17. Cadbury, D. (2015). p.48.
18. Parker, J. (1988). p.155.
19. The Duchess of Windsor. (1980). p.309.
20. Parker, J. (1988). p.154.
21. Morton, A. (2015). p.127.
22. Parker, J. (1988). p.155.
23. King, G. (1999). p.274.
24. Ibid. p.288.
25. Donaldson, F. (1986). p.330.
26. Associated Press Article. 12 October 1937.
27. King, G. (1999). p.274.
28. Ibid. p.279.
29. Allen, P. (1983). pp.95–96.
30. King, G. (1999). pp.280–81.
31. Hichens, M. (2016).
32. Brendon, P. (2016).
33. Morton, A. (2015). p.131.

34. Letter from Duke of Coburg to Duke of Windsor. 10 October 1937. RA. DW3450. Quoted in Petropoulos, J. (2006). p.207.
35. Petropoulos, J. (2006). p.207.
36. Bullitt, O. (1973). p.230.
37. Rothfeld, A. (2002). 'Nazis Looted Art'. *The Holocaust Records Preservation Project, Part 1*, Vol. 34, No. 3. Autumn 2002, The US National Archives and Records Administration.
38. Göring, E. (1972). p.89.
39. Brett, A. (2007). 'Masking Nazi Violence in the Beautiful Landscape of the Obersalzberg'. *Comparative Literature*. Vol. 59, No. 3, Summer 2007. Duke University Press. p.4.
40. Gun, N. (1969). p.167.
41. Parker, J. and Bearne M. (1988). 'Shadier Side of the Windsors'. *Sunday Mail* (QLD). 17 April 1988.
42. The Duchess of Windsor. (1980). p.87.
43. King, G. (2010). p.294.
44. Higham, C. (2016). p.258.
45. Allen, P. (1983). p.97.
46. Higham, C. (2016). p.258.
47. Milton, R. (2007). p.166.
48. King, G. (2011). p.294.
49. Schmidt, P. (2016). p.85.
50. Higham, C. (2016). p.259.
51. Ibid. p.259.
52. Getty, J. (1976). p.149.
53. The Duchess of Windsor. (1980). p.317.
54. Padfield, P. (2014). p.21.
55. The Duchess of Windsor. (1980). p.87.
56. Allen, P. (1983). p.98.
57. Morton, A. (2015). p.134.
58. King, G. (2011). p.294.
59. Schmidt, P. (2016). p.85.
60. Cadbury, D. (2015). p.56.
61. Cazalet Papers. 27 June 1937. Quoted in Roberts, A. (1994). p.10.

Chapter Nine

1. Sandner, H. (2010). p.326.
2. Ibid. p.337.
3. Modin, Y. (1994). p.65.
4. *Bericht unseres Vertrauensmannes* (Report of our Trustee) in London. 11 December 1935 R 43 II 1434 BAB. Quoted in Urbach, K. (2015). p.202.
5. Sir Arnold Wilson MP. (1934). 'Germany in May'. *English Review* (June 1934). Quoted in Urbach, K. (2015). p.205.
6. Hosech Report. R 43 11 1434. BAB. Quoted in Urbach, K. (2015). p.202.
7. Urbach, K. (2015). pp.242–33.
8. DGFP. Doc 531. P1006. January 1936. Quoted in Leibovitz, C. and Finkel, A. (1997). p.145.
9. Brendon, P. and Whitehead P. (2000). p.104.

10. Roberts, A. (1997). p.201.
11. Bouverie, T. (2019). p.151.
12. Sir Ivone Kirkpatrick. (1959). p.95.
13. Lord Halifax's Diary. Quoted in Roberts, A. (1997). p.72.
14. Letter from Henderson to Halifax. 11 March 1938. DBFP. Third Series, Vol. 1, No. 13. (1949). Quoted in Bouverie, P. (2019). p.144.
15. Bouverie, T. (2019). p.145.
16. Nicholson, N. (Ed.) (2004). p.334.
17. Bouverie, T. (2019). p.320.
18. Ibid. pp.138–39.
19. Ibid. p.178.
20. Hesse, F. (1954). p.43.
21. Bouverie, T. (2019). p.151.
22. Lord Templewood. (1976). p.282.
23. Churchill, W. (1948).
24. Bouverie, T. (2019). p.180.
25. Letter from Chamberlain to his sister Hilda. 13 March 1938. The Chamberlain Papers (Birmingham University) 18/1/1041.
26. De Waal, E. (2011). p.237.
27. Snyder, L. (1976). p.320.
28. De Waal, E. (2011). pp.237–47.
29. Handsard. HC Deb. 24 March 1938. Vol. 333. Col. 1454.
30. Shirer, W. (1962). p.351.
31. Eilers, M. (1987). p.113.
32. Ibid. p.116.
33. King, G. (2007). *Twilight of Splendour: The Court of Queen Victoria During Her Diamond Jubilee Year.* John Wiley & Sons.
34. Eilers, M. (1987). p.116.
35. Montgomery Hyde, H. (1991). p.90.
36. Ibid. p.91.
37. Eilers, M. (1987). p.114.
38. Montgomery Hyde, H. (1991). p.91.
39. *Manchester Guardian.* 16 September 1938.
40. Horace Wilson. Notes on Munich. CAB 127/158.
41. Caldecote Papers Diary. *August 26th to September 19th 1928* – Munich. 17 September 1938/ INKP 1. Cabinet Minutes. 17 September 1938/ CAB 23/95/3/72.
42. Cabinet Minutes. 17 September 1938. CAB 23/95/3/72–86.
43. *The Czechoslovakia Crisis.* Notes of Informal Meeting of Ministers. 24 September 1938. CAB 27/646/91–2.
44. Letter from George VI to Queen Mary. 27 September 1938. Quoted in Wheeler-Bennett, J. (1959). *King George VI.* Reprint Society. p.352.
45. Prime Minister's Statement. Hansard. HC Deb. 28 September 1938. Vol. 339. Cols 5–28.
46. Urbach, K. (2015). pp.206–07.
47. Rose, K. (1975). *The Later Cecils.* Weidenfeld and Nicolson.
48. Bouverie, T. (2019). p.280.
49. Ibid.
50. Cadbury, D. (2015). p.66.
51. *Illustrated London News.*

52. Grigg, J. (1989). *The Times*. 11 November 1989.
53. Roberts, A. (1994). p.21.
54. Ibid.
55. Bouverie, T. (2019). p.298.
56. McDonough, F. (1998). pp.124–33.
57. Roberts, A. (1994). p.21.
58. McDonough, F. (1998). pp.106–07.
59. Faber, D. (2008). p.420.
60. Kershaw, I. (2000). p.138.
61. Defries, H. (2001). p.134.
62. Bouverie, T. (2019). p.308.
63. Peak Papers. 19 February 1957. Quoted in Defries, H. (2001). p.134.
64. *Truth*. 11 May 1938.
65. Macmillan, H. (1966). p.587.
66. *The Times*. 28 September 1939.
67. Bouverie, T. (2019). p.308.
68. *The Times*. 11 November 1938.
69. Gilbert, M. (1979). p.223.
70. Roberts, A. (1997). p.70.
71. Cabinet Minutes. 21 December 1938. PS/PSO/GVI/C/47/140.
72. Muggeridge, M. (Ed.) (1939) *Count Ciano*. . p.10.
73. *The Times*. 16 March 1939.
74. Cadbury, D. (2015). p.71.
75. Brendon, P. and Whitehead P. (2000). p.105.
76. Urbach, K. (2015). p.207.
77. James, R. (Ed). (1993). p.207.
78. Cadogan Papers. Diary. 15 and 20 April 1939. ACAD 1/8. Quoted in Bouverie, T. (2019). p.332.
79. Gilbert, M. (1983). *Winston S. Churchill. Vol. V. Companion, Part 3. Major-General James Marshall-Cornwall to Halifax, 'Conversation with Count Schwerin', 6 July 1930*. pp.1553–54.
80. Chamberlain Papers. NC 18.1/1108, 23 July 1939. Quoted in Roberts, A. (1994). p.24.
81. Chamberlain Papers. NC 18.1/1108, 23 July 1939.
82. Bloch, M. (1988). pp.313–14.
83. Roosevelt Library, PSF France. Quoted in Bradford, S. (2011). p.380.
84. Morton, A. (2015). p.145.
85. Petropoulos, J. (2006). p.201.
86. Morton, A. (2015). p.145.
87. Ibid. p.146.
88. Farago, L. (1971).
89. Petropoulos, P. (2006). p.201.
90. Crawford, M. (1952). p.59.
91. Eade, P. (2012). p.126.
92. Parker, J. (1990). p.73.
93. Ibid.
94. King, G. (2003). pp.302–04.
95. Roberts, A. (2018). p.422.
96. Ibid. p.447.
97. Ibid.

98. Dormus, M. and Romane, P. (Ed.) (2007). p.579.
99. Cadbury, D. (2015). pp.75–76.
100. Dietrich, O. (2010). p.47.
101. Cadbury, D. (2015). p.84.
102. The Duchess of Windsor. (1980). pp.329–30.

Chapter Ten

1. Weisbrode, K. (2013). p.108.
2. Roberts, A. (1994). p.13.
3. Weisbrode, K. (2013). p.66.
4. Young, K. (Ed). (1980). Quoted in Roberts, A. (1994). pp.14–15.
5. Bloch, M. (1988). p.144.
6. Higham, C. (2005). p.302.
7. Roberts, A. (1994). p.25.
8. Shawcross, W. (2012). pp.279–80.
9. Parker, J. (1988). p.180.
10. Cadbury, D. (2015). pp.107–08.
11. Higham, C. (2005). p.308.
12. Bielenberg, C. (1998). p.69.
13. Ibid.
14. Bryan, J. and Murphy, C. (1979). p.418.
15. Ziegler, P. (1981). p.199.
16. Higham, C. (2005). pp.304–05.
17. Minister Zech to State Secretary Weizsäcker. 19 February 1940. *Documents on German Foreign Policy 1918–1945* (1954). Series D. Volume VIII. p.785.
18. Costello, J. (1988). pp.413–14.
19. FOIA. FBI File on the Duke and Duchess of Windsor. 13 September 1940.
20. Chamberlain Papers, NC 7/4/10 17 May 1940.
21. *The Quotable Winston Churchill.* (2013). Running Press. p.114.
22. Roberts, A. (1997). p.203.
23. Wheeler-Bennett, J. (1959). p.446.
24. Halifax Diary. 10 May 1940.
25. Cadbury, D. (2015). p.130.
26. Jenkins, R. (2001). p.608.
27. Howard, A. (1987). pp.96–100.
28. Roberts, A. (1991). pp.248–50.
29. Foreign Minister's Secretariat to Foreign Ministry. 30 June 1940. *Documents on Germany Foreign Policy*, Series D., Volume X, No. 66. p.68.
30. Telegram to Cadogan. 26 September 1940. TNO FO 1093/23 C/5023. Quoted in Cadbury, D. (2015). p.154.
31. Bloch, M. (1984). p.59.
32. Morton, A. (2015). p.179.
33. Donaldson, F. (1986). p.374.
34. Higham, C. (2005). p.320.
35. Morton, A. (2015). pp.166–68.
36. Ibid. p.170.
37. MSS 1W4126cFA2. Weddell, A. Box 4. Elizabeth Weddell. Weddell Collection, Virginia Historical Society.
38. Urbach, K. (2015). p.213.

39. Parker, J. (1988). p.193.
40. Bloch, M. (1984). p.144.
41. Cadbury, D. (2015). p.159.
42. Morton, A. (2015). pp.187–88.
43. Parker, J. (1988). p.203.
44. Ibid. p.193.
45. Cadbury, D. (2015). p.159.
46. Huene to Ribbentrop. *2* August 1940. *Documents on German Foreign Policy.* Series D. Volume X, No. 277. pp.398–440.
47. Parker, J. (1988). p.200.

Chapter Eleven

1. Urbach, K. (2015). p.216.
2. Müller-Hill, B. (1999). 'The Blood from Auschwitz and the Silence of the Scholars'. *History and Philosophy of the Life Sciences.* 21 (3). pp.331–65.
3. History of the Kaiser Wilhelm Society. Official Website.
4. Sandner, H. (2010). p.340.
5. Schwartz, M (1998). '"Euthanasie" Debate in Deutschland'. *Vierteljahreshefte für Zeitgeschichte* (Quarterly Bulletins for Contemporary History). 46: 631.
6. Rushton, A. (2018). p.72.
7. Faulstich, H. (1998). *Hungersterben in der Psychiatre* (Starvation Deaths in Psychiatry) *1914–1949.* Lambertus Verlag. p.582.
8. Rushton, A. (2018). p.114.
9. Ibid. p.94.
10. Schloss Hartheim Memorial and Documentation Centre. Official Website.
11. Rushton, A. (2018). p.114.
12. Sandner, H. (2010). p.378.
13. Urbach, K. (2015). p.159.
14. Petropoulos, J. (2006). p.262.
15. Urbach, K. (2015). p.158.
16. Petropoulos, J. (2006). p.251.
17. BAB. RS. File of Prince Wilhelm von Hessen (b. 1 March 1905), Medizinalrat to the Reichsführer-SS. RuSHA. 27 July 1938. (Gsteinbe.instrasun.tcnj.edu).
18. HHStAW, 520 D-Z, Nr 519.563. Statement of von Schlabrendorff on behalf of Prince Philipp. 21 November 1947. Quoted in Petropoulos, J. (2006). p.253.
19. Petropoulos, J. (2006). p.253.
20. Prince Philipp's Testimony. May 1947 and March 1948 in Kempner, Dritte Reich im Kreuzverhör, 145. Quoted in Petropoulos, J. (2006). p.253.
21. Petropoulos, J. (2006). pp.235–36.
22. Ibid. p.233.
23. HHStAW, 520 D-Z, Nr. 519.563. Statement of Princess Sophia. 15 July 1946. Quoted in Petropoulos, J. (2006). p.234.
24. Kahn, D. (1978). p.179.
25. Petropoulos, J. (2006). p.142.
26. Princess Sophie. *Memories.* (Unpublished handwritten manuscript). Quoted in Petropoulos, J. (2006). p.142.
27. Petropoulos, J. (2006). p.219.
28. Ibid. p.220.

29. Crossland, David (2006). 'Nazi Programme to Breed Master Race: Lebensborn Children Break Silence'. *Der Spiegel*. Hamburg. 7 November 2006.
30. 'Thompson, Lebenborn and the Eugenics Policy of the Reichsführer-SS'. *Central European History*, Vol. 4 (1971): 62. Quoted in Petropoulos, J. (2006). p.220.
31. Letter from Christoph to Sophie. 10 July 1940. Quoted in Petropoulos, J. (2006). p.228.
32. Ibid.
33. Ibid.
34. Letter from Christoph to Sophie. 2 September 1940. Quoted in Petropoulos, J. (2006). p.229.
35. Bradford, S. (2011). p.428.
36. Ibid.
37. Spencer Shew, B. (1955). p.76.
38. Letter from Queen Elizabeth to Queen Mary. 13 September 1940. RA QM/ PRIV/C12/135. Quoted in Shawcross, W. (2009). p.524.
39. Bradford, S. (2011). p.428.
40. Ibid. p.234; Parker, J. (1990). p.105; and Petropoulos, J. (2006). p.230.
41. Petropoulos, J. (2006). pp.229–31.
42. Shawcross, W. (2009). p.516.
43. Ibid. p.528.
44. Princess Alice, Countess of Athlone. (1966). p.249.
45. Aronson, T. (2014). p.413.
46. Princess Alice, Countess of Athlone. (1966). p.251.
47. RA GDKH/ENGT/Ao2, 1940. Quoted in Cadbury, D. (2015). p.123.
48. Duke of Kent's Engagement Diary. 20 May 1940. Quoted in Cadbury, D. (2015). p.123.
49. Cadbury, D. (2015). p.105.
50. Watson, S. (1997). p.166.
51. Cadbury, D. (2015). p.105.
52. Ibid. p.145.
53. Ibid. p.167.
54. Balfour, N. and Mackay, S. (1980). p.175.
55. Wheeler-Bennett, J. (1959). p.492.
56. Williams, E. (2013). 'A Royal Quest. Interview with Princess Elizabeth of Yugoslavia'. *The Economist*. 1843: Stories of an Extraordinary World (www.1843magazine.com). March/April 2013. Retrieved 15 April 2020.
57. Weinberg, G. (2004). p.78.
58. Freeman, G. (2008). p.94.
59. James, R. (Ed.) (1993). Diary entry for 25 March 1941. p.296.

Chapter Twelve

1. James, R. (Ed.) (1993). Diary Entry. 21 January 1941.
2. Queen Alexandra of Yugoslavia. (1956). p.68.
3. Macmillan, H. (1984). p.558.
4. Vickers, H. (2000). p.303.
5. Letter from VMH to MtB. KP. 19 November 1943. Quoted in Vickers, H. (2000). p.297.
6. Letter from Alice to Philip. 5 October 1943. Quoted in Vickers, H. (2000). p.297.

7. De Pough, L. (1979). p.104.
8. Vickers, H. (2000). pp.297–98.
9. Morton, A. (2015). p.255.
10. Bloch, M. (1984). p.223.
11. Parker, J. (1988). p.244.
12. Evan, R. and Hencke. D. (2002). 'Wallis Simpson, the Nazi Minister, the Telltale Monk and an FBI Plot'. *The Guardian*. 29 June 2002.
13. Porter, D. (2005). p.603.
14. Letter from Commander Perkins to US Naval Intelligence, Washington. 11 February 1942. NARA/NND 883021/SIS Intelligence Reports/29 November 1941–31 March 1942.
15. McIver, S. (1995). 'Murder in the Tropics'. *The Florida Chronicles. Volume 2. Pineapple Express*. p.28.
16. Morton, A. (2015). p.214.
17. Oursler Jr, F. (1991). 'Secret Treason'. *American Heritage*, Vol. 42. No. 8. December 1991. p.61.
18. Parker, J. (1988). p.236.
19. Evan, R. and Hencke. D. (2002). 'Wallis Simpson, the Nazi Minister, the Telltale Monk and an FBI Plot'. *The Guardian*. 29 June 2002.
20. Rand, H. (2011). 'Wallis Simpson – Style File'. *Vogue*. 13 September 2011.
21. Ziegler, P. (1990). p.401.
22. Parker, J. (1988). p.238.
23. Ibid. p.240.
24. Chan, M. (2018). '"A Date Which Will Live in Infamy." Read President Roosevelt's Pearl Harbor Address'. *Time Magazine*. 6 December 2018. (www.time.com) Retrieved 15 April 2020.
25. Warwick, C. (2016). p.126.
26. Ranter, H. (2016). *ASN Aircraft Accident Short Sunderland III W4026 Dunbeath, Scotland*. (Aviatio-swafety.net).
27. Warwick, C. (2016). p.127.
28. Ibid.
29. Watson, S. (1997). p.179.
30. Macwhirte, R. (1985). *The Crash of W-4026: Wil Bethune and Louise Kennedy Interviews by Robin Macwhirte*. BBC Radio Scotland. 26 August 1985.
31. Watson, S. (1997). p.181.
32. Ibid. p.180.
33. Ibid.
34. Aronson, T. (1994). p.91.
35. Parker, J. (1988). p.244.
36. Watson, S. (1997). p.181.
37. *Crash of a Short S.25 Sunderland in Braemore: 14 killed*. 25 August 1942. Bureau of Aircraft Accidents. (www.baa-acro.com).
38. Hansard Report. 7 October 1942.

Chapter Thirteen

1. Goeschel, C. (2018). p.247.
2. Wiskemann, E. (1966). p.352.
3. Ibid.

4. Ibid.
5. Bianchi, G. (1988), *25 Luglio: crollo di un regime* (25 July: Collapse of the Regime). Mursia. p.668.
6. Ibid.
7. Ibid.
8. Farrell, N. (2003). *Mussolini: A New Life*. Weidenfeld and Nicolson.
9. De Felice, R. (1996). *Mussolini. L'Alleato. 1: L'Italia in guerra II: Crisi e agonia del regime* (Italy at War II: Crisis and Agony of the Regime). (2 Ed.). Einaudi. p.1400.
10. Farrell, N. (2003). *Mussolini: A New Life*. Weidenfeld and Nicolson.
11. Goeschel, C. (2018). p.249.
12. Bianchi, G. (1989). *25 Luglio: crollo di un regime*. (25 July: Collapse of the Regime). Mursia. p.720.
13. Hooper, J. (2011). 'Mussolini "had an affair with Italy's last queen"'. *The Guardian*. 31 August 2011.
14. Mack Smith, D. (1995). p.299.
15. Mussolini, B. (2000). p.235.
16. Goeschel, C. (2018). p.251.
17. Mack Smith, D. (1995). p.299.
18. Ibid.
19. Susmel, E. and Suseml. D. (Eds) (1951). Vol. 34. p.277.
20. Giudice, G. (1971). pp.643–44.
21. Susmel, E. and Suseml. D. (Eds) (1951). Vol. 34. p.285.
22. Mussolini, B. (2000). p 105.
23. Farrell, N. (2003). p.12121.
24. 'The Little King'. *Time Magazine*. 5 January 1948.
25. Goeschel, C. (2018). p.261.
26. Ibid.
27. Ibid. p.260.
28. Petropoulous, J. (2006). p.293.
29. Ley, R. (1944) 'Gott schütze den Führer' (God Protect the Leader). *Der Angriff*. 23 July 1944.
30. 'What Himmler Told His Doctor'. *The Sunday Express*. 30 March 1947.
31. Speer, A. (2009). p.399.
32. Petropoulous, J. (2006). p.293.
33. Goebbels Diary. Entry of 10 August 1943.
34. Evans, R. (2008). p.97.
35. Crankshaw, E. (2002). pp.96–97.
36. Padfield, P. (1990). p.145.
37. Crankshaw, E. (2002). pp.96–97.
38. Gavin, P. (2001). *Triumph of Hitler: The Gestapo is Born*. The History Place (Online).
39. Crankshaw, E. (2002). pp.96–99.
40. HHStaw, 520 D-Z. Nr. 519-563. Statement of Prince Philipp. 21 February 1947. Quoted in Petropoulous, J. (2006). p.294.
41. Petropoulous, J. (2006). p.294.
42. HHStaw, 520 D-Z. Nr. 519-563. Statement of von Schlabrendorff on behalf of Prince Philipp. 21 November 1947. Quoted in Petropoulous, J. (2006). p.298.
43. Trevelyan, R. (1981). *Rome 1944*. Martin Secker and Warburg.
44. HHStaw, 520 D-Z. Nr. 519-563. Statement of von Schlabrendorff on behalf of Prince Philipp. 21 November 1947. Quoted in Petropoulous, J. (2006). p.300.
45. Ibid.

46. Hackett, Buchenwald Report. Quoted in Petropoulous, J. (2006). p.300.
47. Webb, C. Lisciotto, C. (2007). *Buchenwald Concentration Camp.* The Holocaust Research Project.
48. HHStaw, 520 D-Z. Nr. 519.563. Spruchkammer Protocol of Prince Philipp, 15–17 December 1947, 27. *Statement of Adelheid Fliege.* 2 July 1945. Quoted in Petropoulous, J. (2006). p.302.
49. Petropoulous, J. (2006). p.301.
50. Ibid. p.292.
51. Ibid. p.295.
52. HHStaw, 520 D-Z. Nr. 519-563. Statement of von Schlabrendorff on behalf of Prince Philipp.21 November 1947. Quoted in Petropoulous, J. (2006). p.295.
53. HHStaw, 520 D-Z. Nr. 519-563. Spruchkammer Protocol of Prince Philipp, 15–17 December 1947, 27. *Statement of Adelheid Fliege.* 2 July 1945. Quoted in Petropoulous, J. (2006). p.296.
54. Petropoulous, J. (2006). p.296.
55. HHStaw, 520 D-Z. Nr. 519-563. Spruchkammer Protocal of Prince Philipp, 15–17 December 1947, 27. *Statement of Adelheid Fliege.* 2 July 1945. Quoted in Petropoulous, J. (2006). p.302.
56. HHStaw, 520 D-Z. Nr. 519-563. Statement of von Schlabrendorff on behalf of Prince Philipp. 21 November 1947. Quoted in Petropoulous, J. (2006). p.302.
57. Petropoulous, J. (2006). p.301.
58. Hohne, H. (1979). p.579.
59. NARA, M 1204/5; *Record of Testimony in the Trial of the United States versus Friedrich Becker. Et al.* 12 June 1946, pp.3335–36, 3440, 3449–50, 3455.
60. HHStaw, 529 D-Z. Nr. 519-563. Statement of Prince Philipp. 21 February 1947. Quoted in Petropoulous, J. (2006). p.297.
61. Wachsmann, N. (2015). p.163.
62. Ibid. p.119.
63. Ibid. p.165.
64. Morehouse, R. (March 2012). 'Hitler's Dream Capita'l. *History Today* (Online) Vol. 62, Issue 3.
65. Wachsmann, N. (2015). p.561.
66. NARA, M 1204. *Record of Testimony in the Trial of the United States versus Friedrich Becker. Et al.* 12 June 1946, 3335–36, 3440, 3449–50, 3455.
67. IfZG, ZS 918. Interrogation of Philip Hesse. 4 March 19. Quoted in Petropoulous, J. (2006). p.297.

Chapter Fourteen

1. Petropoulos, J. (2006). p.205.
2. *Documents of German Foreign Policy 1918–1945 Series D Volume XIII. The War Years 23 June 1941–11 December 1941.* Published in UK by HMSO.
3. Urbach, K. (2015). p.215.
4. Fjellman, M. (1968). p.125.
5. Petropoulos, J. (2006). pp.305–12.
6. BAB (formerly BDC), SSF 94A. File of Prince Christoph, General Taubert to Himmler. 30 November 1943. Quoted in quoted in Petropoulos, J. (2006). p. 311.

7. Petropoulos, J. (2006). p.312.
8. Alice to Philip, Athens. 23 April 1944, BP. Quoted Vickers, H. (2000). p.302.
9. VMH to NK, KP. 16 October 1943, BA. Quoted in Vickers, H. (2000). p.301.
10. VMH to Mtb, KP. 4 February 1944, BA. Quoted in Vickers, H. (2000). p.301.
11. Wolfgang Prinz von Hessen, Aufzeichnungen, 195. Quoted in Petropoulos, J. (2006). p.312.
12. News Chronicle. April 1945.
13. Lane, P. (1980). p.121.
14. Eade, P. (2012). p.152.
15. Higham, C. (2005). pp.106–07.
16. Parker, J. (1990). p.89.
17. Crawford, M. (1952). p.85.
18. Hart-Davis, D. (2007). p.189.
19. Parker, J. (1990). p.89.
20. Nicholson, Unpublished Diary. Balliol College, Oxford. 12 June 1955. Quoted in Bradford, S. (2011). p.420.
21. Higham, C. (2005). p.107.
22. *Newcastle Journal*. April 1944.
23. Wiltz, J. (2015). 'The Princess in the Contention Camp'. *Royal History* (Online). 4 March 2015.
24. Bailey, C. (2019). p.309.
25. Von Hassell, F. (1987). *Hostage of the Third Reich: The Story of My Imprisonment and Rescue from the SS*. Charles Scribner's Son. p.180.
26. Ibid. p.194.
27. Ibid. p.198.
28. Beevor, A. (2007). pp.249–50.
29. Urbach, K. (2015). p.310.
30. Von Hassell, F. (1987). p.202.
31. Ibid. p.208.
32. Petropoulos, J. (2006). p.316

Chapter Fifteen

1. *Bunte Bühne für die Wehrmacht* (Colorful Stage for the Wehrmacht). Radio programme. 17 April 1945. Quoted in Urbach, K. (2015). p.309.
2. Urbach, K. (2015). p.310.
3. Sandner, H. (2010). p.428.
4. Rushton, A. (2018). p.6.
5. Princess Alice, Countess of Athlone. (1966). p.275.
6. Aronson, T. (2014). p.424.
7. Urbach, K. (2015). p.311.
8. Letter to Sir Brian Robertson. 20 September 1946. Correspondence Regarding the Duke of Saxe-Coburg-Gotha. FO 1030/302.
9. Rushton, A. (2018). p.5.
10. Letter to Sir Brian Robertson. 12 September 1946. Correspondence Regarding the Duke of Saxe-Coburg-Gotha. FO 1030/302.
11. Letter to Sir Brian Robertson. 10 August 1946. Correspondence Regarding the Duke of Saxe-Coburg-Gotha. FO 1030/302.
12. Rushton, A. (2018). p.6.

13. Letter to Sir Brian Robertson. 12 September 1946. Correspondence Regarding the Duke of Saxe-Coburg-Gotha. FO 1030/302.
14. 28 August 1947, FO 371 64689, NA.
15. Urbach, K. (2015). p.312.
16. Eade, P. (2012). p.176.
17. Alford, K. (1994). p.2214.
18. Ibid. p.2416.
19. Petropoulos, J. (2006). p.317.
20. Eade, P. (2012). p.176.
21. 'Obituary: Princess Margaret of Hesse and the Rhine'. *The Independent.* 30 January 1977.
22. Vickers, H. (2000). p.321.
23. Ibid.
24. Petropoulos, J. (2006). p.322.
25. Ibid. pp.324–25.
26. HHStAW, 520, D-Z, Nr. 519.563. Statement of Princess Margaret of Hesse-Darmstadt. Quoted in Petropoulos, J. (2006). p.328.
27. Petropoulos, J. (2006). p.324.
28. Ibid. p.326.
29. Lough, D. (2015). p.216.
30. Ibid.
31. Bradford, S. (2011). p.504.
32. *The Quotable Winston Churchill.* (2013). Running Press. p.123.
33. Chilton, M. (2018). 'From Churchill to Corbyn: The 40 Most Brutal British Political Insults'. *The Daily Telegraph* 15 March 2018.
34. Lord Moran. (1966). pp.311–12.
35. Ibid.
36. Marr, A. (2011). p.109.
37. Hutton, M. (2013). p.99.
38. Morton, A. (2015). p.240.
39. Bradford, S. (2011). p.503.
40. Marr, A. (2011). p.109.
41. 'The German Foreign Ministry's Archives at Whaddon Hall, 1948–58'. *American Archivist.* 24 (1): pp.43–54. (1961).
42. Morton, A. (2015). p.245.
43. Ibid. p.252.
44. Costello, J. (1991). p.368.
45. Ziegler, P. (1990). p.549.
46. Shawcross, W. (2009). p.599.
47. Morton, A. (2015). p.258.
48. Ibid.
49. Bradford, S. (2011). p.172.
50. Carter, M. (2001). p.305.
51. Ibid. p.449.
52. Ibid. p.313.
53. *Edward VIII: Traitor King.* (1996). Television Documentary. Interview Douglas Price. Channel 4.
54. Morton, A. (2015). p.265.
55. Ibid. p.266.
56. Alford, K. (1994). p.2249.

57. Ibid. p.2218.
58. Carter, M. (2001). p.312.
59. Alford, K. (1994). p.2350.
60. Ibid. p.2369.
61. Judge Advocate General's Corps, The Army Lawyer (1975). p.172.
62. Harding, S. (2009). 'The Hesse Jewel Heist, World War II'. *Soldiers of Fortune.* (March 2009).
63. Judge Advocate General's Corps, The Army Lawyer (1975). p.173.
64. Parker, J. (1990). p.106.
65. Ibid. p.106.
66. Alford, K. (1994). p.4093.
67. Boothroyd, B. (1971). p.114.
68. Eade, P. (2012) p.177.
69. Queen Alexandra of Yugoslavia. (1960). pp.85–86.
70. Pimlott, B. (2002). p.103.
71. Corbitt, F. (1956). p.187.
72. Eade, P. (2012). p.179.
73. Pimlott, B. (2002). p.104.
74. Ibid.
75. Turner, G. (2002). 'Elizabeth: The Woman and Queen'. *The Daily Telegraph.* 24 May 2002.
76. Parker, J. (1990). pp.113–14.
77. Brendon, P. and Whitehead P. (2000). p.125.
78. Bedell Smith, S. (2001). 'Love and Majesty'. *Vanity Fair.* 14 December 2001.
79. Pimlott, B. (2002). p.113.
80. Callan, P. (2008). 'Prince Philip and the Nazis'. *The Daily Express.* 20 February 2008.

Chapter Sixteen

1. Eade, P. (2012). p.206.
2. Rhodes, J.R. (Ed.) (1967). p.419.
3. *The Times.* 23 November 1947.
4. Marr, A. (2011). p.111.
5. Pathé News Reel (1947). *The Royal Wedding Collection.*
6. Hicks, P. (2012). p.159.
7. Pimlott, B. (2002). p.140.
8. Eade, P. (2011). p.206.
9. Edwards, A. (1991). p.195.
10. *Country Life Magazine.* November 1947.
11. Hicks, P. (2012). p.162.
12. Eade, P. (2012). p.203.
13. Pimlott, B. (2002). p.124.
14. Bedell Smith, S. (2012). p.42.
15. Colville Diary (Unpublished). 10 July 1947. Quoted in Pimlott, B. (2002). p.123.
16. Pimlott, B. (2002). p.137.
17. Sir Michel Duff writing to Cecil Beaton. 10 December 1947. Quoted in Vickers, H. (1985). p.320.
18. Hartnell, N. (1955). p.112.

19. Fraser, A. (2011). 'Royal Wedding: From Rations to Raptures at the Queen's Austerity Wedding'. *Daily Telegraph* 26 April 2011.
20. Bradford, S. (2011). p.560.
21. Roberts, J. (2007). p.104.
22. King, G. (2999). p.384.
23. Princess Alice, Countess of Athlone. (1966). p.281.
24. Ibid. p.281.
25. Rushton, A. (2018). p.152.
26. Sandner, H. (2010). pp.427–29.
27. Thornton, M. (2007). 'The Nazi Relative that the Royals Disowned'. *Daily Mail.* 1 December 2007.
28. Urbach, K. (2015). p.313.
29. Sandner, H. (2010). p.294.
30. Ibid. p.281.
31. Prince Andreas of Saxe-Coburg and Gotha. (2015). pp.80–81.
32. Princess Alice, Countess of Athlone. (1966). p.1.
33. Prince Andreas of Saxe-Coburg and Gotha (2015). p.81.
34. Petropoulos, J. (2006). p.331.
35. Ibid. p.332.
36. Ibid. p.329.
37. Ibid. p.330.
38. Ibid. pp.330–31.
39. Ibid. p.330.
40. Ibid. p.331.
41. Ibid. p.332.
42. HHStAW, 520 DZ Nr 519.562. Speech for Prince Philipp. 17 December 1947. Quoted in Petropoulos, J. (2006). p.332.
43. Petropoulos, J. (2006). p.333.
44. HHStAW, 520 DZ Nr 519.563. *Minister für politische Befreiung to the Erster öffentliche Kläger der Berfungskammer* (Minister for Political Liberation to the First Public Plaintiff of the Chamber of Appeal). 23 February 1948. Quoted in Petropoulos, J. (2006). p.334.
45. Petropoulos, J. (2006). p.334.
46. Ibid.
47. RvH. *Declaration of the Zentralberufungskammer* in Frankfurt. 17 April 1950. Quoted in Petropoulos, J. (2006). p.336.

Epilogue

1. Petropoulos, J. (2006). pp.355–7.
2. Parker, J. (1990). p.135.
3. Bradford, S. (2011). p.562.
4. Morton, A. (2015). p.275.
5. Letter from the Duchess of Windsor to the Duke of Windsor. 17 February 1952. Quoted in Bloch, M. (1988). p.263.
6. Interview with Atalanta Clifford. *Edward on Edward* (1996). Television Documentary.
7. The Duke of Windsor. (1947). p.279.
8. Lord Kinross. (1974). 'Love Conquers All'. *Books and Bookmen.* Vol. 20. p.50.

INDEX